Tolley's
Data Protection: A Guide to
Legal Compliance for HR and Payroll

by

Lynda A C Macdonald
Susan Singleton
Norman F Green

Members of the LexisNexis Group worldwide

United Kingdom	LexisNexis UK, a Division of Reed Elsevier (UK) Ltd, 2 Addiscombe Road, CROYDON CR9 5AF
Argentina	LexisNexis Argentina, BUENOS AIRES
Australia	LexisNexis Butterworths, CHATSWOOD, New South Wales
Austria	LexisNexis Verlag ARD Orac GmbH & Co KG, VIENNA
Canada	LexisNexis Butterworths, MARKHAM, Ontario
Chile	LexisNexis Chile Ltda, SANTIAGO DE CHILE
Czech Republic	Nakladatelství Orac sro, PRAGUE
France	Editions du Juris-Classeur SA, PARIS
Germany	LexisNexis Deutschland GmbH, FRANKFURT and MUNSTER
Hong Kong	LexisNexis Butterworths, HONG KONG
Hungary	HVG-Orac, BUDAPEST
India	LexisNexis Butterworths, NEW DELHI
Ireland	LexisNexis, DUBLIN
Italy	Giuffrè Editore, MILAN
Malaysia	Malayan Law Journal Sdn Bhd, KUALA LUMPUR
New Zealand	LexisNexis Butterworths, WELLINGTON
Poland	Wydawnictwo Prawnicze LexisNexis, WARSAW
Singapore	LexisNexis Butterworths, SINGAPORE
South Africa	LexisNexis Butterworths, DURBAN
Switzerland	Stämpfli Verlag AG, BERNE
USA	LexisNexis, DAYTON, Ohio

© Reed Elsevier (UK) Ltd 2004
Published by LexisNexis UK

A CIP Catalogue record for this book is available from the British Library.

ISBN 0 75452 4469

Typeset by Columns Design Ltd, Reading, England
Printed and bound in Great Britain by Cromwell Press, Trowbridge, Wiltshire

Visit LexisNexis UK at www.lexisnexis.co.uk

About the Authors

Lynda Macdonald

Lynda Macdonald is a self-employed freelance employment law trainer, advisor and writer. For fifteen years, prior to setting up her own business, she gained substantial practical experience of employee relations, recruitment and selection, dismissal procedures, employment law and other aspects of human resource management through working in industry. With this solid background in human resource management, she successfully established, and currently runs, her own business in employment law and management training/consultancy. She is also appointed as a panel member of the Employment Tribunal service in Aberdeen, where she lives.

Lynda is a university graduate in language and a Fellow of the Chartered Institute of Personnel and Development. Additionally, she has an LLM degree in employment law.

Lynda has to date written nine books on various aspects of employment law, all of which have been published by well-known national publishers.

Contact Lynda at: lyndamacdonald@clara.co.uk

Web site: www.lyndamacdonald.co.uk

Susan Singleton

Susan Singleton LLB, Solicitor, Singletons has run her own London legal practice, Singletons (www.singlelaw.com), since 1994, specialising in data protection, IT, intellectual property, competition and commercial law.

Author of 25 legal books she has written widely on data protection and related areas of law and frequently speaks on this topic. Last year she spoke at over 60 legal conferences. She is author of Tolley's *Data Protection Handbook*. She edits and writes in a number of computer law and data protection newsletters. Since 1994 she has advised over 450 clients from leading public companies to small businesses, from charities to regulatory bodies, from all around the UK and abroad.

She trained at solicitors Nabarro Nathanson before moving to leading City solicitors Slaughter and May when she qualified as a solicitor in 1985 as a competition/IT lawyer. In 1988 she moved to Bristows, a specialist intellectual property law practice with which she remained until founding her own solicitor's firm. She serves on the EC/Laws Committee of the Licensing Executives Society, the Legal Committee of the Chartered Institute of Purchasing and Supply and the

Competition Law Association. She is a member of the Society of Computers and Law.

Susan also has a substantial competition/anti-trust practice and brought the first action for damages for breach of the EU competition rules to reach a trial before an English court (*Arkin*) after a 49-day trial in 2002. Her work covers both non-contentious/contractual work and advice and also litigation. In the data protection area she advises on employee policies, email marketing, data protection handbooks and compliance. According to the Chambers and Partners Guide to the Legal Profession she is one of the UK's leading IT lawyers. She lives in North London and has five children.

Norman F Green

Norman F Green, BSc (Hons), CEng, FBCS, CITP, FIPPM is Legislation Manager at LogicaCMG UK Limited.

Having read mathematics at London University, Norman's first job was in the Finance Department of a local authority preparing for the introduction of what are now called Housing Benefits. This involved monitoring a Bill during its passage through Parliament and revising procedures as the legislation changed.

Before joining CMG (now LogicaCMG) in 1981, Norman had computing jobs with a county council and a university, both of which involved supporting payroll, pensions and personal systems.

Norman is currently responsible for ensuring the legislative correctness of LogicaCMG's payroll products within its Enterprise Services UK business and for interpreting new legislation for inclusion in the products. He provides technical support to LogicaCMG's HR and payroll clients and internally to the managed payroll and personnel service as well as sales, production, development and maintenance teams including the design of bespoke enhancements, payroll consultancy and the investigation of new legislation and requirements specific to various industry groups.

A Fellow of the British Computer Society, Norman is the Chairman of its Payroll Specialist Group, Chairman of its Information Privacy Expert Panel and a member of its 'Top Team'. A Fellow of the Institute of Payroll and Pensions Management, Norman is a tutor and examiner for its Diploma in Payroll Management.

He is in regular discussion with senior civil servants (policy advisors) from various government departments on payroll and employment related issues and participates in formal consultation exercises.

Norman has contributed to a number of data protection books and has chaired a working party developing a Data Protection Code of Good Practice for the Engineering Council. He writes for a number of payroll periodicals and edits guidance material in the HR and payroll sector.

Contents

Table of Cases

References are to paragraph numbers.

Table of Statutes

References are to paragraph numbers.

Table of Statutes

Table of Statutory Instruments

References are to paragraph numbers.

Chapter 1
Overview of the Data Protection Act 1998

Introduction 1.1

The *Data Protection Act 1998* (*DPA 1998* or 'the Act') aims to protect individuals' personal information, or personal data, as it is known. Those involved with human resources (HR) manage large amounts of often very confidential data, from past criminal convictions to health information such as which members of staff carry the HIV virus. The Act sets out the law on how that data can be handled and used. It gives individuals in most cases the right to see the data held about them. They request this by making a 'subject access request'. Data must be handled in accordance with the eight data protection principles which are the subject of **CHAPTER 2** of this book. Anyone holding personal data is called a 'data controller' and they must notify the Information Commissioner that they hold the data and the purposes for which they hold it. This registration process is examined in **CHAPTER 3**.

The Information Commissioner, Mr Richard Thomas, has issued lots of useful guidance on the *DPA 1998*. Copies are all on the IC web site at www.informationcommissioner.gov.uk, which is regularly updated. In the HR field the four-part employment Code of Practice is of most relevance, although part 4 of the code, which is on medical records, at the date of writing is still a draft. Parts 1, 2 and 3, which are examined in **CHAPTERS 5, 6** and **9** respectively, are subject to revision, in particular following an important data protection case decision, *Durant v Financial Services Authority [2003] EWCA Civ 1746*, which clarified what data was caught by the Act. The latest position should always be checked.

Breach of the Act is a criminal offence and fines of up to £5,000 can be imposed. Anyone who has suffered damage through a breach of the legislation can sue for damages. The aim of this chapter is to provide a general overview of the *DPA 1998* and in particular concentrate on how it applies in the payroll and HR area.

Purposes of Data Protection Legislation 1.2

The *DPA 1998* brought an EU directive on data protection into force in the UK. The 1998 Act replaced the *Data Protection Act 1984*. The aim of the legislation is to ensure privacy rights of individuals are respected and that data is processed fairly and lawfully.

1

Importance of Compliance – Penalties and Risks 1.3

Data protection lawyers spend much of their time advising on risks and rewards. Breach of the Act can lead to:

- fines of £5,000 per offence;

- a criminal record;

- requirement to correct a practice which breaches the Act;

- very bad publicity such as 'ABC Bank plc publishes customer bank account details on the internet' or 'Individuals who ordered Viagra find their personal details pasted on the net' etc; and

- actions for damages by anyone who suffers loss through breach of the legislation.

A very important area is claims for unfair dismissal. Often the information needed to prove a case and claim damages of £60,000 and more is found by the ex-employee obtaining copies of their personal data from the ex-employer. Statements in records such as 'will not fit in here', 'three small children' and 'black' in interview notes have many a time been used against the employer in subsequent employment tribunal cases.

Many areas of the Act are vague and it is sometimes difficult to know how the law would be construed. In the Soham murder investigation, for example, one police force unnecessarily destroyed records which would have led to the murderer not having been employed at a school. Some areas are clear. Others require detailed advice and a judgment to be made about where or how data can be used.

Methods of Compliance 1.4

This book aims to provide guidance on how to comply with the legislation. Running through most of the Information Commissioner's guidance is advice that companies should undertake audits – general audits of their data protection policies and procedures and specific audits such as checking the effect if they were to introduce a particular kind of monitoring.

The aim of an audit is:

- to ensure the rules are not breached in the first place; and

- to show where a breach of the rules has occurred.

Audits 1.5

The Information Commissioner has published a substantial 167-page audit manual which companies can use (available on the web site). It contains a methodology for conducting data protection compliance audits and lots of useful checklists to complete in the process of assessing whether or not a business is compliant with the main provisions of the *DPA 1998*. Rather than simply being tailored to the Commissioner's specific needs, it has been written in such a way that any data controller can use it to help judge their own data protection compliance. The Information Commissioner states, 'Similarly, it may also be used by other organisations offering such services to data controllers. Given that potential users may have different levels of existing audit expertise, the manual also includes general guidance on compliance auditing.'

Policies   1.6

Lots of companies have data protection policies. These written documents are given or emailed to all members of staff and the content will vary from company to company. They need to be updated from time to time to reflect changes in regulations and case law. For example, in December 2003 the *Privacy and Electronic Communications (EC Directive) Regulations 2003 (SI 2003 No 2426)* came into force. These Regulations change the law on unsolicited email marketing; have effects on the wording to be given on marketing emails; require individuals to be told if cookies operate on web sites; and provide that employees must give explicit consent to the use of tracking devices such as in cars or even on electronic passes to enter their place of work. Many compliance programmes therefore would need modifying to reflect these changes. On 8 December 2003 in *Durant v Financial Services Authority [2003] EWCA Civ 1746*, the Court of Appeal decided some important issues, principally about what data is caught by the Act at all, with the result that much of the manual data in many offices is outside the Act. As a result of this, data protection policies needed to be revised. It is therefore sensible to have an annual programme so that any such policy informed of the company's data protection rules.

Data protection officers   1.7

Many companies appoint one person as data protection officer. This could be a person from the HR department, or it may be the company secretary or a nominated officer who works on nothing but data protection matters. Much depends on how the company is structured as to who has this role. There are organisations such as the European Privacy Officers Network (EPON) which data protection officers can join. EPON was set up by Privacy Laws and Business (www.privacylaws.com). Membership of EPON is open to privacy/ data protection professionals working for organisations operating in more than one country. Members have European responsibilities for privacy, which may be part of wider regional or worldwide functions.

The Data Protection Forum deals with data protection matters in the United Kingdom. It was set up and is run by practising data protection officers. Forum members represent a cross-section of those involved with data protection and include *private sector members* from financial services, retail, accountancy, travel, charities; *public sector members* from the police, local authorities, universities; as well as lawyers, consultants and consumers. For details see www.dpforum.org.uk.

Enforcement and Complaints Handling   1.8

The Information Commissioner is in charge of data protection enforcement in the UK. If anyone receives a request for information or formal notice from the Information Commissioner it should be taken very seriously indeed and ideally legal advice taken on the implications and what should or should not be said or done by way of response.

There are huge demands on the Information Commissioner's Office's time. In the Annual Report to 31 March 2003 the Commissioner stated:

> 'The considerable, and increasing, demands that have been placed on the Office during the period under review have caused us to look closely at our existing resources and how we can best use them. The challenges have been great. For example, we currently handle some 12,000 requests yearly from members of the public to assess whether the Data Protection Act is being complied with. We deal with many thousands of written requests from businesses and other record holders for advice about how best to comply with the law. In the period under review our enquiry line dealt with nearly 60,000 telephone enquiries, often difficult or complex ones. Although we are satisfied that we generally provide a good service, we intend to improve our service standards across the board.

> 'In response to the pressures described above, we are in the process of reviewing all aspects of the way our Office is run. This involves looking, for example, at staffing issues and at the way we handle information within our organisation. Most importantly, we are reviewing how we deliver our services to the considerable numbers of individuals and businesses who, quite rightly, expect prompt, clear, responses to their enquiries about how to comply with the potentially complex pieces of law we are responsible for promoting compliance with.'

The above quote is important because it illustrates the current state of flux of data protection enforcement and legislation. Procedurally, people can make a request for assessment if they are directly affected by any processing of personal data under the *DPA 1998, section 42. Section 40* gives the Information Commissioner the power to serve enforcement notices on the data controller where there has been a contravention of one of the data protection principles. The notice will specify what the controller must do, such as stop processing data in breach of the Act. The Act gives the Commissioner powers to serve an 'information notice' on a data controller once he has received a request for assessment, or of the Commissioner's own volition. The notice will tell the data controller to provide information to the Information Commissioner and give a time limit by which to do so.

Inspection visits 1.9

If there are reasonable grounds for suspecting that an offence has been or is being committed under the Act, or that any of the data protection principles have been or are being contravened, the Commissioner may apply to a circuit judge for a warrant to enter and search premises on which it is suspected that evidence of the offence or contravention of the principles is to be found.

Before issuing a warrant, the judge will need to be satisfied that there are reasonable grounds for the Commissioner's suspicion *and* that:

- the Commissioner has already demanded access to the premises by giving seven days' written notice to the occupier; and

- access was demanded at a reasonable hour and was unreasonably refused; or

- although entry to the premises was granted, the occupier unreasonably refused to comply with a request by the Commissioner (including the Commissioner's officers or staff) to allow him to carry out any of the procedures mentioned in the list that follows; and

- the Commissioner has notified the occupier of the application for the warrant and that the occupier has had an opportunity to be heard by the judge as to whether or not the warrant should be issued.

However, if the judge is satisfied that the case is urgent or that giving notice would defeat the object of the entry, the judge may issue the warrant without notice having been given to the occupier.

The warrant will authorise the Commissioner or any of the Commissioner's officers or staff to:

- enter and search the specified premises at any time within seven days of the date of the warrant;

- inspect, examine, operate and test any equipment found there which is used or intended to be used for the processing of personal data; and

- inspect and seize any documents or other material found there which may be evidence of an offence or contravention of the principles.

Communications made for the purpose of proceedings under the Act between a professional legal adviser and his or her client are also exempt from inspection and seizure. This means that if external advice is obtained from solicitors this cannot be seen on a visit and should be kept separately and marked as such.

It is a criminal offence, try-able only in the Magistrates Court or the Sheriff Court of Scotland:

- intentionally to obstruct a person in the execution of a warrant; or

- to fail, without reasonable excuse, to give anyone executing a warrant such help as may reasonably be required to execute the warrant.

On conviction an offender is liable to a maximum fine of £5,000.

In Scotland, warrants to enter and search premises in this context are issued by the Sheriff and in Northern Ireland by a county court judge (see **CHAPTER 9**).

If an inspection visit is proposed or takes place employers should seek legal advice right away.

Compensation   1.10

Compensation can in addition be claimed. In the Legal Guidance (October 2001) on *DPA 1998*, the Commissioner poses the question: 'How much will the court award if a claim for compensation is successful?' The reply is as follows:

> 'There are no guidelines as to appropriate levels of compensation for a claim under the Act and the Commissioner is not routinely advised of the outcome of cases where individuals have made a successful claim for compensation under the Act. The judge hearing the case has discretion in these matters and would have to take into consideration many factors including the seriousness of the breach and the effect upon the claimant, particularly when considering damages for distress.'

In the case of *Campbell v Mirror Group Newspapers Plc (QBD, 27 March 2002)* the High Court awarded £3,500, but the decision was overturned on appeal in October 2002. An appeal to the House of Lords began in early 2004.

Personal Liability   1.11

Under *DPA 1998, section 61*, if a company commits a criminal offence under the Act, any director, manager, secretary or similar officer or someone purporting to act in any such capacity is personally guilty of the offence in addition to the corporate body if the offence:

- was committed with his or her consent or connivance; or
- is attributable to any neglect on his or her part.

Where the affairs of a corporate body are managed by its members, any member who exercises the functions of management as if he or she were a director can also be guilty of the offence that results from any of his or her acts or omissions.

Government departments are not liable to prosecution under the Act, but individual civil servants may be prosecuted if they personally are believed to be guilty of an offence under *DPA 1998, section 55* (the unlawful obtaining or disclosure of personal data), or obstructing or failing to assist in the execution of a warrant issued in accordance with the Act (*Schedule 9, para 12*).

Offences include:

- processing without notification (*section 21(1)*);
- failure to notify the Commissioner of changes to the notification register entry (*section 21(2)*);
- processing before expiry of assessable processing time limits or receipt of assessable processing notice within such time (*section 22(6)*);
- failure to comply with written request for particulars (*section 24*);
- failure to comply with an enforcement notice, or information notice, or special information notice (*section 47(1)*),
- knowingly or recklessly making a false statement in compliance with an information notice or special information notice (*section 47(2)*), and
- intentional obstruction of, or failure to give reasonable assistance in, execution of a warrant (*Schedule 9*).

Also, under *section 55* it is an offence for a person, knowingly or recklessly, without the consent of the data controller, to:

- obtain or disclose personal data or the information contained in personal data; or
- procure the disclosure to another person of the information contained in personal data.

The Act provides specific exceptions to liability for this offence where the person can show that:

- the obtaining, disclosing or procuring:
  - was necessary to prevent or detect crime; or
  - was required or authorised by law;
- he or she acted in the reasonable belief that they had the legal right to obtain, disclose or procure the disclosure;
- he or she acted in the reasonable belief that the data controller would have consented to the obtaining, disclosing or procuring if the data controller had known; or
- in the particular circumstances the obtaining, disclosing or procuring was justified as being in the public interest.

A person will not be guilty of this offence if the personal data in question fall within the national security exemption at *section 28*.

It should be noted that an offence under this section cannot be committed by a data controller in respect of data of which he or she is the data controller. However, a data controller who discloses personal data of which he or she is the data controller may breach the first principle if the disclosure is unfair or unlawful.

Where employees of a data controller organisation have authority to obtain and disclose personal data in the course of their employment (for example bank employees who can access customer accounts for bank purposes), they will commit these offences if they use their position to obtain, disclose, or procure disclosure of personal data for their own purposes.

If a person has obtained personal data in contravention of *section 55(1)* (see above), it is an offence to sell or offer to sell personal data. Often errant employees do this. Private investigators will pay employees to pass on data to them. Data protection policies and procedures should seek to ensure this does not happen.

It is also an offence to offer to sell personal data which the person subsequently obtains in contravention of *section 55(1)*. An advertisement indicating that personal data are or may be for sale is an offer to sell the data. 'Personal data' includes information extracted from personal data for the purposes of these offences. A person will not be guilty of this offence if the personal data in question fall within the national security exemption at *section 28* (see **CHAPTER 5**).

Under *section 56*, unless one of the statutory exceptions apply it is an offence for a person to require another person or a third party to:

- supply him or her with a relevant record (see below); or
- produce a relevant record to him or her;

in connection with:

- the recruitment of that other person as an employee;
- the continued employment of that other person;
- any contract for the provision of services to him or her by that other person; or
- where a person is concerned with providing (for payment or not) goods, facilities or services to the public or a section of the public, as a condition of providing or offering to provide any goods, facilities or services to that other person.

The statutory exceptions to liability for such offences are:

- that the imposition of the requirement was required or authorised by law; or
- that in the particular circumstances the imposition of the requirements was justified as being in the public interest.

The Act provides that the imposition of the requirement is not to be regarded as being justified in the public interest on the ground that it would assist in the prevention or detection of crime.

The term 'relevant record' is defined in the *DPA 1998, section 56* by reference to a table which lists data controllers and the subject matter of subject access requests that may be made to them by data subjects. Generally, the term relates to records of cautions, criminal convictions and to certain social security records relating to the data subject.

The Payroll Perspective   1.12

The payroll function has always handled employees' personal information, passing some of that information back to the employee, using it elsewhere in the employer's organisation and forwarding some of it to third parties. Most employees working within the payroll function understand the need for confidentiality and privacy when processing this personal data through the payroll and the procedures for the payroll function will, typically, meet most of the requirements of the *DPA 1998*. However, the procedures may pre-date this legislation because any given payroll function will have been in existence for as long as the organisation has been an employer. Thus a review of payroll procedures against the requirements of the Act is a worthwhile exercise.

All personal data held in a computer-readable format or in structured manual files are covered by the *DPA 1998*. The only data not covered by the Act are data held in unstructured manual files. It can be argued that all data needed by the payroll function must be held in some structured way in order to render it usable within the payroll function. It is, in any case, better and easier to apply sound data protection principles to all personal data processed within the payroll function than to expend resources on distinguishing between what data are and are not covered by the legislation.

Disclosures   1.13

The primary purpose of the payroll function is to pay employees. However, the payroll function is much broader than this and, because it maintains considerable financial information, there are many 'customers' of the payroll function requiring the data held within payroll systems. These disclosures fall into four broad categories:

- personnel elsewhere in the organisation;

- the contract with the employee;

- legal obligations; and

- other, usually ad hoc, requests.

These are discussed in turn at **1.14** to **1.17** below.

Personnel elsewhere in the organisation   1.14

This is not strictly a disclosure as the personal data remains internal to the organisation of the data controller. However, in an international organisation, this may involve transfers of data outside the European Economic Area. Where the data are not personal, eg the total cost of overtime worked in a unit of the organisation, this is not covered by the data protection legislation. Where the data does relate to an individual, however, the purpose of the processing elsewhere in the organisation must be recorded in the notification.

Contract with the employee   1.15

As well as the contract of employment, employees often enter into other contacts such as Save As You Earn schemes and pension schemes. In order to fulfil such contracts, it may be necessary to disclose personal data to a third party such as pension scheme administrators.

Legal obligations   1.16

All employers operating a PAYE scheme must make end-of-tax-year returns to the Inland Revenue. The legal obligation to do this means that no other authority (as may otherwise be required under the Act) is needed for the disclosure.

Other requests   1.17

The payroll function frequently receives requests from third parties to provide information about an employee's earnings; there is no legal obligation upon the employer in such cases. This could, for example, be a request from a mortgage lender to confirm an individual's earnings. Such a disclosure would be against the data protection legislation unless the employee asked for the data to be disclosed.

Sensitive personal data   1.18

The *DPA 1998* does identify a number of categories of personal data that are different from other personal data. These are called 'sensitive personal data' in the Act. Two categories of sensitive data are likely to be processed by the payroll function:

- trade union membership; and

- an employee's mental or physical health.

It is common in organisations where a number of the employees are members of a trade union for the union subscriptions to be deducted from pay. Employment rights legislation does require the individual to authorise such a deduction in writing. It would be reasonable to assume that a written authorisation is also authority to pass the details to the trade union (ie when the subscriptions are paid over). However, it would be against the principles of data protection for a list of union members to be drawn up by the payroll department for distribution to line managers.

All employers must operate the Statutory Sick Pay scheme or an occupational one that is at least as good as the State scheme. For any such sick pay to be payable, it is necessary to know that the employee is sick. No matter how superficial the data contained in a notification of sickness, it is data about the physical or mental health of the employee and thus sensitive data. This subject is discussed in more detail in **CHAPTER 7**.

Outsourced processing   1.19

Many employers make use of a third party to provide some or all elements of the payroll function. This can vary from using a computer bureau to process the payroll to outsourcing all payroll functions. Under the *DPA 1998* the outside organisation is referred to as a 'data processor', whatever the degree of processing carried out. The employer is the 'data controller'. When a data controller uses a data processor, the responsibility for data protection remains with the data controller. In particular, the contract for the processing of the payroll must be in writing and must restrict the data processor to processing personal data only on the instructions of the data controller. The data controller must verify that the data processor used has the required level of technical and organisational security. These points arise from the seventh data protection principle and are discussed further in **CHAPTER 2**.

An important issue can arise here. Any obligations imposed on the data controller by law do not pass to the data processor. Thus the data processor cannot undertake this disclosure unless it has been written down as part of the contract between the data controller and the data processor. For example, the Child Support Agency has the powers to demand details about an employee and his or her earnings from an employer. Were such a request sent direct to the outsource organisation, they would not be able to provide the details unless there were written instructions from the data controller to respond to requests from the Child Support Agency.

The HR Perspective   1.20

The *DPA 1998* creates many responsibilities and liabilities for HR managers and practitioners. In most organisations (other than small businesses), it will be the HR department that is expected to manage and control employment records and advise line managers as to the implications of data protection legislation in the context of people management and the recording and use of employee information.

The issue of data protection should of course be viewed not only as an HR responsibility, but rather as an integral part of good general management. The aim should be to mainstream data protection into all the organisation's policies, procedures and practices in order to promote openness and transparency in the collection and use of personal information about employees, whilst at the same time ensuring security of the information held, the protection of confidential information and respect for employees' right to privacy. It will usually fall to HR to strive to achieve a coordinated approach to data protection, since the topic demands input and cooperation from people in a range of different posts throughout the organisation.

This matter should not, however, be left to chance. The employer should allocate clear responsibility for every aspect of data protection to a senior person within the organisation, ideally an HR director or senior HR manager who has sufficient authority to challenge any policies or practices that might risk being in breach of legislation. This senior manager should have sufficient authority to make and enforce decisions about data protection compliance. He or she should also be charged with ensuring that all the employer's policies and procedures are regularly checked against the Act and the recommendations contained in the Employment Practices Data Protection Code. An equally important responsibility will be to ensure that policies and procedures are consistently put into practice by all staff, especially by those whose jobs take them into contact with personal data held about employees (or customers, suppliers, etc).

It will be up to HR to make sure that all staff, and in particular line managers, fully understand their responsibilities under the Act and that those whose jobs take them into contact with personal data receive full training in data protection matters. In particular, employees who deal with personal data in the course of their jobs should be made aware that they can personally be held liable for a breach of the Act, for example if they use personal data for an illegitimate purpose or disclose it without the authority to do so. This could be in addition to the employer's liability to pay compensation to any employee who has suffered damage as a result of a breach of the Act.

HR managers will also be responsible in most organisations for handling requests from employees for access to data held about them. It will be important for HR to devise and implement a reliable and efficient system for handling such requests, having previously ensured that all locations where personal information is held are known and that all personal information, whether held manually or on computer, is readily accessible.

CHAPTERS 4 to 9 of this book (inclusive) explore the practical application of the Act, taking into account also the recommendations contained in the Employment Practices Data Protection Code. **CHAPTER 4** provides a general introduction to the Act in practice and this is followed by five other chapters that focus on specific issues of relevance to both HR and line managers. **CHAPTER 5** concentrates on data protection in recruitment and selection, ie the collection and retention of records about job applicants throughout the recruitment process, including the thorny issue of subject access to references. **CHAPTER 6** focuses on the management and control of employee records generally, including sensitive data, whilst **CHAPTER 7** deals with health records and issues such as medical examinations and drugs and alcohol screening. **CHAPTER 8** branches out to review the topics of equality and equal opportunities monitoring, tackling such matters as records created for the purposes of equal opportunities monitoring and dealing with equal pay questionnaires. Finally, **CHAPTER 9** concentrates on other aspects of monitoring, principally of employee communications and ensuring the information obtained from such monitoring is used lawfully. This latter chapter touches also on the implications of the *Telecommunications (Lawful Business Practice) (Interception of Communications) Regulations 2000 (SI 2000 No 2699)* and the *Human Rights Act 1998*.

Definitions 1.21

The *DPA 1998* applies to personal data only. Company names on their own are not caught. Commercial data such as formulae are not caught. Nor is any other data except to the extent it relates to 'living individual'. Most HR data of course is personal data.

What manual data is caught? 1.22

The *DPA 1998* applied data protection to manual files for the first time. However, in a decision in the *Durant v Financial Services Authority [2003] EWCA Civ 1746* case, the Court of Appeal took the view that the Act intended to cover manual files 'only if they are of sufficient sophistication to provide the same or similar ready accessibility as a computerised filing system'.

It is the view of the Information Commissioner that most manual files are outside the *Data Protection Act* following the *Durant v FSA* decision.

Any manual filing system is one,

> 'which, for example, requires the searcher to leaf through files to see what and whether information qualifying as personal data of the person who has the made the request [for access to his personal data] is to be found there, would bear no resemblance to a computerised search.'

It would not, therefore, qualify as a relevant filing system.

The judgment concluded that:

> 'a "relevant filing system" for the purposes of the Act, is limited to a system:

1 in which the files forming part of it are structured or referenced in such a way as to clearly indicate at the outset of the search whether specific information capable of amounting to personal data of an individual requesting it under *section 7* is held within the system and, if so, in which file or files it is held; and

2 which has, as part of its own structure or referencing mechanism, a sufficiently sophisticated and detailed means of readily indicating whether and where in an individual file or files specific criteria or information about the applicant can be readily located.'

The judgment includes some helpful statements as to the effect of this interpretation as follows which are quoted in February 2002 guidance on the Case by the Information Commissioner:

- 'the protection given by the legislation is for the privacy of personal data, not documents';

- 'if the [DPA] statutory scheme [for the handling of manual personal data] is to have any sensible and practical effect, it can only be in the context of filing systems that enable identification of relevant information with a minimum of time and costs, through clear referencing mechanisms within any filing system potentially containing personal data...';

- 'to qualify [as a relevant filing system] under ... the Act ... requires ... a file to which [a] search [for personal data] leads to be so structured and/or indexed as to enable easy location within it or any sub-files of specific information about the data subject that he has requested'; and

- '... it is only to the extent that manual filing systems are broadly equivalent to computerised systems in ready accessibility to ... personal data that they are within the system of data protection'.

In the Information Commissioner's view it follows, therefore, that when a subject access request is received for information held in manual form (other than information contained in an 'accessible record'), the statutory right to be given access to personal data will only apply if the filing system is structured as a 'relevant filing system'. That is to say, the filing system is structured in such a way as to allow the recipient of the request to either:

(a)   know that there is a system in place which will allow the retrieval of file(s) in the name of an individual (if such file(s) exists); and

(b)   know that the file(s) will contain the category of personal data requested (if such data exists);

or:

(i)   know that there is a system in place which will allow the retrieval of file(s) covering topics about individuals (eg personnel type topics such as leave, sick notes, contracts etc); and

(ii)   know that the file(s) are indexed or structured to allow the retrieval of information about a specific individual (if such information exists) (eg the topic file is subdivided in alphabetical order of individuals' names).

Where manual files fall within the definition of 'relevant filing system', the content will either be so sub-divided as to allow the searcher to go straight to the correct category and retrieve the information requested without a manual search, or will be so indexed as to allow a searcher to go directly to the relevant page(s).

Example

A set of legal files containing files divided into sections for legal aid, pleadings, orders, correspondence by year, instructions to counsel and counsel's advice, will not be a relevant filing system because the divisions/referencing do not assist a searcher in retrieving the required personal information without the need to leaf through the file contents.

It is important to note that the *Freedom of Information Act 2000* (*FOIA 2000*) will, in 2005, amend the *DPA 1998* to expand the definition of 'data'. As a result of the expanded definition, public sector bodies caught by *FOIA 2000* must ensure that the personal data they hold (including unstructured manual personal data *except* unstructured manual personnel records) must be accurate, up to date and accessible under *DPA 1998, section 7*. They should also note that the compensation and rectification provisions of the *DPA 1998* will apply in respect of such data although so far as subject access fees are concerned, the charges under *FOIA 2000* will apply.

Where information is filed in a system using individuals' names as file names, the system may not qualify as a relevant filing system if the indexing, referencing, and/or sub-division is structured otherwise than to allow the retrieval of personal data without leafing through the file.

A filing system containing files about individuals, or topics about individuals, where the content of each file is structured purely in chronological order *will not be a relevant filing system* as the files are not appropriately structured, indexed, and/or divided or referenced to allow the retrieval of personal data without leafing through the file.

Personnel files and other manual files using individuals' names or unique identifiers as the file names, which are sub-divided or indexed to allow retrieval of personal data without a manual search (such as sickness, absence, contact details, etc), are likely to be held in a 'relevant filing system' for the purposes of the *DPA 1998*. However, following the *Durant* judgment it is likely that *very few manual files will be covered by the provisions of the DPA 1998*. Most information about individuals held in manual form does not, therefore, fall within the data protection regime.

Following the *Durant* case and the February 2004 guidance of the Information Commissioner on this, the guidance on employment in the data protection Code relating to that area will have to be revised in 2004. The case makes it easier for those involved with HR to argue that manual files are outside the *DPA 1998* and thus helps reduce the regulatory burden.

CCTV systems

1.23

The *DPA 1998* applies to CCTV used in the workplace. **CHAPTER 9** examines employee monitoring and Part 3 of the data protection code on employment includes sections on CCTV. In addition there is a 30-page data protection Code of Practice on CCTV generally.

In the 2004 Guidance on CCTV, the Information Commissioner concluded, following *Durant v Financial Services Authority [2003] EWCA Civ 1746*, that those with a basic CCTV system would probably no longer be covered by the Act.

This depends on what happens in practice. For example, small retailers who:

- only have a couple cameras;

- cannot move them remotely;

- just record on video tape whatever the cameras pick up; and

- only give the recorded images to the police to investigate an incident in their shop;

would not be covered.

Shopkeepers need to make sure that they do not use the images for their own purposes, such as checking whether a member of staff is doing their job properly. If CCTV was used for such a purpose, the employee would be the focus of attention and the employer would be trying to learn things about him or her, so the use would then be covered by the *DPA 1998*. Those now outside the Act in relation to CCTV who were within it before are advised in the guidance:

> 'If you have already notified the Information Commissioner of your CCTV activities you will not have to renew this when it is due. Just let us know when you get your renewal reminder.'

Data controller

1.24

A data controller is the person (ie in most cases a company) who controls data – in most cases relevant here, the employer. Several subsidiaries in a group may need individually to notify their holding of personal data. Take advice in cases of doubt.

Individual rights

1.25

There are seven individual rights under the Act:

- right of access to personal data;

- right to prevent processing likely to cause damage or distress;

- right to prevent processing for purposes of direct marketing;

- rights in relation to automated decision taking;

- rights of data subjects in relation to exempt manual data;

- right to seek rectification, blocking, erasure and destruction of inaccurate data; and

- right to make a request for assessment – see **1.8** above. Such requests are made to the Information Commissioner's Office.

Direct marketing is outside the scope of this book. Automated decision taking is relevant if decisions are taken such as to hire, sack or promote an employee solely on the basis of data generated by automated methods such as how fast he or she scans goods over a supermarket checkout till etc.

Employees have a right to have inaccurate data held about them removed. If there is a dispute and the employer is sure the data is accurate then both the employer's and the employee's views can be kept on the record.

Exemptions 1.26

There are several exemptions from the Act, some of which apply to all of its provisions and some just to certain of them. They are too numerous to list here but are usefully summarised in the Information Commissioner's Introduction to the DPA, part 5. Many are not relevant to HR in any event.

Exemptions include those relating to national security (*section 28*) and crime and taxation (*section 29*) Sometimes employers are approached by the police asking to be given data about employees. The natural inclination of most HR officers is to cooperate with the police; however it is better to take legal advice on the legality of the approach in case the employee's rights under the *DPA 1998* are breached and the employer is held liable. There are also exemptions for health and social work and regulatory activities purposes.

Some disclosures made by law or because of legal proceedings (*section 35(2)*) also apply. Domestic purposes is a further exemption – thus someone's personal Christmas card list held on his or her home computer is outside the Act, whereas their Christmas card list on the firm's computer for clients' cards is caught.

References exemption 1.27

Those working in the HR field should also bear in mind *DPA 1998, Schedule 7*. Personal data which consist of a confidential reference given, or to be given, by the data controller for specified purposes (education, training or employment, appointment to office or provision of any service) are exempt from subject access.

This exemption is not available to the data controller who receives such references.

The Information Commissioner explains this as follows:

'Where company A provides an employment reference concerning one of its employees to company B, if the employee makes a subject access request to company A, the reference will be exempt from the disclosure. If the employee makes the request to company B, the reference is not automatically exempt from disclosure and the usual subject access rules apply.'

(See **CHAPTER 4**.)

Right of Subject Access   1.28

The *DPA 1998, section 7* gives individuals a right of access to their personal data. This means they can request it by written notice to the data controller. A fee usually up to £10 must be paid. Where this is done an individual is entitled to be told by the data controller whether they or someone else on their behalf is processing his or her personal data, and if so, to be given a description of:

- the personal data;
- the purposes for which they are being processed; and
- those to whom they are or may be disclosed.

The individual is also entitled to have communicated to him or her, in an intelligible form, all the information which forms any such personal data. This information must be supplied in permanent form by way of a copy, except where the supply of a copy in permanent form is not possible or would involve disproportionate effort, or the data subject agrees otherwise.

In its guidance the Information Commissioner states:

'"Disproportionate effort" is not defined in the Act. Accordingly, it will be a question of fact in each case as to whether the supply of information in permanent form amounts to disproportionate effort. Matters to be taken into account by the Commissioner may be the cost of provision of the information, the length of time it may take to provide the information, how difficult or otherwise it may be for the data controller to provide the information and also the size of the organisation of which the request has been made. Such matters will always be balanced against the effect on the data subject.'

Subject access and emails   1.29

There is a separate set of Information Commissioner's guidance notes on subject access rights to information contained in emails. This guidance looks at what effort is required and when even a 'deleted' email may have to be retrieved from a hard drive by an IT expert in response to a subject access request.

Third party data   1.30

Employers should be very cautious about disclosing third party data. If a husband makes a request he must not be given information about his wife, for example. If a request is made and the data to be disclosed will reveal not only information about the data subject but also another person, that other information may have to be obscured – crossed out ('redacted' is the word lawyers use for this). There is guidance on 'Subject access and Third Party Data' on the Information Commissioner's web site.

Summary   1.31

This chapter has examined the principal data protection rights which exist under the *Data Protection Act 1998*. It has examined the consequences of breach of the Act including fines and the criminal offences which can be committed where the rules are broken. It has shown that those who control personal data must notify/register with the Information Commissioner's office and should comply with the important individual rights of data subjects under the legislation, including the right of an individual to 'subject access'. The next chapter examines the eight data protection principles themselves.

Further Reading   1.32

● Tolley's *Data Protection Handbook* (3rd edition, 2004) has an A–Z format which deals with many of the issues addressed in this chapter in more detail.

● The web site of the Information Commissioner contains copies of all the guidance mentioned in this chapter – www.informationcommissioner.gov.uk

● Those exporting data to the US where the recipient is registered under the Safe Harbor Agreement can find further information at www.export.gov./safeharbor

Chapter 2
The Data Protection
Principles

Introduction

The *Data Protection Act 1998* (*DPA 1998*, or 'the Act') requires that businesses holding personal data must follow eight data protection principles. How they apply in the HR area is summarised in the Data Protection Office's Code of Practice in the employment area and examined in more detail in **CHAPTER 5** (Part 1 of the code – recruitment), **CHAPTER 6** (Part 2 of the Code – records) and Chapter 7 (health records – Part 2 and also Part 4 of the Code on medical records). **CHAPTERS 9** and **10** look at equal opportunity monitoring and employee monitoring respectively, which are the subject of Part 3 of the Code of Practice. This chapter seeks to provide a general overview of the eight principles.

This chapter examines the data protection principles under the Act and in particular the obligations which they impose on data controllers and data processors. As under the *DPA 1984*, the Act imposes general and, in some cases fairly loosely worded, obligations on those handling data as to how they obtain and use it. *DPA 1998, section 4(4)* provides that it is the duty of the data controller to comply with the data protection principles in relation to all personal data with respect to which he or she is the data controller. This applies to the data controller and not the data processor. This is subject to *section 26*, which exempts data which is covered by an exemption. Some data is entirely exempt and some is exempt from certain of the obligations only. The exemptions are in *Part IV* of the Act.

The data protection principles are set out in *DPA 1998, Schedule 1*, which also elaborates on what the principles mean. This is the heart of the Act.

The First Principle: Fair and Lawful Processing

2.2

The first principle provides:

'1. Personal data shall be processed fairly and lawfully and, in particular, shall not be processed unless—

(a) at least one of the conditions in Schedule 2 is met, and

(b) in the case of sensitive personal data, at least one of the conditions in Schedule 3 is also met.'

Schedule 1, Part II provides that regard should be paid to the method by which the data are obtained, including whether any person from whom they are obtained is deceived or misled as to the purpose(s) for which they are to be processed. Data controllers therefore have to be ever vigilant to ensure they do not deceive data subjects about the use to which their data will be put. Data is deemed to be fairly obtained if they consist of information obtained from a person who is authorised by a law (enactment) to supply it, or from an international obligation.

Data that are obtained from the data subject are not fairly obtained *unless* the data controller ensures 'so far as practicable that the data subject has, or is provided with, or has made readily available to him' information specified in *DPA 1998, Schedule 1, para 3.*

In order for the obtaining of information from data subject to be fair, the following details should be supplied:

- the identity of data controller;

- the identity of any representative appointed for the purposes of the Act, if any, by that data controller;

- the purpose or purposes for which the data are intended to be processed; and

- any further information which is necessary, having regard to the specific circumstances in which the data are to be processed to enable the processing in respect of the data subject to be fair.

Where the data is obtained other than from the data subject it must be provided as soon as is reasonably practicable before the relevant time – the time the data is first processed. The 'relevant time' is when data is disclosed to that third party within the time envisaged. If the data controller becomes aware that the data will not be disclosed in that period of time then the relevant time is the time when the data controller becomes aware of this delay or should have become aware of it, or at the latest at the end of the reasonable period after which the data is to be disclosed to a third party.

The Second Principle: Purposes   2.3

The second principle provides:

> 'Personal data shall be obtained only for use for one or more specified and lawful purposes, and shall not be further processed in any manner incompatible with that purpose or those purposes.'

The information about the purposes to which the data will be put can be notified to the data subject by way of a notice or in a notification to the Commissioner under *Part III* of the Act (on registration etc – see **CHAPTER 3**). In deciding whether a disclosure of personal data is compatible with the purpose or purposes for which they were obtained, regard is paid to the purpose or purposes for which the personal data are intended to be processed by any person to whom they are disclosed. For example, a company may obtain data from mail order customers so it can supply goods, market them every year with its catalogue, and send out details of special offers throughout the year. The company may also sell on its list to non-competitors. Customers therefore need to be informed of all the purposes for which the data may be used.

Recital 278 of the Data Protection Directive requires that the purposes for which the data are held must be: 'explicit and legitimate and must be determined at the time of collection of the data.'

The Third Principle: Adequate, Relevant and Not Excessive Data   2.4

The third principle provides:

> 'Personal data shall be adequate, relevant and not excessive in relation to the purpose or purposes for which they are processed.'

Unlike the other principles, there is no explanation of this provision in *Schedule 1, Part II*. It means data controllers must make sure that they obtain enough data, but not too much, and nothing that is irrelevant. Data controllers need to ascertain the minimum amount of information which they require in order to carry out the purpose for which the data is to be held. In *Runnymede Borough Council CCRO and Others v The Data Protection Commissioner (November 1990) (unreported)*, the Data Protection Tribunal, under the 1984 Act (which contains similar provisions), held that where information is required in relation to certain individuals, that does not mean it is reasonable to hold such additional data in relation to *all* individuals. As the Commissioner states in the *Guidelines* under the 1984 Act (November 1994 issue), page 62:

> 'Where a data user holds an item of information on all individuals which will be used or useful only in relation to some of them, the information is likely to be excessive and irrelevant in relation to those individuals in respect of whom it will not be used or useful and should not be held in those cases. It is not acceptable to hold information on the basis that it might possibly be useful in the future without a view of how it will be used. This is to be distinguished from holding information in the case of a particular foreseeable contingency which may never occur, for example, where a data user holds blood groups of employees engaged in hazardous occupations.'

Some of the factors the Commissioner considered under the 1994 Act in relation to this principle, where data is held for all but not *required* for all data subjects, are:

- the number of individuals on whom it is held;
- the number of individuals for whom it is used;

- the nature of that item of personal data;

- the length of time for which it is held;

- the way it was obtained;

- the possible consequences for individuals of its holding or erasure;

- the way in which it is used; and

- the purpose for which it is held.

Regard is had to Codes of Practice under the current law for particular industries and the Commissioner has taken an objective view on whether information is relevant. This is likely to continue under the new law.

The Fourth Principle: Accurate and Up to Date   2.5

The fourth principle provides:

'Personal data shall be accurate and, where necessary, kept up to date.'

Whether data is incorrect or misleading is a matter of fact in each case. Data is not treated as inaccurate for these purposes where the data subject supplied the inaccurate information or a third party did so where the data controller has taken reasonable steps to ensure the accuracy of the data. Where the data subject tells the data controller of the data subject's view that the data are inaccurate, then the data controller must put a note with the data which says so.

In deciding what action to take, the Commissioner will examine whether the data controller has taken the necessary steps to ensure inaccuracies do not occur in the data. Factors include:

- The significance of the inaccuracy. Has it caused or is it likely to cause damage or distress to the data subject?

- The source from which the inaccurate information was obtained. Was it reasonable for the data user to rely on information from that source?

- Any steps taken to verify the information. Did the data user attempt to check its accuracy with another source? Would it has been reasonable to ask the data subject, either at the time of collection or at another convenient opportunity, whether the information was accurate?

- The procedures for data entry and for ensuring that the system itself does not introduce inaccuracies into the data.

- The procedures followed by the data user when the inaccuracy came to light. Were the data corrected as soon as the inaccuracy became apparent? Was the correction passed on to any third parties to whom the inaccurate data may already have been disclosed? Did the inaccuracy have any other consequences in the period before it was corrected? If so, what has the data user done about those consequences?

The obligation to keep data up to date only applies where necessary. It is sensible for mail order companies, for example when they send mailings to customers, to include a slip or notice for customers to send in their change of address. This is normal practice. In the HR area, a note to employees once a year containing their current contact details asking them to confirm that they are up to date is regarded as good practice by many British companies. If the data is supposed to be some sort of a historical record only then updating would defeat the object of the exercise. The Commissioner will look at whether there is any record kept of the date when the information was recorded or last updated. He will also examine whether those involved will be aware or made aware that the data does not necessarily reflect the current position. Whether the data controller takes steps at regular intervals to update data and whether those steps are adequate are also examined when the Commissioner considers compliance with this principle. Finally relevant is whether the fact that data may be out of date is likely to cause damage or distress to the data subject.

The Fifth Principle: Data not to be Kept Longer than Purposes Require 2.6

The fifth principle provides:

> 'Personal data processed for any purpose or purposes shall not be kept for longer than is necessary for that purpose or those purposes.'

There is no elaboration on this principle in the *DPA 1998, Schedule 1, Part II*. The wording, however, is the same as in the sixth principle of the 1984 Act so does not change the law. Under the 1984 Act, and thus under the old law, there was an obligation to review data regularly and delete what was no longer required. The Commissioner recommended that users have a systematic policy of data deletion. There could be a standard life for particular categories of data.

The length over which information and data should be kept is a difficult and important subject. The Institute of Chartered Secretaries and Administrators has issued guidance on the topic but all companies should take advice from their solicitors. Some types of records must be held for very long periods. If there is fraud, for example, the Inland Revenue can go back to records dating back for longer than the normal six-year period. Where documents are signed as a deed, there is a twelve-year limitation period after which legal actions cannot be brought; therefore the documents in this category must be held for at least this period. There are different rules for information such as health and safety records and employee records generally. If the data has only a short-term value to the data controller then it may be right for the data to be deleted after a matter of days or months. The important point is that the data controller must analyse the situation and decide what is an appropriate period and what is not in each case.

The Commissioner has always recognised that even where the relationship between the data subject and the data controller has come to an end there are good reasons for retaining data, for example because a legal action may be mounted thereafter. However only information relevant to the claim should be kept and the rest should be destroyed. Once the possibility of a claim has passed then the data should be deleted unless there is another good reason why it should be retained. Remember that although the *Limitation Act 1980* period of contract actions is six years from when the contract was made in tort for actions such as negligence, it can be much later and time may run from the time of the damage occurring. Therefore retention policies should be assessed on the basis of the longest running time period that could apply to that particular data.

The Sixth Principle: Data Processed in accordance with Data Subjects' Rights   2.7

The sixth principle provides:

> 'Personal data shall be processed in accordance with the rights of data subjects under this Act.'

This provision is contravened if, but only if, a person contravenes:

- *DPA 1998, section 7* by failing to supply information which has been duly requested in accordance with that section;

- *sections 9* or *10* by failing to comply with a notice duly given under that section; or

- *section 13* (automated decision making).

These provisions are considered later in this book.

The Seventh Principle: Measures to Stop Loss – Security Measures   2.8

The seventh principle provides:

> 'Appropriate technical and organisational measures shall be taken against unauthorised or unlawful processing of personal data and against accidental loss or destruction of, or damage to, personal data.'

This principle means that those holding data must take steps to stop it being unlawfully processed. They should try to stop hackers getting into their system and other breaches of their security measures. *DPA 1998, Schedule 1, Part II* provides that regard is had to the state of technological development and the cost of implementing measures. A large company with lots of highly secret data would be expected to have more expensive protective measures in place than a one-man garage in a back street with a set of index cards. However even a local newsagent must take measures to ensure its computer screens and paper records with details of the names and home addresses of data subjects cannot be seen by other customers (this led to censure by the Commissioner under the 1984 Act in an earlier case involving visibility of a computer screen by other customers).

Having regard to technical and costs factors, the data controller must ensure a level of security which is appropriate to the data. This should be based on the likelihood of unauthorised or unlawful processing or accidental loss; destruction or damage as in the seventh principle; and the nature of the data to be protected. Data controllers must also take reasonable steps to ensure that staff who have access to the personal data are reliable. For example, it would be sensible to take up references before recruiting anyone and check whether they have a police record.

The following points should be checked:

- Is proper weight given to the discretion and integrity of staff when they are being considered for employment or promotion, or for a move to an area where they will have access to personal data?

- Are the staff aware of their responsibilities? Have they been given adequate training and is their knowledge kept up to date?

- Do disciplinary rules and procedures take account of the Act's requirements and are they enforced?

- If an employee is found to be unreliable, is their authority to access personal data immediately withdrawn?

Much processing is done by a data processor rather than the data controller. Where the processing is carried out by a data processor on behalf of a data controller then the data controller must, in order to comply with the seventh principle, choose a data processor who provides sufficient guarantees in respect of the technical and organisational security measures governing the processing to be carried out and take reasonable steps to ensure compliance with those measures. Therefore there remain duties on the data controller. He or she cannot simply blame the data processor, though could escape liability for breach of the seventh principle if it can be shown that the controller has check-on measures in place at the processor. Indeed *Schedule 1, para 13* provides that where a data processor is entrusted with the processing, the data controller is not to be regarded as complying with the seventh principle unless:

- the processing is carried out under a written contract under which the data processor is to act only on instructions from the data controller; and

- the contract requires the data processor to comply with obligations equivalent to those imposed on a data controller by the seventh principle.

This provision has implications for those involved in the drafting of contracts in this field. First there must be a written contract. Secondly it must require the data processor to act on behalf of the data controller in these matters and the contract should provide that the data processor complies with the seventh principle. Those with contracts with data processors should revise them now to ascertain whether they need alteration to ensure compliance with this provision.

Data controllers might like to formulate a survey or questionnaire to be sent to prospective data processors asking them questions such as these and then decide who wins a tender based in part on the security measures that they use. Other questions might be about what precautions they have taken against burglary, fire or natural disaster, and whether casual passers-by can read data from screens or print-outs. Check always on back-up copies and whether they are stored off site.

The following questions should be asked:

- Are passwords known only to authorised persons and are passwords frequently changed?

- Does a password allow one access to all parts of a system or just to the personal data with which the employee is concerned? Clearly it is better if there is limited access only, though whether this is possible or practicable depends on the nature of the data controller/processor and the data itself.

- Is the system able to check that the data are valid and does it produce back-up copies? Also check whether full use is made of the facilities on the system. It is not enough that the system can produce back-up copies if no one bothers to make them.

- Will the system will keep an audit trail so that all access to personal data can be logged and traced back to an individual?

Other measures include whether there is a procedure for cleaning tapes and disks before they are re-used or whether they are simply over-written. It is safer and better to clean rather than overwrite. If they are not cleaned there may be a risk, which should be assessed, that the data may reach someone who is not authorised to have access to it. This becomes even more important under the *DPA 1998*, which covers manually stored data.

Companies also need to assess their waste disposal arrangements. News stories appear on a regular basis about particular building societies or banks whose waste contractors have for whatever reason dumped confidential papers in a street or at a tip when they should have been shredded or disposed of in some other more confidential way. The data controller should look carefully at the contractual conditions it has with waste disposal companies and ensure that they are strong and well drafted. It is unlikely to be sufficient to contract with no written conditions or on the contractor's standard conditions of supply. The standard conditions of supply will favour the contractor and may exclude most liability or severely limit it. It is much better for the data controller to have a clear contract with the waste disposal organisation which addresses data protection issues. Similarly if this function is outsourced under an outsourcing or facilities management ('FM') agreement, ensure that the contract for such outsourcing addresses these issues and imposes on the outsourcing company obligations in this field. In 2004 the British Standards Institution issued a warning about allowing computer software companies working for businesses to run tests on 'live payroll data' which might involve disclosure in breach of the Act. Clauses on data protection law are quite common in FM contracts. The Commissioner believes that often shredding is the best means of disposing of documents which contain personal data.

A very important security issue where personal data is given over the telephone is the steps taken to ensure that the identity of the caller is correct. Asking them questions about their date of birth and mother's maiden name or requiring them to give a particular password may suffice; however there may be some types of data so secret that a telephone enquiry is not allowed at all. Staff need a lot of education in this field. They should not assume that it is acceptable for a husband to be given information about his wife. They may be estranged or simply want to keep their financial affairs separate. A jealous husband might call the office to find out if his wife is in work (when she has taken a day's holiday to spend with another man). Would the office/HR department disclose that she was not there?

It is also wise to have one named individual who is responsible for security in this area otherwise employees have a tendency to 'pass the buck'. Many larger companies have a data protection manager or officer, as mentioned in **CHAPTER 1**. They must be allocated sufficient funds to carry out their functions and allowed enough time to do so considering the other work which they may be required to do. That person may perform some of the education of staff in this field. Data protection law is not very well known in the UK despite the efforts of the Data Protection Commissioners over the years. Staff, for example, should be told that although they may have a right to check data on an individual for business purposes, they cannot look up the name of someone who happens to live down their road or whose wife works with their spouse. As a further example, they cannot help out a friend who is running an investigation bureau by checking information on the computer at work.

Some staff now work on data at home with the increase in teleworking. In many ways, jobs relating to processing and use of personal data are very well adapted to new ways of working. However the employer needs to ensure there is sufficient security in place as well. If the employee is working at the kitchen table with people coming in and out all day and able to read screens, then home working for certain particularly sensitive data may not be permissible. Staff homes may need to be checked for these purposes and perhaps the staff made to work at a local 'telecottage' if there is one, or set aside a room for their work at home. Locks and other security measures should also be checked at the employee's home.

There should also be a full investigation of security breaches. Where there is a contract with a data processor, the contract should make it clear which of the parties is responsible for security of the data. In organising training for staff or externally the Commissioner has said:

> 'Data users should also ensure that their contracts with computer suppliers and maintenance organisations, with regard to the supply and maintenance

of equipment and development of programmes, contain adequate safeguards regarding access to personal data by such organisations and their
subsequent dealing with it.'

Data controllers need to assess the harm which may be caused by particular security breaches. In some cases very little harm will be caused and in others considerable damage will result: security measures taken should reflect these
consequences.

The Eighth Principle: Transfer of Data Abroad   2.9

The eighth principle provides:

> 'Personal data shall not be transferred to a country or territory outside
> the European Economic Area unless that country or territory ensures an
> adequate level of protection for the rights and freedoms of data subjects
> in relation to the processing of personal data.'

This was also discussed in **CHAPTER 1**, to which reference should be made. The
DPA 1998, Schedule 1, para 14 provides that protection must be adequate, having
regard in particular to the nature of the data; the country or origin of the information contained in the data; the final destination; the purposes for which and
period during which the data are intended to be processed; the law in force in the
country in question; international obligations of that country; any relevant codes
of conduct or other rules in force in that country; and security measures taken in
respect of the data in that country.

Schedule 4   2.10

The eighth principle does not apply to data covered by *Schedule 4*. These broad
and important exclusions are as follows:

- The data subject has given consent to the transfer. It is not clear if this can
  be express consent or consent by default. Is it enough to write: 'By supplying this information you consent to its being processed in the USA. If you
  object tick the box below'?

- There is a contract between the data subject and data controller and to perform that contract the export of the data is necessary. This also applies
  where the transfer is necessary for the taking of steps at the request of the
  data subject with a view to his entering into a contract with the data controller.

- The transfer is necessary to conclude a contract, between the data controller
  and someone other than the data subject, which the data subject has asked
  the data controller to enter into or which is in the interests of the data subject – this is rather broad wording. There is also an exception where the
  transfer is necessary for the performance of such a contract.

- The transfer is necessary for reasons of substantial public interest. The Secretary of State is given powers to formulate orders which set out what may fall within this category.

- The transfer is necessary for the purpose, or in connection with, any legal proceedings including prospective legal proceedings, for the purpose of obtaining legal advice or otherwise necessary for the purposes of establishing, exercising or defending legal rights.

- The transfer is necessary to protect the vital interests of the data subject.

- The transfer is of part of the personal data on a public register and any conditions subject to which the register is open to inspection are complied with by any person to whom the data are or may be disclosed after the transfer.

- The transfer is made on terms which are of a kind approved by the Commissioner as ensuring adequate safeguards for the rights and freedoms of data subjects.

- The transfer has been authorised by the Commissioner as being made in such a manner as to ensure adequate safeguards for the rights and freedoms of data subjects.

As discussed in **CHAPTER 1**, the European Commission has begun approving countries outside the EEA for export, and model agreements issued by the Commission can be signed in other cases.

Chapter 3
Notification

Introduction 3.1

The Information Commissioner maintains a public register of data controllers. Each register entry includes the name and address of the data controller and a general description of the processing of personal data that the data controller undertakes. For an entry to be made, the data controller must notify the Information Commissioner. This is a requirement of the *Data Protection Act 1998* (*DPA 1998*, or 'the Act'), unless the data controller is exempt. Failure to notify is a criminal offence.

Only one register entry is held for each data controller. It follows that in order that the register entry is complete, the notification must be complete.

Notification lasts for one year and must be renewed each year (unless the data controller no longer has to notify). There is a fee for notification and renewal, currently £35.00 (VAT nil).

As the register is a public document, individuals can consult it to see what processing a data controller does with personal data. It is available online through the Information Commissioner's web site at www.informationcommissioner.gov.uk by following the quick link to 'Public Register of Data Controllers'.

Changes from the 1984 Act 3.2

Under the *Data Protection Act 1984* there was a similar process to notification called registration, which lasted three years. This has been replaced with the process of notification to the Information Commissioner so that an entry can be made on the register. Notification lasts for just one year and there can be only one register entry for each data controller. These two terms – 'registration' and 'notification' – are often used for the requirement under the current legislation to notify. Indeed, the Information Commissioner's web site uses both terms to refer to notification.

Under the old Act, computer bureaux were required to register. Under the current Act, computer bureaux, which are now covered by a wider classification of data processors, do not have to notify. If any part of an organisation's HR and payroll functions are outsourced to third parties, those suppliers or data processors do not need to notify the processing of their clients' personal data. This stems from the concept of the data controller being fully in control of all the processing of the personal data that he or she chooses to gather and process for whatever purpose.

The following points apply:

- Under notification, register entries contain a description of the processing of personal data in very general terms. The detailed coding system of the old 1984 Act no longer exists.

- Sources of the personal data that the data controller processes no longer need to be described. The registration of disclosures has been replaced by the requirement to notify about recipients.

- Transfers of personal data outside the European Economic Area must be described in the notification.

- The notification must contain a statement about the data controller's security measures.

- The notification does not need to give an address for the receipt of data subject access requests.

- Some exemptions from notification are provided under the current legislation but the data controller may choose to notify anyway.

- Head teachers and governing bodies of schools may notify jointly in the name of their school rather than separately.

What Needs to be Notified?   3.3

The notification must contain details of:

- the data controller (see **3.4**);

- the purpose or purposes for which data are processed (see **3.5**);

- recipients of the data (see **3.8**);

- details of transfers outside the European Economic Area (see **3.9**); and

- a statement about the data controller's security measures (see **3.10**).

Data controller   3.4

The details required here are the name and address of the data controller. The correct legal title of the organisation must be given. In the case of limited companies, including public limited companies and limited liability companies, it must be the full name of the company and not any trading name that may be used. Although these are often the same, trading or business names are governed by the *Business Names Act 1985* and company names by the *Companies Act 1981*. For partnerships, the trading name should be given.

In the case of schools, the notification can be in the name of the school and this will cover both the headteacher and the board of governors.

A group of companies must ensure that each company in the group notifies. There cannot be a single notification for the group as a whole. In practice, it is quite likely that several companies within a group carry out the same or very similar trade and thus will have very similar notifications.

Purposes   3.5

The Information Commissioner's Office provides a list of standard purposes and purpose descriptions for use on the register of data controllers. It is stated that wherever possible these purposes must be used and for that reason, the list is reproduced below.

A: The standard business purposes

Staff administration

Appointments or removals, pay, discipline, superannuation work management or other personnel matters in relation to the staff of the data controller.

Advertising, marketing and public relations

Advertising or marketing the data controller's own business, activity, goods or services and promoting public relations in connection with that business or activity or those goods or services.

Accounts and records

Keeping accounts relating to any business or other activity carried on by the data controller, or deciding whether to accept any person as a customer or supplier, or keeping records of purchases, sales or other transactions for the purpose of ensuring that the requisite payments and deliveries are made or services provided by him or to him in respect of those transactions, or for the purpose of making financial or management forecasts to assist him in the conduct of any such business or activity.

B: The other purposes

Accounting and auditing

The provision of accounting and related services; the provision of an audit where such an audit is required by statute.

(cont'd)

Administration of justice

Internal administration and management of courts of law or tribunals and discharge of court business.

Administration of membership records

The administration of membership records.

Advertising marketing and public relations for others

Public relations work, advertising and marketing, including host mailings for other organisations and list broking.

Assessment and collection of taxes and other revenue

Assessment and collection of taxes, duties, levies and other revenue. You will be asked to indicate the type of tax or other revenue concerned.

Benefits, grants and loans administration

The administration of welfare and other benefits. You will be asked to indicate the type(s) of benefit you are administering.

Canvassing political support amongst the electorate

The seeking and maintenance of support amongst the electorate by the data controller.

Constituency casework

The carrying out of casework on behalf of individual constituents by elected representatives.

Consultancy and advisory services

Giving advice or rendering professional services. The provision of services of an advisory, consultancy or intermediary nature. You will be asked to indicate the nature of the services which you provide.

Credit referencing

The provision of information relating to the financial status of individuals or organisations on behalf of other organisations. This purpose is for use by credit reference agencies, not for organisations who merely contact or use credit reference agencies.

Crime prevention and prosecution of offenders

Crime prevention and detection and the apprehension and prosecution of offenders. This includes the use of most CCTV systems which are used for this purpose.

Debt administration and factoring

The tracing of consumer and commercial debtors and the collection on behalf of creditors. The purchasing of consumer or trade debts, including rentals and instalment credit payments, from business.

Education

The provision of education or training as a primary function or as a business activity.

Fundraising

Fundraising in support of the objectives of the data controller.

Health administration and services

The provision and administration of patient care.

Information and databank administration

Maintenance of information or databanks as a reference tool or general resource. This includes catalogues, lists, directories and bibliographic databases.

(cont'd)

Insurance administration

The administration of life, health, pensions, property, motor and other insurance business. This applies only to insurance companies doing risk assessments, payment of claims and underwriting. Insurance consultants and intermediaries should use provision of financial services and advice.

Journalism and media

Processing by the data controller of any journalistic, literary or artistic material made or intended to be made available to the public or any section of the public.

Legal services

The provision of legal services, including advising and acting on behalf of clients.

Licensing and registration

The administration of licensing or maintenance of official registers.

Pastoral care

The administration of pastoral care by a vicar or other minister of religion.

Pensions administration

The administration of funded pensions or superannuation schemes. Data controllers using this purpose will usually be the trustees of pension funds.

Policing

The prevention and detection of crime; apprehension and prosecution of offenders; protection of life and property; maintenance of law and order; also rendering assistance to the public in accordance with force policies and procedures.

Private investigation

The provision on a commercial basis of investigatory services according to instructions given by clients.

Processing for not for profit organisations

Establishing or maintaining membership of or support for a body or association which is not established or conducted for profit, or providing or administering activities for individuals who are either members of the body or association or have regular contact with it.

Property management

The management and administration of land, property and residential property and the estate management of other organisations.

Provision of financial services and advice

The provision of services as an intermediary in respect of **any** financial transactions including mortgage and insurance broking.

Realising the objectives of a charitable organisation or voluntary body

The provision of goods and services in order to realise the objectives of the charity or voluntary body.

Research

Research in any field, including market, health, lifestyle, scientific or technical research. You will be asked to indicate the nature of the research undertaken.

Trading/sharing in personal information

The sale, hire, exchange or disclosure of personal data to third parties in return for goods/services/benefit.

A data controller can use his or her own words to describe a purpose for which he or she processes personal data, but only where none of the descriptions that are provided properly describe the purpose.

The list of purposes is divided into standard business purposes and other purposes. The reason for this distinction is that the standard business purposes are considered common across all businesses and therefore there is no need to notify those purposes. If a data controller needs to notify another purpose, these three purposes need not be notified but the data controller may choose to do so. See **3.21** below.

Data subjects   3.6

Data subjects are the individuals on whom the data controller holds information. The Information Commissioner's Office provides a set of standard descriptions of data subjects; this is set out in the box below.

By examining this part of the register, a member of the pubic can establish whether his or her personal data are likely to be processed by the data controller.

S100	Staff including volunteers, agents, temporary and casual workers
S101	Customers and clients
S102	Suppliers
S103	Members or supporters
S104	Complainants, correspondents and enquirers
S105	Relatives, guardians and associates of the data subject
S106	Advisers, consultants and other professional experts
S107	Patients
S108	Students and pupils
S109	Offenders and suspected offenders

Each description includes past or prospective data subjects as well as current ones. So, for example, S100 will include former employees and job applicants as well as current staff. In the case of deceased employees, the data protection legislation ceases to apply as only living individuals are covered by the Act.

Data classes   3.7

The list of data classes within the register entry specifies the type of personal data that are processed by the data controller. Again, the Information Commissioner's Office provides a list of standard descriptions of data classes.

C200 – Personal details

Included in this category are classes of data which identify the data subject and their personal characteristics. Examples are names, addresses, contact details, age, sex, date of birth, physical descriptions, identifiers issued by public bodies, eg National Insurance number.

C201 – Family, lifestyle and social circumstances

Included in this category are any matters relating to the family of the data subject and the data subject's lifestyle and social circumstances. Examples are details about current marriage and partnerships and marital history, details of family and other household members, habits, housing, travel details, leisure activities, membership of charitable or voluntary organisations.

C202 – Education and training details

Included in this category are any matters which relate to the education and any professional training of the data subject. Examples are academic records, qualifications, skills, training records, professional expertise, student and pupil records.

C203 – Employment details

Included in this category are any matters relating to the employment of the data subject. Examples are employment and career history, recruitment and termination details, attendance record, health and safety records, performance appraisals, training records, security records.

C204 – Financial details

Included in this category are any matters relating to the financial affairs of the data subject. Examples are income, salary, assets and investments, payments, creditworthiness, loans, benefits, grants, insurance details, pension information.

C205 – Goods or services provided

Included in this category are classes of data relating to goods and services which have been provided. Examples are details of the goods or services supplied, licences issued, agreements and contracts.

The examples given are not an exhaustive list of what may be included in each category.

The following eight classes of personal data are classified as sensitive personal data by the Act. Any processing of any of these classes of data must be specified in the notification.

C206	Racial or ethnic origin
C207	Political opinions
C208	Religious or other beliefs of a similar nature
C209	Trade union membership
C210	Physical or mental health or condition
C211	Sexual life
C212	Offences (including alleged offences)
C213	Criminal proceedings, outcomes and sentences

Recipients of the data   3.8

Recipients are individuals or organisations to whom the data controller intends to or may wish to disclose personal data. It does not include any person to whom the data controller may be required by law to disclose in any particular case, for example if required by the police under a warrant. Again, the Information Commissioner's Office provides a standard classification of recipients, which is reproduced below. Some examples of typical HR and payroll functions that have recipients in the different classifications are also given.

R400	Data subjects themselves
R401	Relatives, guardians or other persons associated with the data subject. If you hold details of someone to contact in case of an emergency, then you will need this class of recipient
R402	Current, past or prospective employers of the data subject. For example, giving references for former employees
R403	Healthcare, social and welfare advisers or practitioners. For a group private health insurance scheme or occupation health care scheme
R404	Education, training establishments and examining bodies. Almost all career development involving outside organisations
R405	Business associates and other professional advisers. Are external advisors used for matters relating to employment law?
R406	Employees and agents of the data controller. The HR and payroll functions must be carried out by one or the other of these
R407	Other companies in the same group as the data controller. If you are part of a group of companies and personal data are transferred between the companies, you will need this class of recipient. Remember that each company, as a legal entity in its own right, must notify individually; a group notification cannot be made on behalf of all the companies within the group
R408	Suppliers, providers of goods or services. If the HR or payroll functions are outsourced. Other employment related work done by third parties such as pensions administration, travel arrangements
R409	Persons making an enquiry or complaint
R410	Financial organisations and advisers. Are external advisors used for matters relating to employment law?
R411	Credit reference agencies
R412	Debt collection and tracing agencies
R413	Survey and research organisations
R414	Traders in personal data
R415	Trade, employer associations and professional bodies. If your employees belong to such organisations and you deduct subscriptions from pay
R416	Police forces
R417	Private investigators
R418	Local government
R419	Central government
R420	Voluntary and charitable organisations
R421	Political organisations

R422 Religious organisations
R423 Ombudsmen and regulatory authorities
R424 The media
R425 Data processors. If you use a third party such as a computer bureau to process your payroll or personnel data, then you will need this class of recipient

Transfers outside the European Economic Area   3.9

The eighth data protection principle restricts transfers of personal data outside the European Economic Area (EEA). This part of the notification requires data controllers to state whether any such transfer takes place. Merely passing through a country as part of a transfer elsewhere is not deemed to be a transfer. This could occur where a file server is housed in, for example, the Channel Islands and the data are transferred from England to France via that server. However, if the data are stored on the server in the Channel Islands, then the data have been transferred outside the EEA (as the storing of data is processing and the Channel Islands are not part of the EEA).

In the notification, data controllers must declare the information relating to transfers using one of three options:

- none outside the EEA (if there are none);

- naming up to ten individual countries outside the EEA; or

- worldwide (in all other cases).

If personal data are posted on a web site that can be accessed from countries outside the EEA, 'worldwide' should be stated in the notification.

Security measures   3.10

The seventh data protection principle is concerned with the protection of the personal data against unauthorised or unlawful processing and against accidental loss or destruction or damage to personal data.

Data controllers are required as part of the notification to make some statements about the security measures that are in place in the data controller's organisation. This is done by responding to a number of questions that are asked as part of the notification application. The questions are of a general nature but cover some of the key requirements of effective information security management and can thus be treated as a checklist designed to encourage good information security within the organisation.

This part of the notification is not placed on the public part of the register.

The questions are:

- Have you taken any measures to guard against unauthorised or unlawful processing or personal data and against accidental loss or damage?

- Do the measures include:

  - adopting an information security policy?

  - taking steps to control physical security?

  - putting in place controls on access to information?

  - establishing a business continuity plan?

  - training your staff on security systems and procedures?

  - detecting and investigation breaches of security should they occur?

  - adopting the British Standard on Information Security Management BS7799?

Ideally, the answers should all be yes, but each of the 'measures' questions is discussed below. It is possible to say no to all the questions but as this shows little regard for the seventh data protection principle, the notification may be queried by the Information Commissioner's Office.

Adopting an information security policy   3.11

Having an information security policy means that an organisation has taken its responsibilities seriously and at the correct level of authority within the organisation. The policy should be endorsed at the most senior level within the organisation. It should provide direction to all employees on security matters and indicate individuals' responsibilities for data security.

Taking steps to control physical security   3.12

The physical security of personal data includes access to buildings, computer rooms and offices where the data are used as well as access to computer and other equipment where unauthorised access could have a detrimental effect on security. If personal data are processed in a single office that is locked from the rest of the staff during normal office hours, are the records put away at night in locked filing cabinets before the cleaners arrive? Are team passwords used and just kept in an unlocked desk draw? Is access outside normal office hours recorded (with an electronic security system, using manual records, or both)?

Putting in place controls on access to information   3.13

If there are rules about what personal information can be seen by which employees then there probably are controls on access to information. Is, for example, the information that line managers can see about their staff different to that which a local personal manager can view? In small organisations, it is often difficult to make such distinctions as the different roles may be performed by a single person. In larger organisations, where job roles are well defined, the distinction should be clear. If there is no segregation as to what personal data can be seen by which employees it should be questioned if that is necessary for the operation of the business. This is especially true if sensitive personal data is processed. If personal records are held on a computer system, who has access to that system – is it just HR and payroll staff, or is it available to all? If individual staff have been empowered to change address and bank account details, is the security in place to prevent one employee seeing another's details and how does an employee 'prove' to the system his or her true identity?

Some form of access monitoring or logging will probably be required as this will assist in detecting breaches of security (see **3.16** below).

Establishing a business continuity plan   3.14

A business continuity plan is a set of procedures to minimise the disruption to the business when things go wrong. There should be one overall plan with each function within the organisation contributing to that plan. During a disaster, not all functions will need to continue. For example, the annual pay review is less essential than continuing to pay employees. How will employees get paid if the pay records become inaccessible? This could be because they are held in a computer system and there has been a electricity power failure or it may be a fire or flooding of the payroll office.

Some of the steps to resolve these issues will be applicable to all the organisation's functions that are similarly affected. There may be a standby generator for all essential equipment at a particular location. Where a whole office building is inaccessible, there may be contingency plans to use another building, possibly already equipped with office furniture and computer equipment. HR and payroll can use these general plans but will need to develop them further to address the specific requirements of equipment and data used in the HR and payroll function. Are back-ups of data held on computers taken and are they held at a different location? What arrangements are in place with the payroll software or service provider to support the organisation in such circumstances?

Training your staff on security systems and procedures   3.15

There is little point in developing a good security policy unless it is known and used by everyone in the organisation. Employees cannot put any policy into action unless they both know and understand the policy. It follows that they must have training for staff on the policy either as part of their induction or at specialist sessions appropriate for their job function.

Detecting and investigating breaches of security should they occur   3.16

In the sense that no house is burglar-proof, any anti-burglary precautions are merely deterrents or delaying devices. Whatever security measures are put in place, there will be someone who can break that security. It is thus important to have mechanisms to detect any breach of security and procedures in place to investigate the breach. Investigation allows for security measures to be reviewed and improved, but without detection of breaches there can never be any investigation or subsequent improvement.

BS7799   3.17

BS7799 is a standard of best practice in security. It is *not* a requirement on data controllers and is seen by many experts in the field as being appropriate only for large organisations. However, as with any best practice, it provides useful and meaningful direction towards good security and is thus worthy of consideration by organisations of any size. Some organisations work to the standards of BS7799 but do not have formal certification to the standard.

BS7799 has ten areas of control:

- security policy;
- organisation of assets and resources;
- asset classification and control;
- personnel security;
- physical and environmental security;
- communications and operations management;
- access control;
- systems development and maintenance;
- business continuity management; and
- compliance.

Further details of BS7799 (including costs) can be found on the BSI group's web site at www.bsi.org.uk

Trading names   3.18

If the organisation has one or more trading names they can be included here. Although not mandatory, the information will make it easier for individuals to find the entry in the register by using the name they are familiar with rather than having to know the formal legal title.

As previously stated, each legal entity must have its own register entry and make its own notification. There cannot be a single notification for the group as a whole.

In the case of partnerships, it is not necessary to list the names of all the partners.

Exempt processing 3.19

Because not all processing of personal data needs to be notified, the register entry must alert anyone examining the register to un-notified processing. Data controllers can include in their notification details of all their processing, both what has to be notified and that which is exempt from notification. If this is done, then the register entry will be complete and nothing further is required. If a data controller chooses to make use of the exemption and not notify processing where there is no obligation to do so, the notification (and thus the register entry) must contain a statement about exempt processing. The statement is prescribed by the Information Commissioner's Office:

'This data controller also processes personal data which are exempt from notification.'

Data controllers are not required to notify:

- any processing of structured manual records; or, subject to certain conditions which are described at **3.25** below:

- processing for the purpose of staff administration;

- processing for the purpose of advertising, marketing and public relations (in connection with your own business activity);

- processing for the purpose of accounts and records; and

- processing by a body not established for profit for the purpose of membership administration and other activities.

Representatives 3.20

Where the data controller is not established in the UK and not in any other state within the EEA, the name and address details of a representative in the UK must be provided. The details will be on the public part of the register. Non-UK-based data controllers would not normally be caught by the UK data protection legislation but where a data controller outside the EEA is using equipment in the UK for processing personal data (other than just for transit through the UK) the UK legislation will apply and notification becomes necessary.

Where the data controller is in the EEA, this can be used to provide a contact point which will be used, for example, by individuals wishing to contact the data controller or to make a data subject access request. If no details are given here, data subjects are expected to contact the data controller using the details given at the beginning of the notification.

Voluntary Notification   3.21

All data controllers are required to notify unless they are exempt from notification. This is discussed at **3.25** below.

A data controller who is exempt from notification can choose to notify voluntarily. As a data controller may be required to give some of the details contained in the register entry to an inquirer, it may save some administrative work to notify voluntarily.

There is a section on the notification form which asks the data controller to indicate whether the notification is voluntary.

Do I Need to Notify?   3.22

Every data controller who is processing personal information must notify unless there is an exemption from notification.

A data controller is a person who determines the purposes for which, and the manner in which, any personal information is, or is to be, processed.

Personal information means data that relates to a living individual who can be identified from those data or from those data and other information that is in the possession of the data controller.

How to Notify   3.23

Notification has to be done in writing in the form prescribed by the Information Commissioner. There are three ways of starting the process:

- Internet www.informationcommissioner.gov.uk; click on 'Register online');

- sending (by post or fax) a Request to Notify Form; and

- telephoning the Notification help line at the Information Commissioner's Office (01625 545 740).

Using the Internet is described at **3.32** below.

In completing the Request to Notify Form, some details of the data controller and his or her business are given. The same details are requested if the Notification help line is called. The details are used to pre-populate the Notification Form that is then sent to the data controller. Part 1 of the form needs to be checked and the appropriate sections of Part 2 of the form should then be completed.

Once the details in the notification have been placed on the register, the Information Commissioner's Office will write to the data controller enclosing a copy of the register entry. The data controller will also be provided with a security number that has to be quoted in all future dealings with the Information Commissioner's Office about the register entry. In effect this is a mechanism to stop people other than the properly authorised person within the data controller's organisation from making changes to the register entry.

Notification Fee   3.24

Every notification must be accompanied by a fee of £35.00 (nil VAT).

The period of notification is one year. The Information Commissioner's Office does not send invoices but will acknowledge receipt of payment. After this time a continuation fee of £35.00 must be paid.

It is possible to pay by direct debit, cheque or BACS.

● **Direct debit** — Complete a direct debit form as part of the notification process.

● **Cheque** — Make the cheque payable to the Information Commissioner and cross it A/c Payee only. Write your reference number on the back of your cheque.

● **BACS** — Ensure that you provide your reference number when submitting a BACS payment.

Exemptions from Notification   3.25

Exemptions are possible for:

● some not-for-profit organisations (see **3.26** below for further details);

● processing of personal data for personal, family or household purposes (including recreational purposes);

● data controllers who only process personal data for the maintenance of a public register;

● data controllers who do not process personal data on a computer; and

● data controllers who only process personal data for any one or more of the following purposes for their own business:

  –   staff administration;

  –   advertising, marketing and public relations; and

  –   accounts and records.

There is no requirement to notify processing of manual records that come within the scope of the *DPA 1998*. However, the data controller can choose to notify voluntarily.

It must be remembered that an exemption to notify is not an exemption from the Act. All data controllers, whether they have to notify of not, must operate within the requirements of the Act.

The Information Commissioner's Office has produced a Self-Assessment Guide to Notification Exemptions. This is an easy-to-follow guide with simple yes/no questioning. It is available from the Information Commissioner's web site at www.informationcommissioner.gov.uk

As the purposes of the HR and payroll functions within any organisation are to undertake staff administration, at the first level notification would seem unnecessary. However, if an organisation has to notify, then the staff administration purpose, or a reference to it, will have to be included in the notification. Either the purpose has to be included in the notification, or a statement made that the data controller also processes personal data for purposes that are exempt from notification.

If an organisation is not processing personal data and not using a computer (or similar equipment capable of automated processing), the organisation will be exempt from notification. The very existence of an HR or payroll function in an organisation is a clear indication that personal data are processed by the organisation.

Only data controllers are to notify. Those who are not data controllers do not have to notify and there is no mechanism for them to notify. Someone or some organisation that processes personal data for a data controller is called a data processor under the Act. If any part of the HR or payroll functions has been outsourced to a third party, the third party cannot notify in respect of the processing of personal data on behalf of its clients. This is a change from the old 1984 act; the current law places the full responsibility for the processing of personal data on the data controller. It is the data controller who chooses what personal data to process and for what purposes. Under the seventh data protection principle, the data controller must have a written contract with any data processor and the data processor is limited to only the processing specified in writing by the data controller. The data controller is also responsible for ensuring that the data processor's security measures are adequate.

Individuals who process personal data only for their own domestic, family or household purposes are exempt from notifying (and indeed, the requirements of the Act). So, a list of friends' and relatives' addresses and dates of birth, even if it was held on a computer, would not create a need to notify. This does not extend to an individual running a business from home as this is beyond the domestic purposes exemption. However, the domestic exemption does extend to an individual's recreational activities, such as sports and hobbies.

Not-for-profit organisations   3.26

Not-for-profit organisations are exempt provided the processing is limited to the following description.

- The *processing* is only for the purposes of either establishing or maintaining membership or support for a body or association not established or conducted for profit, or providing or administering activities for individuals who are either members of the body or association or have regular contact with it.

- The *data subjects* are restricted to any person the processing of whose personal data is necessary for this exempt purpose.

- The *data classes* are restricted to data that is necessary for this exempt purpose.

- The *disclosures* other than those made with the consent of the data subjects are restricted to those third parties that are necessary for this exempt purpose.

- The *data is retained* only until the relationship between the data controller and the data subject ends, unless and for so long as it is necessary to do so for the exempt purpose.

Common purposes requiring notification   3.27

The Self-Assessment Guide to Notification Exemptions provides a list (reproduced below) of common purposes that *do* require notification:

- accountancy/auditing;
- administration of justice and legal services;
- canvassing political support amongst the electorate;
- constituency casework;
- credit referencing;
- crime prevention and prosecution of offenders (including use of CCTV for these purposes);
- debt administration and factoring;
- education;
- health administration and provision of health services;
- mortgage/insurance broking/insurance administration;
- pastoral care;
- private investigation;
- provision of financial services and advice;

- research;

- trading and sharing in personal information;

- pensions administration; and

- accounts and records (where personal data are processed by or obtained from a credit reference agency).

Amending Notification 3.28

Once an entry has been made on the register of data controllers, it may need changing to reflect any changes in the business needs of the data controller's organisation. Although notification lasts for only one year and must be renewed annually, there is an obligation on data controllers to keep their register entry up to date.

When any part of the register entry becomes inaccurate or the entry is incomplete, the data controller has a maximum of 28 days to notify the changes or additions. Failure to do so is a criminal offence.

The security number that was given when the original notification was made will need to be quoted.

No additional fee is payable for amendments.

Renewing the Notification 3.29

Notification last for one year only and must be renewed annually. The notification year starts on the day the Information Commissioner's Office receives a complete and correct notification form and the notification fee. Currently the renewal fee is the same as the initial notification fee. Data controllers will be written to before their notification expires.

Even if there are no changes that have to be made to the register entry, the renewal fee must be received before the old notification expires. For this reason, the Information Commissioner's Office promotes the use of direct debit.

If a notification expires, it cannot be renewed and a new notification must be made.

Once the renewal has been made the data controller will be sent a letter confirming the renewal together with a copy of the renewed entry in the register.

Removing the Register Entry 3.30

Once an entry has been made on the register of data controllers and it becomes no longer necessary for the data controller to notify, the register entry can be removed.

The data controller should write to the Information Commissioner's office explaining the change in circumstances and providing the security number. Any direct debit instruction will need to be cancelled.

Change of Legal Entity 3.31

A register entry is not transferable from one data controller to another. If there is a change in the legal entity of the data controller a new entry must be made in the register for the new legal entity. The register entry for the old legal entity may then become unnecessary and may need to be removed.

If the change is such that a new company number is given to the legal entity by Companies House, a new notification will be needed.

It is recommended that the Notification help line is contacted in the first instance.

Completing the Notification Form on the Internet 3.32

It is possible to complete the Notification Form on the Internet. However, after completing the form online it must be printed, signed and sent to the Information Commissioner's Office by post together with the notification fee or a direct debit instruction. It is not possible, currently, to send the form electronically. Data controllers will be deemed notified on the day the Information Commissioner's Office receives the correctly completed forms and fee.

Completing the Notification Form online is a step-by-step process. You are asked to answer certain questions and provide information before continuing to the next question. At the end of the form it can be printed off and sent to the Commissioner's Office.

The first questions on the form are about the data controller who is notifying, for example his or her name, address and contact details.

The next stage of the online process involves choosing an appropriate nature of business template. Each notification must include a general description of the processing of personal data being carried out. On the register this description is structured by reference to purposes. A selection of templates are provided that describe the processing which is likely to be being carried out by a range of different businesses. After selecting the template appropriate to a business it needs to be checked to ensure that it accurately describes the processing which is being carried out. The template may be amended and supplementary purposes added to it. If a relevant template cannot be found, the one that best matches the actual processing can be used and amended as necessary. Alternatively, the Notification help line should be contacted.

The following stage of the online process involves providing additional information, for example the security statement and statement of exempt processing.

Some of this information is mandatory, so failure to return this part of the form renders the notification invalid and it will be returned to you.

The final stage is to print the form, sign the declaration and return it to the Information Commissioner's Office together with the notification fee or completed direct debit instruction. If after printing the form it is found to be missing, then the omission can be written in ink directly onto the form and it will be included in the notification.

Summary 3.33

Check on the Information Commissioner's Office's web site to see if the organisation has an entry on the register of data controllers.

If there is an entry, you should find out who within the organisation is responsible for data protection and, specifically, for notifying the Information Commissioner. This person could be in the company secretariat, legal department or information technology department. Discuss with whoever has the responsibility to ensure that all the processing undertaken by HR and payroll are covered by the register entry. Because HR and payroll are likely to process sensitive personal data, this may have been overlooked in the notification. If the register entry is incomplete, it will need to be amended to include the processes of the HR and payroll functions. Equally, they may have been treated as being exempt from notification so the register entry should contain a note about exempt processing.

If there is no register entry, again it is worth investigating who in the organisation should be responsible for this. Remember that there is a time delay between the Information Commissioner's Office receiving a notification and the corresponding register entry appearing on the web site. Draw up a draft notification for processing within the HR and payroll function. This chapter goes through the process in the order required in the documentation provided by the Information Commissioner. It may be useful to use the online notification process to build the purposes from the templates and print out the document ready for submission. If nothing else, securing a signature for the notification and the fee will alert someone in the organisation to the issue of data protection notification and help lead you to the area with responsibility for this within the organisation. Clearly, with smaller organisations this is easy to establish quickly.

The person with responsibility for data protection within the organisation will need to decide if processing that is exempt from notification is to be notified. If all the processing of personal data are exempt, then no notification is necessary. If other processing takes place, then the exempt processing can either be included or a reference to exempt processing included in the notification. The expression 'exempt processing' is used in respect of exemption from notification and it must be remembered that an exemption to notify is not an exemption from the Act.

Chapter 4
The Data Protection Act 1998 in Practice

Introduction   4.1

The *Data Protection Act 1998* (*DPA 1998*, or 'the Act') was introduced largely to promote openness and transparency of information held about individuals in filing systems, whether manual or computerised. The Act is not an employment law as such, but has considerable impact in every area of the employment relationship.

Key Features of the Act   4.2

In relation to employment, the Act is designed to:

- require employers to determine how and why they process personal information about their employees and others;

- require employers to comply with eight data protection principles, with a view to protecting all personal information held about individuals;

- protect the privacy and other rights of individuals in respect of information held about them by the employer;

- strike a balance between the reasonable needs of employers to keep records about their staff and the rights of employees to have respect for their private life;

- eliminate any collection of personal information that is irrelevant or excessive to the employment relationship; and

- allow individuals to gain access to any information held about them.

The issue of data protection should be viewed as an integral part of good management and should, arguably, be mainstreamed into the employer's policies, procedures and practices. Employers should therefore seek to incorporate data protection principles into all their policies and procedures, including those on recruitment, references, record keeping, discipline, sickness absence, security, computer use and monitoring. In this way issues such as security, confidentiality of information and privacy will become the norm within the workplace and the employer will be in a much stronger position to ensure compliance with the *DPA 1998*.

As the law stands at present, there is no duty to consult trade unions or workers' representatives on data protection matters. Despite this absence of a duty to consult, consultation is to be recommended in that it can help the employer to ensure that their data processing practices are fair, transparent and acceptable to their employees, thus increasing trust and respect in employment relationships.

Personal data 4.3

'Personal data' for the purposes of data protection legislation means simply any personal information held in a filing system that relates to a living individual who can be identified from the data, whether by name or otherwise. This includes information that:

- is held manually (ie on paper) in a 'relevant filing system' (see below);

- is stored in a computer, and information stored in such a way that it can be fed into a computer;

- is contained in the text of an email;

- is stored on microfiche;

- is stored on telephone logging systems, or on audio or video systems; or

- forms part of an 'accessible record'. This would include health records.

In addition, information that is recorded in any format with the intention that it will be put on file or on to computer is regarded as personal data. Where information is stored manually, however, it must be stored in a 'relevant filing system' if it is to fall within the definition of 'personal data'. This means that the file in which the information is stored must be structured in such a way that specific information relating to a particular individual is readily accessible (see also the *Durant* case at **4.4** below).

There is no legal duty on an employer to obtain employees' consent to the collection of personal data, although they must inform employees whenever any record about them is set up or held. There are also further strict rules in place that govern what the employer may, or may not, do with personal data once they have collected it.

Certain information relating to individuals is regarded as 'sensitive data' under the Act and such data is subject to special provisions and restrictions (see **4.6** below).

The Durant case 4.4

In *Durant v Financial Services Authority [2003] EWCA Civ 1746,* the Court of Appeal held that for a manual record to be part of a 'relevant filing system' for the purposes of the *DPA 1998*, it must be one in which the information is structured by reference to the individual or criteria relating to the individual. The Court pointed out that the purpose of the *DPA 1998* was to protect the privacy of personal data, and not documents. The file must also have a structure or referencing mechanism that allows specific information about the individual to be easily found, eg information about the employee's contract, or on topics such as appraisal, holiday leave or sickness absence. Furthermore, the file must be part of a system in which the files are structured or referenced in a way that specific files about individuals can be readily identified and located within the system without searching through the content of each file.

The Information Commissioner subsequently issued guidance on the *Durant* decision. The guidance notes state that where a filing system contains files about individual employees, or topics about individual employees, and where the files or the information contained within them are structured purely in chronological order, they will not constitute a 'relevant filing system' for the purposes of the Act. This is because the structure or referencing system of the files would not allow the retrieval of personal data without someone having to leaf through the file and search for the data they were looking for. Without some form of indexing or other mechanism to assist with the location of specific data, the file would not be sufficiently structured to fall within the ambit of the Act.

The Court of Appeal also held in the *Durant* case that in order for information to be 'personal data' for the purposes of the *DPA 1998*, it must not only name or directly refer to an individual, but must also be biographical in a significant extent and have the data subject as its focus (rather than, for example, focusing on some transaction or event in which the individual may have been involved). This would suggest that letters or emails that merely mention an employee's name, for example as one of a list of people who attended a meeting, would not constitute personal data since the individual concerned would not be the focus of the correspondence. In contrast, if the individual's name was mentioned together with other information about him or her, eg his or her address, salary details or medical history, it would constitute personal data under the Act. In short, the Court of Appeal took the view that for information to constitute personal data, it must relate in some way to information affecting the individual's privacy, whether in their personal or family life, business or professional capacity.

Data processing   4.5

The *DPA 1998* uses the term 'data processing'. The word 'processing' in this context has a wider meaning than its dictionary definition and covers any and all activities that relate to the collection, holding, use and destruction of information that is about an individual. Thus 'data processing' covers all the routine aspects of handling personal information, including:

- the initial collection of personal information about an individual, howsoever the information is obtained;

- holding the information in a file or on computer;

- organising or reorganising the information;

- making changes to the information, for example as part of an updating exercise, or changing the way in which it is stored;

- retrieving the information, for example as part of a computerised report;

- conveying the information, for example by passing an employee's details to a line manager;

- disclosure of the information by any means or making it publicly available (for example on a company web site);

- erasing, deleting or destroying some or all of the information held; and

- using the information in any other way.

Sensitive data   4.6

The *DPA 1998, section 2* sets out a list of personal information which is to be regarded as 'sensitive data'. The list includes the following:

- racial or ethnic origin;

- political opinions;

- religious beliefs or other similar beliefs;

- membership of a trade union;

- physical or mental health or condition;

- sexual life;

- the commission or alleged omission of any offence; and

- anything related to any proceedings for an offence committed or alleged to have been committed.

Information related to a number of the items listed above may in practice be frequently found in an employee's (or job applicant's) file, for example:

- records set up for the purpose of equal opportunities monitoring may contain details of individuals' racial or ethnic origins or religious beliefs;

- a record that an employee of overseas nationality has the right to work in the UK may be held in the individual's file together with copies of documents that prove this right;

- information may be available on file about individuals' trade union membership in order to enable employers to deduct members' subscriptions from their pay at source;

- an email from an employee to a trade union representative may reveal that the employee is a member of that trade union;

- sickness records may contain information about an employee's physical or mental health;

- emails sent from an employee to an occupational doctor may contain information about that employee's health or illness;

- personnel files may contain details of an employee's disability and how it affects them so as to enable the employer to meet their duty under the *Disability Discrimination Act 1995* to make reasonable adjustments for that employee;

- an employee's file may contain information about health collected in order to allow the employer to process Statutory Sick Pay;

- information may be contained in an employee's personal file in connection with an allegation of discrimination or harassment, which may reveal that employee's sexual orientation;

- files may contain information about employees' previous criminal convictions where the employee's job involves, for example, security or work of a sensitive nature such as the supervision of children.

Conditions for the processing of sensitive data 4.7

Schedule 3 of the *DPA 1998* sets out a series of conditions, at least one of which must be met before an employer can process sensitive data about an individual. The conditions that are potentially relevant to data protection in employment are listed below.

- **Where processing is necessary in order for the employer to comply with a legal obligation in connection with employment.**

  Such a legal obligation may arise as a result of statute or common law, ie decisions of courts and tribunals which interpret the law. The scope of this condition is fairly wide and it is the most likely condition to be relevant to the processing of personal data in the context of employment. The condition could apply whether the legal duty in question related to the individual about whom the sensitive data was held, or to another employee. For example, it may be necessary to record details of a particular employee's mental illness in order to be able to ensure the safety of other workers. There are many legal obligations on employers that may require the processing of sensitive data, for example:

  - health and safety legislation;

  - anti-discrimination legislation, including the duty to make reasonable adjustments under the *Disability Discrimination Act 1995*;

  - the duty on public authorities to monitor the racial background of their staff under the *Race Relations Act 1976 (Statutory Duties) Order 2001 (SI 2001 No 3458)*;

  - the duty under the *Social Security Contributions and Benefits Act 1992* to process Statutory Sick Pay for employees who are absent from work due to sickness;

- unfair dismissal rights contained in the *Employment Rights Act 1996*;

- duties and rights under the *Rehabilitation of Offenders Act 1974* which relates to individuals' criminal convictions;

- the duty to ensure continuity of employment under the *Transfer of Undertakings (Protection of Employment)) Regulations 1981 (SI 1981 No 1794)* (the 'TUPE' Regulations).

This list is, of course, not exhaustive.

- **Where processing is necessary to protect the vital interests of the employee or another person in circumstances where the employee cannot give consent.**

This condition is likely to be satisfied only in cases that represent a matter of life or death.

- **Where the information has been made public as a result of steps taken by the employee.**

An example of this could be where an employee has taken part in a radio programme in the context of promoting trade union rights, and it is therefore public knowledge that the employee is an active trade union member. In these circumstances, it will not be unlawful for the employer to record the employee's trade union membership and activities on his or her file.

- **Where processing is necessary in connection with any legal proceedings, including the defence of a legal claim against the employer, or necessary for the purpose of obtaining legal advice.**

This means that if an employee or job applicant has brought a complaint against their employer to court or tribunal, it would be legitimate for the employer to retain the complainant's personal data (and possibly personal data relating to others) in order to facilitate the employer's defence against the claim. An example could be the retention of a group of job applicants' details, including their respective racial backgrounds, in order to defend a claim of race discrimination brought to tribunal by one of the applicants alleging that their rejection was on racial grounds.

- **Where processing is necessary for the exercise of any functions conferred under an enactment or any functions of the Crown, a Minister of the Crown or a government department.**

This condition would be relevant mainly to public sector employers who may have special statutory duties conferred on them to ensure the qualifications or probity of employees who fill certain posts. This condition may, for example, justify the processing of information about employees' criminal convictions or any proceedings relating to an offence the employee is alleged to have committed.

- **Where processing is necessary for medical purposes and is undertaken by a health professional or someone with an equivalent duty of confidentiality.**

This condition would apply where health information about employees was held by a company doctor or similar person (see **CHAPTER 7**).

● **Where processing of information about individuals' racial or ethnic origin, religious beliefs or physical or mental health is for the purpose of carrying out equal opportunities monitoring.**

If the sole purpose of retaining this type of data is to promote and maintain equality of treatment, and provided the information is necessary in order to achieve this purpose, it will be lawful to retain the data (see **CHAPTER 8** for details of equal opportunities monitoring).

One common thread in most of the above conditions is that it must be *necessary* for the employer to hold the sensitive data in order to fulfil the condition. This means that it is not, for example, open to employers to retain sensitive data about individuals in circumstances where the reason for doing so is convenience or 'just in case' a particular situation might arise.

Gaining employees' consent to the processing of sensitive data   4.8

If none of the conditions for processing sensitive data at **4.7** above apply, the only course of action open to an employer who thinks they need to collect and hold sensitive data about an individual is to obtain that individual's consent to the processing of sensitive data. However, under data protection principles, consent to the processing of sensitive data must be 'explicit', and 'freely given'. 'Explicit' in this context means that the employee must have signed a document indicating his or her agreement, having first been clearly informed how the information will be used. 'Freely given' is defined as giving the employee a genuine choice as to whether or not to consent to the processing, and operating a policy of not subjecting anyone who declines to give their consent to any detriment. Part 2 of the Employment Practices Data Protection Code (on Employment Records) points out that the extent to which individuals' consent can be relied on in the context of employment is limited on account of this requirement for consent to be freely given.

Despite the fact that it may not always be a sound prospect for an employer to rely on consent as a means of justification for the processing of sensitive data about their employees, it is nevertheless a sensible precaution for an employer as a matter of course to seek employees' (and job applicants') consent to the collection and use of sensitive data about them.

Employers should always consider carefully whether they actually need to collect and hold sensitive data about their employees. If justification exists, they should still aim to keep such data to a minimum. Apart from information gathered for the purpose of equal opportunities monitoring, the only sensitive personal information that the employer is realistically likely to need would be information relating to individuals' trade union membership (for the purpose of deducting subscriptions from wages at source), health and (in some, but not all jobs) criminal records.

Individuals' rights under the Act   4.9

Employees (and others – see below) have considerable rights under the *DPA 1998*. These can be summarised as follows:

The right to:

- be informed if personal data about them is being processed;

- be given a description of the data;

- be informed of the purpose for which the data is held;

- be told to whom the data may be disclosed and for what purpose (for example disclosure of pay information to the Inland Revenue for taxation purposes);

- have any inaccuracies corrected or removed – if necessary by applying to the courts to obtain an order;

- seek compensation if they have suffered any damage or distress as a result of any breach of the DPA 1998; and

- be given a copy of the information held about them on written request (see **4.23** below).

The rights listed above would be available to:

- employees of the organisation;

- other workers, for example contractors or casual staff where the employer held personal information about them;

- agency staff;

- ex-employees, including pensioners of the company;

- job applicants, whether past or present, successful or unsuccessful;

- volunteer workers;

- apprentices and trainees;

- customers and clients; and

- suppliers.

Responsibilities under the Act   4.10

It is important for all employers to identify who within their organisation will hold overall responsibility for data protection issues, and for ensuring that all the employer's policies, procedures and practices comply with legislation, including the *DPA 1998*.

The person appointed to hold such responsibility should ideally be a senior manager who has sufficient authority to challenge any practices that might risk being in breach of legislation or associated Codes of Practice and make decisions about data protection compliance. In a large organisation, a senior HR manager would be an ideal candidate for such responsibility, whilst in a small business it may be appropriate for the owner or managing director to hold responsibility.

The responsible person should aim to achieve a coordinated approach to the issue of data protection, since the topic demands input and cooperation from people in a range of different posts throughout the organisation. In effect, data protection is a multi-disciplinary matter. The responsible person should therefore take steps to ensure that all line managers receive appropriate training to enable them to understand their responsibilities under data protection legislation.

The responsible manager should also be charged with ensuring that all the employer's policies and procedures are regularly checked, in particular against the *DPA 1998* and the Employment Practices Data Protection Code (see **4.22** below). The responsible person should also be made accountable for ensuring that policies and procedures are consistently put into practice by all staff, and especially by those whose jobs take them into contact with personal data held about employees. In particular, HR staff, line managers and possibly IT staff may have access to personal information about individuals and the responsibility for ensuring the ongoing training of these individuals in data protection matters will have to be ensured.

Someone who is newly appointed to the role that involves responsibility for data protection issues may wish to review and deal with the following matters:

- whether the organisation has a valid notification in the register of data controllers;

- what personal data about employees (and others) exists within the organisation and where and by whom it is held;

- whether it is necessary or appropriate for individuals other than HR staff to hold personal data about staff;

- the type of information held and whether it is genuinely appropriate and necessary in light of the needs of the organisation;

- whether any information routinely collected about employees or job applicants is irrelevant or excessive when viewed against the employer's legitimate needs and whether the employer should consequently refrain from collecting it (or destroy it);

- whether reliable processes are in place for ensuring the proper destruction of paper and computerised files when they are no longer needed by the organisation;

- where sensitive data is collected, whether one of the conditions for the processing of sensitive data is satisfied;

- whether those who have access to personal data are aware of their legal responsibilities under the *DPA 1998*, including the fact that they may be held personally liable for any breach of the Act;

- whether clear data protection guidelines have been devised and communicated to all staff who may have access to personal data in the course of performing their jobs;

- whether staff who have access to personal data in the course of their jobs have received proper training in the provisions of the *DPA 1998*;

- whether employees who have access to personal information in the course of their work have signed confidentiality and security clauses;

- whether newly recruited staff are properly informed of the employer's data protection rules and guidelines during induction.

One of the tasks of the senior person in charge of data protection matters might be to select an 'off-the-shelf' computer package to manage the employer's personnel records. In this eventuality, the employer should ensure the computer system they purchase is fully data protection compliant. It will not be open to an employer to 'blame the computer' if their data protection measures fail to conform to the Act, nor to argue that the responsibility for their failure to comply with the Act rests with the supplier of the computer system. The responsibility for compliance with the Act rests plainly with each employer, rather than with any organisation that has supplied them with a computer system or that manages data on their behalf.

When purchasing a computerised personnel records system, the employer may also wish to satisfy themselves that the system will readily enable them to retrieve all the information about any individual employee on receipt of a subject access request (see **4.22** below).

Individuals' responsibilities   4.11

Data protection issues should not be viewed as the responsibility of only one senior manager within the organisation. Arguably all staff have a duty to comply with the *DPA 1998*, including responsibility for the type of personal data they collect and how they use the information. All workers will have a duty:

- to use personal data to which they have access in the course of their work only for legitimate business purposes;

- to keep personal data about others secure and confidential at all times;

- not to use personal data about others for their own personal purposes; and

- not to disclose personal information about others except when authorised to do so.

It is up to the employer to take the appropriate steps to make sure that all staff, and in particular line managers, understand their responsibilities under the Act and, if necessary, that staff are reminded of these responsibilities from time to time.

In particular, staff should be made aware that they can personally be held liable for a breach of the Act, for example if they knowingly or recklessly disclose personal information outside their employer's organisation without authority to do so. This could be in addition to the employer's liability to pay compensation to any employee who has suffered damage as a result of a breach of the Act. Breach of the *DPA 1998* should be quoted as a disciplinary offence in the employer's disciplinary procedure in order to draw to the attention of all staff to the fact that the employer views such breaches seriously.

A useful way of achieving these objectives would be for the employer to prepare written rules and guidelines to be distributed to line managers and others whose jobs take them into contact with personal data, explaining the key duties and responsibilities under the Act and the consequences of individuals' actions.

Legal requirement to disclose personal data about employees 4.12

As a general principle, employers are obliged to keep employees' personal data secure and confidential and not disclose it other than to authorised persons. There are, however, a number of exceptions to this general principle where the employer may be required by law to disclose personal data relating to their employees to outside bodies or agencies. The organisations to whom such disclosures must be made on demand would include the:

- Inland Revenue;
- Child Support Agency;
- Benefits Agency;
- Department of Work and Pensions; and
- Financial Services Authority.

Prior to disclosing information about any of their employees to an outside body or agency, employers should, however, check that there really is a legal duty to do so. Assuming that this has been established, the employer should still only provide the information that they are legally obliged to disclose and no more. Furthermore, in normal circumstances the employee concerned should be immediately informed that a disclosure has been made, to whom it has been made, why it has been made and what information about him or her has been disclosed.

The data protection principles in practice 4.13

The *DPA 1998* contains eight data protection principles that form the core of the Act. In the event of an employer failing to comply with the principles, the Information Commissioner can serve an enforcement notice on the employer. A failure to comply with the enforcement notice would be a criminal offence.

The eight data protection principles compel employers to ensure that personal information about individuals is:

1   processed fairly and lawfully;

2   obtained only for one or more specified and lawful purposes, and not processed for any purpose(s) that is incompatible with those stated purposes;

3   adequate, relevant and not excessive in relation to the purpose(s) for which it was obtained;

4   accurate and, where necessary, kept up to date;

5   not kept for longer than is necessary in relation to the purpose(s) for which it was obtained;

6   processed in accordance with individuals' rights under the *DPA 1998*;

7   protected by appropriate technical and organisational measures against unauthorised or unlawful processing, accidental loss or destruction, and damage;

8   not transferred outside the European Economic Area unless the country or territory to which it is transferred has in place an adequate level of protection for individuals' rights and freedoms in relation to the processing of personal data.

The principles are explored more fully at **4.14** to **4.21** below in the context of their practical application in employment.

The first principle   4.14

The duty to process data fairly and lawfully

The first data protection principle creates the obligation on employers to process personal data 'fairly and lawfully'. This duty is subject to the proviso that personal data must not be processed unless one of a number of conditions is fulfilled. The conditions are that:

- the employee has given his or her consent to the processing, ie has signified their agreement by some positive means; or

- data processing is necessary for one of the following reasons:

    - for the performance of a contract, for example the processing of employees' wages;

    - in order to ensure compliance with a legal obligation, for example information about an employee's working hours may be necessary in order to comply with the *Working Time Regulations 1998 (SI 1998 No 1833)*;

    - to protect the vital interests of the employee, for example the disclosure of an employee's medical details to a hospital casualty department on discovering that the employee had been admitted following an accident would be legitimate;

– for the administration of justice or for the exercise of any public functions (this condition has no general application to employers);

– for the purposes of legitimate interests pursued by the employer, for example if the business was about to be transferred.

Further conditions are imposed on the processing of data where it is classed as 'sensitive data' under the Act (see **4.6** above).

It is important to note the word 'necessary' used in this part of the Act. If the employee's consent has not been obtained, data about that person can be processed only if one of the relevant conditions is necessary for the business, and not just because (for example) management would find it convenient.

Where data processing is being done in order to comply with a legal obligation, or is done for any purpose authorised by legislation, it will be lawful. An example could be the processing of data obtained as a result of an exercise to monitor employees' use of the organisations' email or telephone system. Provided the monitoring was conducted for one of the purposes authorised by the *Telecommunications (Lawful Business Practice) (Interception of Communications) Regulations 2000 (SI 2000 No 2699)*, it would be lawful (see **CHAPTER 9** for a full discussion of this topic).

Fairness, however, is quite another matter. It is theoretically possible for data processing to be lawful but unfair. If, for example, the processing of personal data is excessive or carried out without good cause, it could be unfair even though it may not overtly be in breach of any statutory provisions. Similarly the obtaining of personal data through deception might not be against the law, but would almost certainly be unfair.

The second principle   4.15

The duty to obtain data only for one or more specified and lawful purposes, and not process the data for any purpose(s) that is incompatible with those stated purposes

The second data protection principle requires employers:

● to obtain and use information about individuals only for one or more specified and lawful purposes; and

● not to use the information for any other purposes.

It follows that the employer should firstly be clear as to the (lawful) purpose to be served by the collection of personal information about employees. Then, once an employer has specified the purpose(s) for which they wish to collect information about employees, they must not subsequently use any of the information they hold for any purpose that is incompatible with or vastly different from the purpose for which it was collected.

One example of this principle in practice could be in organisations that use the contact details of their employees (or ex-employees, eg pensioners) for marketing purposes, for example to market the employer's own products or services or advertise any special deals on offer from another organisation. It would not be permissible under the *DPA 1998* to do this without first informing employees that there was an intention to use their personal details for this purpose and giving them a reasonable opportunity to object and decline to have their details used in this way. According to the Employment Practices Data Protection Code, Part 2 (Employment Records), this could be done in one of two ways:

- by informing new employees if the employer wishes to use their personal details to deliver advertising or marketing information to them and giving them a clear opportunity to 'opt out' by notifying the employer that they do not wish to receive such material; or

- by actively seeking employees' consent to the use of their personal details for this purpose, ie asking them to indicate in writing whether they wish to 'opt in'.

The Code of Practice recommends that the first method (opting out) would be appropriate in two circumstances, the first of which would be for new employees. The matter could sensibly be dealt with during induction by simply providing the employee with the information and advising them how to opt out. The employer should, of course, respect any objections and ensure that the details of those persons objecting are not included on any list of names and contact details used for marketing purposes.

The other circumstances in which an 'opt-out' rather than an 'opt-in' may be appropriate would be where employees expected their details to be used for marketing purposes, for example where there was a general, accepted practice in the organisation, or within the particular industry as a whole, of offering staff discounts on the employer's products or services and advertising these to individuals through the use of their personal contact details. So long as any communications of this nature included an explanation of how an individual could opt out, there would be no infringement of the data protection principles.

The second method (opting in), according to the Code, should be used in circumstances where the employer wished to begin marketing or advertising (having not previously carried out any direct marketing to its staff) and employees had not previously been made aware that their personal details might be used in this way. Each employee should be informed of precisely what the employer plans to do and invited to send an email or written note confirming that they wish to opt in. Only those who opt in should have their names put on the marketing list. A similar approach should be taken in the event that the employer wished to pass on employees' contact details to another organisation, for example a sister company. The Code of Practice points out that the disclosure of employees' details for this purpose would require individual employees' express consent because such a disclosure would otherwise be intrusive and could amount to a breach of the employer's duty of confidence.

The third principle 4.16

The duty to ensure data is adequate, relevant and not excessive in relation to the purpose(s) for which it was obtained

The third data protection principle states that personal information must be adequate, relevant and not excessive in relation to the purpose or purposes for which it is processed. The employer should therefore, as a starting point, carry out a review of all existing personal data they hold to ensure that the information they keep about their employees in personnel files is not excessive. Essentially, if there is no clear and obvious reason why particular information is being retained in employees' files, the employer should take the appropriate steps to delete or destroy the information.

Another useful action point for employers would be to review carefully all forms and questionnaires they use (for example in recruitment) to check whether the information they request is relevant to the achievement of a legitimate business aim, and is not excessive when viewed in relation to that aim. Any questions that require individuals to provide information that is not strictly relevant and necessary to the employer's needs should be removed or amended. Equally, the wording of the questions should be reviewed to ensure the questions are clear and that they are likely to secure only the information that the employer legitimately requires.

The fourth principle 4.17

The duty to ensure personal information is accurate and, where necessary, kept up to date

The fourth data protection principle obliges employers to ensure personal data is accurate and kept up to date. No employer can ever guarantee that all their staff will automatically cooperate with a request to keep them informed as to any changes to their personal data, for example changes of address, family circumstances or health, but so long as the employer has taken reasonable steps to ensure the accuracy of the information they hold, that should be sufficient to comply with the *DPA 1998*.

One way to increase the chances of personal data being kept up to date is for the employer routinely to issue all the personal data they hold on an annual basis to individuals, and ask for any changes or corrections to be communicated back to HR department within a given timescale. This approach will have the added advantage that it may reduce the number of subject access requests.

The fifth principle   4.18

The duty not to keep personal data for longer than is necessary in relation to the purpose(s) for which it was obtained

Neither the *DPA 1998* nor the Employment Practices Data Protection Code prescribes any time limitation on the retention of personal data. It is therefore up to each employer to decide for themselves what time periods are appropriate in relation to the needs of their business. Decisions on this matter should be made objectively, and records should not be maintained 'just in case' they might be needed at some future point in time. Proper policy decisions should be made and adhered to as to the specific retention periods for different types of records, for example the retention of leavers' files (see **CHAPTER 6**) or recruitment files (see **CHAPTER 5**).

The sixth principle   4.19

The duty to process data in accordance with individuals' rights under the *DPA 1998*

This is self-explanatory, and would include the duty on the employer to ensure that subject access requests were treated properly and in accordance with the provisions of the *DPA 1998* (see **4.23** below).

The seventh principle   4.20

The duty to protect personal data by putting in place appropriate technical and organisational measures against unauthorised or unlawful processing, accidental loss or destruction, and damage

The seventh data protection principle requires employers to put in place proper measures, eg security measures, to protect personal data against unauthorised or unlawful processing, accidental loss or destruction, or damage. This will include adequate protection for computer systems, eg proper use of passwords, and possibly the use of encryption and establishment of firewalls.

One of the simplest and cheapest methods of ensuring the protection of personal data is to formulate and implement a rigorous system of employee passwords. Rules should be devised for employees governing the choosing of a password and for the regular changing of passwords. There should also be a clear written rule forbidding the disclosure of passwords to any unauthorised person, and this rule should be consistently enforced. Disciplinary rules and procedures should make it clear that any unauthorised access to files or misuse of passwords will be regarded as misconduct and render the employee liable to disciplinary action up to and including summary dismissal.

Another simple step that employers can take is to advise all employees that they must not use email or fax to communicate personal data. These methods of communication are not secure or confidential. Alternatively, confidential messages that the employer wants to send by email could be encrypted. Encryption simply means the process of translating normal text into a series of letters and/or numbers that can be deciphered only by someone with the correct password or key. It is a useful tool to prevent outsiders from reading confidential, sensitive or personal information.

Employers can further protect employees' personal data by using 'firewalls' and other security technology which can help to keep would-be external hackers at bay to a great extent. The purpose of a firewall is to provide protection against unauthorised access to computer systems and receipt of unwanted correspondence. Technical advice should be sought from computer experts on this subject.

Over and above any breach of the Act, it will be a criminal offence under the *Computer Misuse Act 1990* for an individual to secure unauthorised access to a computer system or to computer material in certain circumstances, or to modify the contents of a computer system without authority. 'Unauthorised modification' of computer material includes deliberate erasure or corruption of programmes or data, modifying or destroying a system file or another user's file or the addition of any programme or data to the computer's contents. It may be advisable for employers to communicate this fact to all staff so that they understand fully the seriousness of any conduct of this nature.

Another point to consider and guard against, in particular in larger organisations, is the possibility of false subject access requests made by an employee in order to gain access to information about another employee for illegitimate or malicious purposes. The employer should put in place the appropriate measures for ensuring that any request for access to personal data is valid, ie that the identity of the person making the subject access request matches that of the subject of the files requested.

The eighth principle   4.21

The duty not to transfer personal data outside the EEA unless the country or territory to which it is transferred has in place an adequate level of protection for individuals' rights and freedoms in relation to the processing of personal data

The European Economic Area (EEA) consists of all EU countries plus Iceland, Norway and Liechtenstein. The transfer of data to any country or territory outside these countries, for example to the United States, should be subject to the employer satisfying themselves that the data, once transferred, will be properly protected.

Key Features of the Employment Practices Data Protection Code   4.22

The Employment Practices Data Protection Code was published in four separate parts by the Information Commissioner during 2003. The Code, which is available on www.dataprotection.gov.uk, represents the Information Commissioner's interpretation of the steps employers should take to ensure compliance with the *DPA 1998*. The Code consists of four parts in total, the first three of which have been published in their final form at the time of writing. The fourth part is currently available in draft form. The four parts are:

- Part 1: Recruitment and selection – This covers personal data held in the context of recruitment, including carrying out checks on job applicants (see **CHAPTER 5**);

- Part 2: Employment records – This covers a range of information about staff likely to be held on file by employers (see **CHAPTER 6**);

- Part 3: Monitoring at work – This covers mainly monitoring of employees' communications but also some other forms of monitoring (see **CHAPTER 9**);

- Part 4: Information about workers' health (in draft form at the time of writing) – This covers occupational health data, medical testing, drugs screening and genetic testing (see **CHAPTER 7**).

Neither the *DPA 1998* nor the Code of Practice prevents employers from processing data about employees. Instead they set out to ensure that employers process personal data in a fair and proper way and regulate when and how processing is carried out. The key stated aims of the Code of Practice are to:

- strike a balance between an employer's legitimate need to run its business and their employees' legitimate right to respect for privacy; and

- assist employers to comply with the Act by helping them to establish good practice in the handling of personal data.

The Code, like other Codes of Practice, is not legally binding on employers, but a failure to follow its recommendations can be used in evidence against an employer in the event of a court or tribunal claim. It is therefore in every employer's interests to adhere to the recommendations given in the Code, which in any event is a useful source of information and practical guidance in an area that can sometimes by quite complex.

The Code of Practice identifies a range of examples of the types of personal information that would be likely to be covered by the provisions of the *DPA 1998*, including:

- details of a named employee's pay, whether held manually or on computer;

- an email in which a named member of staff was discussed;

- information written in a supervisor's notebook where different sections contained information about various named employees;

- information on one individual written in a supervisor's notebook where the supervisor planned to put that information into the employee's file; and

- a set of completed job application forms.

This list is of course illustrative and not exhaustive. Essentially, whenever a record is created about an individual (or the individual's activities), it is liable to fall within the scope of the *DPA 1998* and the Code of Practice.

The Code points out that in general, information will be covered by the Act and the Code of Practice if an individual can be identified (whether by name or by other means, for example a reference number). Where, however, information is held about a group of people in such a way that individuals are not named or otherwise identifiable, the information will not constitute personal data, and hence will not be covered by either the Act or the Code of Practice.

Dealing with Requests for Access to Employees' Personal Files 4.23

One of the cornerstones of the Act is that it gives individuals the right to contact any organisation that they believe holds information about them personally and request access to that information. Such a request is known as a 'subject access request'. Requests for access may be made in respect of manual files, microfiche records, audio or video tapes, computer files and email correspondence that contains information about the individual. The individual making the subject access request is not obliged under the Act to give any reason for seeking the information.

A fee of up to £10 per access request may be charged if the employer so chooses. Many employers will, in practice, grant their employees one free subject access request per year, but then charge £10 for any or all further requests within the same year. This approach strikes a reasonable balance, ie it allows employees to see, at regular intervals, what information the employer holds about them on file, without creating a situation where the employer might otherwise be inundated with frequent requests for access to data, compliance with which could be time-consuming and disruptive.

The Act lays down strict rules as to how subject access requests should be made and dealt with. For a subject access request to be valid, it must be in writing (email is acceptable) and must identify the data to which the person seeks access.

When an employer receives a subject access request, they should:

- verify the identity of the person requesting access to the data, if necessary (ie to ensure that personal information is disclosed only to the person who is its subject);

- inform the person making the application if the employer does in fact keep any personal information about them, and if so provide a description of the type of information held, the purposes for which the information is used and to whom it may be disclosed;

- inform the person making the application whether a fee is to be charged for the provision of a copy of the information;

- (once any fee has been paid and identity verified) produce copies of the relevant information in an intelligible permanent form promptly and at least within 40 calendar days and provide these to the individual. If any codes or reference numbers are used, an explanation of these should be provided; and

- give the employee any additional information that the employer has about the sources of the information provided (unless this would involve the unauthorised disclosure of confidential information relating to another individual).

The employer is not obliged to comply with an employee's request for access unless the employee has supplied such information as the employer may reasonably require in order to locate the information requested. In the event of an unspecific request, the employer would be advised to ask the employee to limit their request by defining it in some way, for example by date range, or by specifying authors, recipients or subject matter.

The employer may refuse to comply with a subject access request if the same employee has previously made a similar or identical request and a 'reasonable time interval' has not yet elapsed between compliance with the previous request and the making of the current request. 'Reasonable time interval' is, however, not defined in the Act and so a common sense approach should be taken.

As a result of these provisions, employees have the right to see documents such as:

- performance reviews or appraisals;

- sickness records;

- warnings or minutes of disciplinary interviews;

- training records;

- statements about pay;

- emails or word-processed documents of which they are the subject; and

- expressions of opinion or intention about (for example) promotion prospects.

Employees may also request access to information generated by computer systems involved in automated decision making on matters such as performance and conduct.

In requesting access to personal data held about themselves, employees may seek access to copies of any emails in which their name appears. The Employment Practices Data Protection Code, Part 3, Monitoring at Work states that workers will not usually be entitled to be granted access to all emails just because they were the sender or recipient, but that access would normally have to be granted to emails in which the employee was the subject of the email. If the employee's name was merely mentioned in the email, for example as one of a list of people who attended a meeting, it is unlikely that disclosure would be required under the Act.

It would be advantageous for employers to:

- nominate a senior person in the organisation who is to be responsible for ensuring that subject access requests are properly dealt with;

- establish a system and procedure for responding to subject access requests, including how any requirement for employees to pay a fee for subject access will be administered;

- ensuring that all information is readily accessible; and

- create a checklist that lists the locations where personal data is held.

Exceptions to an employee's right of access to personal data 4.24

There are some limited exemptions to the general duty to comply with a subject access request. These include circumstances where the information held relates to:

- management planning or forecasting;

- negotiations with employees;

- the price of a company's shares;

- the prevention or detection of crime or the apprehension or prosecution of offenders;

- the assessment or collection of any tax or duty;

- references; and

- data about another person.

A partial exemption also exists where the provision of a permanent copy of the information requested would require disproportionate effort.

These exemptions are discussed further at **4.25** to **4.32** below.

Information relating to management planning 4.25

Information relating to management planning or forecasting may be withheld if its disclosure would be likely to prejudice the employer's business. Examples of the type of information that could potentially be withheld under this heading would be plans to promote or transfer an employee, or a proposal to make a group of staff redundant. Employers should note, however, that employers may be under a statutory duty to consult employees over proposed redundancies, depending on the numbers of staff involved.

Negotiations with employees   4.26

If the employer has information on file that, if disclosed, would reveal its intentions in relation to negotiations with an employee, a group of employees or a trade union, and if such a disclosure would be likely to prejudice the negotiations, the information may be withheld. An example could be information that stated how far the employer was prepared to go in forthcoming or current pay negotiations.

Information on the price of a company's shares   4.27

This limited exemption (known as the 'corporate finance exemption') could apply where disclosure of information might affect the price of a company's shares or other financial instrument.

Information held for the prevention or detection of crime or the apprehension or prosecution of offenders   4.28

Employers would be entitled to refuse to disclose personal information about any of their employees if the disclosure would be likely to prejudice the prevention or detection of crime or the apprehension or prosecution of an offender.

Information held for the assessment or collection of any tax or duty   4.29

Refusal to disclose personal data under this heading would be legitimate if the grounds for the refusal were similar in principle to those given at **4.28** above, ie if disclosure would be likely to prejudice the legitimate collection of income tax or other tax or duty.

References   4.30

There is an exemption in respect of references given in confidence in relation to the organisation that gave the reference. Such references may be for the purpose of the person's employment (a job reference), appointment to any office, their education or training, or for the purpose of any service to be provided to the person.

The exemption for references no longer applies, however, once the reference is in the hands of the recipient employer. Thus references contained in employees' or job applicants files are subject to disclosure, but may nevertheless be withheld on the grounds that the reference would reveal information about a third party (see **4.31** below).

Data that would reveal information about a third party 4.31

A general exemption applies to any information the disclosure of which would reveal information about another person (a third party), such that the third party could be identified from it. Disclosing the document could in some cases lead to a breach of confidence and a violation of the third party's rights under the *DPA 1998*. Examples of such information could include a written statement of complaint about an employee, signed by a colleague, or a confidential job reference received from another employer and signed by an individual manager. In this case, the employer should first of all consider whether either of the following options would be a reasonable course of action:

- to request permission from the third party to release the data to the employee who has requested it; or

- to blank out the details of the third party before making the data available to the employee who has requested it (if doing so would be sufficient to conceal their identity).

The case of *Asda Stores Ltd v Thompson & Ors EAT [2002] IRLR 245* endorses the approach suggested above of blanking out the third party's identity from a document. In this case, the Employment Appeal Tribunal ruled that, for the purpose of disposing of the employees' complaint of unfair dismissal, the employer had to disclose confidential witness statements involving allegations of drugs dealing, but that they could conceal the identity of the witnesses, or if necessary edit parts of the statements, in order to prevent the witnesses from being identified.

Before refusing to release a document that would disclose details of a third party, the employer should take a reasoned decision on whether it is reasonable to disclose it, by balancing the third party's right to privacy against the employee's right to know what information is held about them and its source.

Employers should bear in mind, however, that even though a third party may be identified in a document to which an employee has requested access, the information may not be confidential. If, for example, the document states facts of which the employee is already aware, then there would be no valid reason to refuse disclosure of the document to the employee notwithstanding that it contained the names of one or more third parties.

Part 2 of the Employment Practices Data Protection Code (Employment Records) endorses this point by suggesting that employers should normally be prepared to disclose information that identifies work colleagues, provided the colleagues provided the information in a business capacity and so long as the information is not of a particularly private or sensitive nature. The Code also provides a list of factors that employers should consider when conducting the balancing exercise. These are:

- whether the disclosure of the document as it stands would actually be in breach of the duty of confidence owed to the third party – automatic assumptions about this should be avoided;

- whether the information identifies the third party in a business or personal capacity – the right to privacy will be greater if the third party is identifiable in a personal capacity, for example where a personal, rather than a corporate, reference has been provided;

- the nature of the information and whether its disclosure could potentially be damaging to the third party, for example if the document contained a complaint about the employee made by a colleague, the colleague may fear (reasonably or unreasonably) that the employee might seek revenge on them if their identity as the author of the complaint was disclosed;

- whether the information is already known to the employee either in total or in part, in which case the release of the document should not risk being in breach of the duty of confidence owed to the third party;

- whether the documents contains information that the employee would have a right to know or would have a right to dispute, for example allegations about poor job performance or misconduct;

- whether it is feasible to edit the document in such a way as to remove the identity of the third party without significantly changing its content or relevance to the employee who requested access to it (for example the employer should consider whether it is possible to photocopy the document in such a way that the third party's name does not appear on the copy);

- whether the third party has expressly refused consent to the disclosure of the document, and if so the reasons given and whether they are considered reasonable;

- what information the third party was given when consent was requested, and what their reasonable expectations would be, for example it would not be appropriate to take the view that references can be kept confidential in all circumstances since a court or tribunal can order their disclosure where they consider that it is in the interests of justice to do so;

- the impact the disclosure of the information might have on the employee, for example whether disclosure would be likely to have a negative or damaging effect on them.

Where the provision of a permanent copy of the information requested would require disproportionate effort   4.32

A partial exemption to the duty to respond to a subject access request exists in circumstances where the provision of a permanent copy of the information requested would require disproportionate effort. Even if this is the case, however, the employer must do all they reasonably can to provide the employee with access to the information he or she has requested, for example by allowing them to inspect a file rather than providing a copy of everything in the file. Alternatively, the employer may be able to deal with the problem effectively by asking the employee to redefine his or her request, for example to specify a date range for a set of documents, specify authors or recipients of information, or provide more detail of the subject matter of the data that they wish to access.

The *DPA 1998* does not define 'disproportionate effort' but it is likely that matters affecting what would or would not be disproportionate could include:

- the time needed to locate all the information requested by the individual;

- the cost of providing the information in permanent form; and

- any particular difficulty involved in locating or providing the information.

Part 2 of the Employment Practices Data Protection Code (Employment Records) suggests that employers should only decline to provide an employee with a permanent copy of the files requested on the basis of the disproportionate effort exemption in exceptional circumstances. A better course of action would be to provide as much information as the employer reasonably can and explain why the remainder of the information requested is delayed, or cannot be provided.

An example of this provision coming into play could be if an employee requested access to all the emails on the employer's computer system that contained information about him or her. It would in all likelihood be an unwieldy task to search through all the company's email records just in case there might be a message that contained information about the employee in question. This would involve disproportionate effort. The employer should, however, check locations that are reasonably likely to contain emails about the employee, the most obvious example being the employee's line manager's inbox and outbox. Alternatively, the employee could be asked to provide more information as to the likely location of any email messages, so that the search could be narrowed down.

Chapter 5
Data Protection in
Recruitment and Selection

Introduction 5.1

The recruitment and selection of new staff represents one of the most important activities of any organisation. An organisation that attracts and retains talented people will in all likelihood perform well. In contrast, if recruitment is not carried out effectively and within the law, the results can be poor performance, the need for increased supervision, excessive training, frustration for the colleagues of the new recruit, and ultimately the possibility that the employer will have to dismiss the new employee and begin the recruitment process all over again.

The key aim of this chapter is to explore the subject of recruitment in light of the data protection provisions contained in the *Data Protection Act 1998* (*DPA 1998* or 'the Act') and the Employment Practices Data Protection Code, Part 1: Recruitment and Selection (the Code of Practice).

Creating and Maintaining Records of Job Applicants 5.2

The recruitment process will inevitably lead to the need to create a set of records for each job applicant and to maintain these records throughout the process of recruitment and for at least a short period of time after the recruitment exercise has been concluded. Some of the data held on file will be information provided by the job applicant, whilst other papers will be those created by the employer. Relevant documents may include:

- the applicant's CV and/or application form;

- letters from the employer to the job applicant acknowledging the person's application, inviting them to interview and providing a response post-interview;

- letters from the applicant to the employer relating to interview arrangements;

- a copy of the job description and employee specification;

- interview notes made at or after the interview (see **5.19** below);

- copies of any psychometric or other tests completed by the applicant and their results/interpretation;

- personal information about the applicant's racial or ethnic background, obtained for monitoring purposes (see **5.17** below);

- interview expense claim forms;

- references obtained about the applicant from third parties (see **5.25** below);

- medical information about the applicant, for example a medical questionnaire completed by the applicant or a report from an occupational doctor (see **5.18** below);

- copies of certificates or proof of qualifications supplied by the job applicant (see **5.27** below);

- copies of documents that prove the individual has the right to work in the UK (required under the *Asylum and Immigration Act 1996*) (see **5.28** below);

- statements from the Criminal Records Bureau concerning any criminal records appertaining to the applicant (see **5.29** below);

- a copy of a letter from the employer offering the individual employment, and a copy of the applicant's acceptance or rejection;

- a written statement of the individual's key terms and conditions of employment.

Not of all of the above documents will constitute 'personal data' under the Act; for example the job description and employee specification will not be specific to any one job applicant.

The extent to which information held about job applicants constitutes 'personal data' under the DPA 1998
5.3

If some or all of the information created about a job applicant is input to a computer, it will automatically constitute personal data, defined in the *DPA 1998* as 'data which relate to a living individual who can be identified either from the data, or from the data together with other information which is in the possession of the data controller.'

If, as is more likely, the information is held manually, it will fall under the Act if it is contained in a 'relevant filing system'. A relevant filing system is a set of information that is 'structured, either by reference to individuals or by reference to criteria relating to individuals, in such a way that specific information relating to a particular individual is readily accessible'.

In *Durant v Financial Services Authority [2003] EWCA Civ 1746,* (see also **4.4**) the Court of Appeal interpreted the scope of this provision quite narrowly. The Court stated that, in order for information to be 'personal data' for the purposes of the Act, it must not only name or directly refer to an individual, but must also be biographical to a significant extent and have the data subject as its focus. The

Court of Appeal took the view that for information to constitute personal data, it must relate in some way to information affecting the individual's privacy, whether in their personal or family life, business or professional capacity. This would suggest, for example, that letters sent between the employer and the applicant concerning interview arrangements would not necessarily constitute personal data since the focus of the letters would be the interview arrangements and not the applicant.

Despite the *Durant* decision, it is advisable for employers to assume in the first instance that much of the information held on file about a job applicant will fall within the scope of the Act and thus be subject to the subject access provisions (see **5.5** below).

Information about a job applicant that constitutes 'sensitive data'   5.4

Clearly records appertaining to job applicants should be treated as strictly confidential. Some of the data in the applicant's file may constitute 'sensitive data' under the *DPA 1998*, defined as:

'personal data consisting of information as to:

(a)   racial or ethic origin;

(b)   political opinions;

(c)   religious beliefs or other beliefs of a similar nature;

(d)   whether the person is a member of a trade union;

(e)   physical or mental health or condition;

(f)   sexual life;

(g)   the commission or alleged commission of any offence;

(h)   any proceedings for any offence committed or alleged to have been committed, the disposal of such proceedings or the sentence of any court in such proceedings.'

Some of the information gathered during the recruitment process may qualify as sensitive data such as:

● information about the applicant's health, or disability, obtained as a result of a pre-employment medical examination or following the completion by the applicant of a medical questionnaire;

● information about criminal convictions or other information obtained from the Criminal Records Bureau in respect of the applicant;

● information provided for monitoring purposes on the applicant's racial or ethic origin.

The issue of sensitive data in relation to job applications is explored further at **5.13** below.

Job Applicants' Right of Access to Records   5.5

Job applicants about whom information is held on a file by a prospective employer will have the right to request access to the information held about them, subject to the request for access being in writing (email is acceptable) and to the payment of any fee prescribed by the employer (up to a maximum of £10). This is known as a subject access request. A job applicant will have the right to submit a subject access request irrespective of whether their application was in response to a job advertisement or unsolicited, and irrespective of whether the application has been successful or unsuccessful. So long as a record about the job applicant still exists, the person will have the right of access to it. In the event of a valid request, the employer must comply by providing the job applicant with:

- a description of the type of information held about the applicant, the purpose(s) for which it is held and any types of organisation that the information may be passed on to;

- a copy of the data itself in permanent and intelligible form.

This information must be provided promptly and within a timescale of no more than 40 calendar days.

The right of access may include access to information about the applicant contained in the text of emails, for example internal emails from an HR officer to the line manager of the department in which the vacancy exists providing information about the applicant. By contrast, an email that simply listed the names of a group of job applicants would not constitute personal data.

Requests for access to data must be sufficiently precise to enable the employer to locate the right information, otherwise, under the principle of proportionality, the employer will not be obliged to comply. In the case of requests for access from job applicants, it would not be difficult for the applicant to make their subject access request precise. It is likely that it would be sufficiently precise for the applicant to identify the job vacancy (for example by referring to the job title or any reference number provided by the employer) and the date his or her application was submitted and state that they were seeking access to any file containing personal information about them in relation to recruitment into that job.

If any of the information held in the recruitment file identifies a third party, the employer must take care not to breach that third party's rights under the Act. The most obvious example of this would be in relation to any references held on the applicant's file provided in confidence by a previous employer or other contact which would, if disclosed, reveal the identity of the author of the reference. Paragraph **5.25** below deals fully with this issue.

The Code of Practice on Recruitment   5.6

The Information Commissioner published a Code of Practice in 2003, Part 1 of which provides guidance on how employers can comply with the *DPA 1998* in the context of recruitment. The full name of the Code is the Employment Practices Data Protection Code, Part 1: Recruitment and Selection (referred to hereafter as 'the Code of Practice').

The Code of Practice is not legally binding, but represents the Information Commissioner's recommendations as to how employers should fulfil their legal requirements under the Act in relation to recruitment and selection. In the event of a legal challenge, however, a court or tribunal can take the Code of Practice into account, and evidence of non-compliance can operate to the employer's detriment.

One key stated aim of the Code of Practice is 'strike a balance between a worker's (or a job applicant's) legitimate right to respect for his or her private life and an employer's legitimate need to run its business'. Much of the Code is concerned with proportionality, ie whether a particular course of action carried out by the employer is appropriate and necessary for the achievement of a legitimate aim when balanced against the needs of the individual, including the right to privacy.

The Code of Practice provides guidance on every stage of the recruitment process from advertising the job through to the retention of recruitment records. Some of the general principles advocated by the Code of Practice are that employers should:

- disclose the organisation's identity to all job applicants as soon as possible (for example if the post is advertised via an employment agency);

- restrict the information they collect about job applicants to that which is relevant to the job in question;

- refrain from collecting information about job applicants' personal lives unless it is necessary for the purpose of the specific recruitment exercise;

- collect sensitive data only where the job applicant's explicit consent has been obtained or in circumstances where the collection of such data is in order to fulfil a legal obligation (for example a check carried out via the Criminal Records Bureau in relation to a sensitive post);

- inform job applicants as to how the information held about them is to be used unless this is self-evident;

- ensure any tests used as part of the assessment process are carried out by properly trained and qualified personnel;

- retain recruitment records for as short a period of time as necessary, based on business needs;

- notify the applicant if the employer wishes to retain their details on file after the conclusion of the recruitment exercise, explaining how the information will be used and how long it will be kept, and giving the applicant the option to ask the employer not to retain it;

- ensure the security of all job applications, including devising a secure method for individuals to send in their applications online;

- not automatically transfer all the data relating to the recruitment of the successful job applicant to a permanent employee file, but instead transfer only the data that is relevant and necessary for the ongoing employment relationship.

The points listed above are explored further in the following sections.

Ensuring Advertising Complies with Data Protection Provisions 5.7

The Code of Practice identifies a number of key actions required of employers in relation to job advertising. The underlying principle is that the advertising process should be open and transparent, making it clear to anyone who may wish to respond to the employer's advertisement how the information they supply will be used and to whom it may be disclosed.

The key principles contained in the Code of Practice relating to job advertising are that employers should:

- identify themselves in the advertisement rather than (for example) providing only a PO box number for replies or a web site address that does not make it clear who the employer is;

- include information in the advert as to how job applicants' information will be used in circumstances where the employer intends to use such information for any purpose other than recruitment into the post in question, for example if the employer intends to pass on applicants' details to another organisation or use it for marketing purposes. This is in line with the second data protection principle which requires employers to obtain personal data only for one or more specified and lawful purposes and not to process personal data in any manner incompatible with those purposes.

Where, following an advertising campaign, an agency passes individuals' job applications on to a prospective employer, the employer should, as soon as possible, take steps to inform each applicant of their identity and how they intend to use the applicant's details (unless this is self-evident). This information can be supplied directly to applicants or the task delegated to the recruitment agency to pass the information on to the applicants.

Where an employer wishes to remain anonymous to job applicants until a later stage in the recruitment process, they may do so only if they arrange to receive candidates' applications from the recruitment agency in an anonymous form. In this way, fairness is maintained because neither party will know the identity of the other unless and until the employer decides to take forward an individual's application to the next stage of the recruitment process, at which time they should disclose their identity to the applicant.

Advertising by recruitment agencies   5.8

Where the organisation placing the job advertisement is a recruitment agency, the Code of Practice suggests that the agency should (in addition to the points at **5.7** above):

- identify itself clearly, although there is no duty on the agency at this stage to disclose the identity of the employer on whose behalf it is advertising;

- make it clear in the job advert if the agency intends to pass on applicants' details to one or more of their clients;

- inform potential applicants of any use they intend to make of applications that is not self-evident, for example if the agency plans to retain applicants' details for use in connection with future vacancies.

Some general guidelines for good practice in job advertising are:

- Draft advertisements so that they provide a clear and accurate picture of the organisation's activities, the duties and level of seniority of the job, and the type of candidate the organisation is seeking.

- Make sure that advertisements do not contain any material that could be construed as sexist or racist.

- Ensure that the language used in the advertisement is specific and unambiguous.

- Refrain from specifying age limits or age-related criteria in job advertisements.

- Make sure that any job-related requirements included in an advertisement are necessary for the performance of the job, and not excessive or overstated.

- Check that any employment agency to be used is reputable and ask for a statement from the agency that they will comply with all legal provisions, including the *DPA 1998*.

- Make job applicants sourced from employment agencies aware of the employer's identity as soon as possible.

Using Application Forms and Dealing Lawfully with the Data Obtained, including Sensitive Data   5.9

With the publication of the Employment Practices Data Protection Code of Practice, Part 1: Recruitment and Selection, employers would be well advised to review, and if necessary, amend their application forms if they have not already done so recently. A further beneficial course of action might be to devise different versions of the application form for use for recruitment into different types of jobs.

Job applications may be received in several ways:

- on company-designed application forms;

- in CVs written by individual job applicants;

- online applications; and

- summaries provided by recruitment agencies in the agency's style and format.

Security of job applications   5.10

Whatever method of receiving applications is chosen, the employer has a duty under the seventh data protection principle to ensure that any personal data they hold about job applicants is held securely and in such a way that it is protected against unauthorised or unlawful processing, accidental loss, or destruction or damage. The Code of Practice suggests the following measures:

- ensuring that a secure method of electronic transmission is used where applications are sought online;

- limiting access to electronic applications by ensuring they are saved in a directory or drive to which only authorised personnel have access;

- ensuring that paper applications (whether postal or faxed) are stored under lock and key;

- ensuring that paper applications can be accessed only by those who are actively engaged in the process of recruitment; and

- taking steps to ensure that line managers who review job applications are made aware of the necessary data protection provisions in relation to job applications.

Company application forms   5.11

Whilst an employer may not have much control over the design of an individual's CV, they will be able to control the information provided by applicants on in-house application forms to a significant extent. Apart from the importance of designing applications forms to ensure the collection of all the necessary information for the purpose of effective recruitment, the form should:

- identify the employer clearly, ie provide the employer's name, address and other contact details;

- advise applicants if the information they provide on the application form is to be used for any purpose other than recruitment into the post for which they are applying (for example applicants should be informed if their information may be retained for recruitment into different posts, or is likely to be passed on to another organisation);

- include a statement asking candidates to choose (perhaps by ticking a yes/no box) whether to apply for only a specific post, or to opt to have their details kept on file (in the event that they are unsuccessful in their application) in case other positions arise in the future;

- request only information that is appropriate, relevant and necessary for the job being considered – this ties in to the third data protection principle which requires employers to ensure that personal data is 'adequate, relevant and not excessive in relation to the purpose or purposes for which they are processed';

- ensure the scope of the information requested is proportionate to the employer's aim – the Code of Practice provides a clear example by pointing out that the extent and nature of the information required of an applicant for the post of head of security at a bank would be very different from the information required of an applicant to work in the same bank's canteen;

- be designed so that the applicant's personal details (ie address, gender, marital or family status, age, nationality, etc) can be separated from the remainder of the form (normally by HR department) before the application is passed through to line managers for short-listing (in order to promote equality of opportunity and the avoidance of discrimination);

- not include any questions that request information that will become relevant only if the applicant is subsequently employed (for example information about a job applicant's partner or children, which might become necessary after employment has commenced for insurance purposes, but would not be relevant to the recruitment decision);

- only ask for information about an applicant's criminal convictions if this information is necessary in relation to the post to be filled;

- make a statement on the form about any checks that the employer routinely makes at a later stage of the recruitment process in order to verify information provided by the applicant;

- ensure there is justification for seeking any sensitive data from the applicant, and if there is justification, explain the reason(s) why the information is being sought (see **5.13** below).

In order to comply with the *DPA 1998* and the Code of Practice, employers should, if they have not already arranged to do so, use more than one version of their application form and customise each version to the type of post in question. The principle behind this is to ensure that job applicants are not asked questions that are irrelevant to the post for which they are applying. Each version of the form can nevertheless contain the same core questions. Distinctions may be drawn in a number of ways, including the following examples (which are not, of course, exhaustive):

- manual and non-manual jobs (so-called 'blue collar' and 'white collar' posts);

- support staff jobs and professional jobs;

- managerial and non-managerial posts;

- office-based and travelling jobs, for example sales executives.

The aim should be to ensure that, insofar as is possible and practicable, the employer should not seek information from job applicants that is not directly relevant to the specific post for which they are applying. Examples of information that might be relevant to some jobs, but not others, could, for example, include information on whether the applicant holds a driving licence, information on criminal convictions, degree of computer literacy, etc.

It is advisable for employers to devise and implement a policy on the handling, retention and disposal of applications for employment, including unsolicited applications. The policy should include the length of time that the employer will retain application forms (see **5.31** below), the method and frequency of destroying out-of-date applications and the circumstances in which an application may be held for longer than the default period.

Online applications   5.12

The principles outlined at **5.11** above would apply equally to job applications sent online. Where this method of receiving applications is used, the employer should take steps to ensure that applications can be sent securely, for example by using encryption-based software.

Sensitive data in relation to job applications   5.13

The *DPA 1998* states that sensitive data may not be gathered about an individual unless either the person has consented to processing, or one of a restricted number of conditions is fulfilled. One of these conditions is if the data is necessary in order for the employer to comply with a legal obligation in connection with employment.

Where data is necessary to comply with a legal obligation   5.14

As stated at **5.13** above, one of the conditions justifying the collection and use of sensitive data is where the data is necessary in order for the employer to comply with a legal obligation. This can be an obligation imposed by statute or by common law (ie as a result of court and tribunal decisions that set binding precedents as to how the law should be interpreted). Thus employers that wish to seek information about job applicants' previous convictions; information about the applicant's physical or mental health racial or ethnic origins; or religion could justify doing so if they were confident that the data was necessary in order to fulfil a legal duty.

Although there is a fairly wide scope for employers to use compliance with a legal obligation as a condition to justify the collection of sensitive data during recruitment and selection, it should be noted that the wording of the law requires the processing of sensitive data to be *necessary* for compliance with a legal obligation (ie not just desirable or convenient for the employer).

Legal reasons why it may be necessary for an employer to collect sensitive data about job applicants could include the following duties:

- to check, prior to appointment, whether a job applicant has the right to work in the UK (see **5.28** below);

- not to discriminate on the grounds of sex, trans-gender status, marital status, sexual orientation, race, religion or (unless there is justification) disability which may justify gathering information about (for example) applicants' racial background and origin;

- to make reasonable adjustments under the *Disability Discrimination Act 1995* (see **5.18** below) which may justify the collection of information about a job applicant's health;

- to ensure the security of employees' and customers' personal data under the *DPA 1998* and the consequent need to ensure that applicants for posts in which personal data is handled are honest, reliable and trustworthy – this may justify collecting information about applicants' previous convictions (see **5.16** and **5.29** below);

- to ensure the health, safety and welfare of people at work, which would justify the collection of information about job applicants' health.

The above list is, of course, not exhaustive.

Gaining employees' consent to the processing of sensitive data **5.15**

It is advisable for employers to design their application forms so that they contain a statement to be signed by the applicant to signify their consent to the sensitive data contained in the application form being processed by the employer. An example of such a statement could read:

> 'Information from this application may be processed for purposes registered by the Company under the Data Protection Act 1998. I hereby give my consent to [company name] processing the data supplied in this application form for the purpose of recruitment and selection.'

The Code of Practice points out, however, that consent to the processing of sensitive data must be 'explicit', and 'freely given'. 'Explicit' in this context is defined as meaning that the applicant must have signed a document indicating his or her agreement, having first been clearly informed how the information will be used. 'Freely given' is described as giving the applicant a real choice whether or not to consent to the processing, and operating a policy of not subjecting any applicant who declines to give their consent to a significant detriment.

It can be seen from the above interpretation of the phrase 'freely given' that the extent to which employers may rely on job applicants' consent to the processing of sensitive data is somewhat limited. Although individuals obviously have a free choice as to whether or not to apply for a particular job and, as part of their application, to choose whether or not to provide any sensitive data that the organisation has requested, consent to the processing of sensitive data as a condition of a job offer is less likely to fall into the category of 'freely given'.

As stated above, employers should always assess properly whether there is justification for seeking any sensitive data from job applicants, in line with the requirements of the post in question. If there is justification, the application form should clearly explain the reason(s) why the information is being sought.

Information about job applicants' criminal convictions   5.16

Information about a job applicant's criminal convictions constitutes sensitive data under the *DPA 1998*. Job applicants also have certain rights under the *Rehabilitation of Offenders Act 1974*. Under this Act, a conviction becomes 'spent' after the elapse of a defined period of time, which in turn depends on the type of conviction and the length of time that has elapsed since it occurred. Where a conviction is spent, this allows a job applicant to be treated for most purposes as if it had never happened and to decline to disclose it during the recruitment process. There are, however, a large number of jobs that are exempt from the non-disclosure principle (listed in the *Rehabilitation of Offenders Act 1974 (Exceptions) Order 1975 (SI 1975 No 1023)*).

Because the right to conceal a spent conviction is a statutory right conferred on job applicants by the *Rehabilitation of Offenders Act 1974*, it is unlawful for an employer to refuse to employ someone because they have declined to disclose a spent conviction. Equally, if a job applicant elects to disclose a spent conviction voluntarily, or if the employer happens to find out about it from another source, the employer must disregard it when making the decision as to whom to employ.

Questions about an applicant's criminal convictions should of course be asked if this information is necessary in relation to the post to be filled. This would be the case, for example, if the job was one covered by the *Rehabilitation of Offenders Act 1974 (Exceptions) Order 1975*, in which case the employer would be entitled to ask for all convictions (including spent convictions) to be declared in order to comply with the law in this area. Where this is the case, this fact should be clearly stated on the application form or accompanying letter.

For most jobs, however, applicants would (under the provisions of the *Rehabilitation of Offenders Act 1974*) be under no obligation to disclose spent convictions and, if a question asking whether the applicant had any previous convictions was contained in the form, would be entitled to answer 'no'.

The Code of Practice recommends that employers should not be tempted to gather information about *all* job applicants' criminal convictions, but instead should restrict any enquiries of this nature to the successful applicant only (unless there are special circumstances justifying a different approach).

Employers may also apply to the Criminal Records Bureau (CRB) for information about a job applicant's previous convictions. This matter is dealt with at **5.29** below.

Information gathered for monitoring purposes   5.17

Many organisations carry out monitoring of job applicants in order to promote equality of opportunity as between people of different racial groups and both sexes and protect against any inequalities that may otherwise creep into the recruitment process. Although information about an individual's racial or ethic origin is classed as sensitive data under the *DPA 1998*, it is legitimate for an employer to request this information from job applicants if the purpose of doing so is equal opportunities monitoring. Once again this purpose should be clearly stated on the application form in such a way that it is made clear that the racial background of the applicant will not in any way influence the selection decision (which would in any event be in breach of the *Race Relations Act 1976*).

The Code of Practice suggests that, even though equal opportunities monitoring is a legitimate reason to collect information about applicants' racial or ethnic origin, the processes used to conduct such monitoring should if possible be based on anonymous or aggregated information.

Information about a job applicant's disability   5.18

Any information gathered about a job applicant's physical or mental health or condition will fall into the category of 'sensitive data'. There are, however, sound legal reasons to ask job applicants whether they have any disability on account of the employer's duty under the *Disability Discrimination Act 1995* to make 'reasonable adjustments' to working arrangements to accommodate the needs of a disabled applicant (or employee) in order to reduce the substantial disadvantage that the applicant would otherwise have in seeking employment. This subject is explored fully in **CHAPTER 7**.

There may also be solid grounds of requesting information about applicants' physical and mental health in order to comply with the employer's duty under the

Health and Safety at Work Act 1974 to ensure, in so far as is reasonably practicable, the health, safety and welfare of all staff at work.

Dealing with Interview Records 5.19

Keeping a record of each job applicant's interview will be an important and necessary part of the recruitment process in order for the employer to be able to objectively review and assess each candidate's suitability for the job in question. It will be especially important to keep a record of the reason(s) for the selection of the successful applicant and the reasons for the rejection of the unsuccessful candidates. The Code of Practice states in relation to interview records that the retention of personal data created following an interview is justifiable, ie it is relevant to and necessary for the process of recruitment and for defending the process against possible legal challenge.

The records should be objective and should focus on factors such as the extent to which a candidate's qualifications, skills and experience match up to the requirements of the job, as defined in the employee specification. Aspects of the applicant's personal background such as family circumstances should not form part of the record as this may, for example, be perceived as discriminatory against a female candidate.

The existence of clear records will be helpful also in the event that one of the unsuccessful candidates brings a claim for unlawful discrimination to an employment tribunal. The record will assist the employer to convince the tribunal that its recruitment practices were objective, that the recruitment exercise was approached in a professional manner and that the selection decision was based on the successful candidate's merit and not on personal factors such as sex or race. If, on the other hand, no records are kept, it will be extremely difficult for the employer to convince a tribunal that the recruitment exercise was carried out fairly and objectively, and the tribunal may infer, in the absence of a satisfactory explanation, that the selection decision was discriminatory.

The first data protection principle states that personal data must be processed fairly and lawfully. 'Lawfully' in this context is likely to be interpreted widely. It would follow that any form of unlawful discrimination, ie unfavourable treatment of an applicant (at any stage of the recruitment process) on grounds of sex, marital status, sexual orientation, trans-gender status, colour, race, nationality, ethic origin, national origin, religion or belief, or disability would be likely to breach this principle.

The right of access to interview records 5.20

When making interview notes, whether on a pre-designed form or not, it should be borne in mind that the job applicant will have the right of access to this information on request (under the subject access provisions of the *DPA 1998*). The interviewer should therefore take care not to record any observations that they would be uncomfortable with the applicant reading. The best guideline is to record only observable facts, or else personal opinions that are backed up by facts. It may, for example, be acceptable to state that the job applicant was 'hesitant' when asked questions on a particular topic, but unwise to record that they would 'not fit in' as this latter observation would tend to be a highly subjective and judgmental statement (and could possibly be influenced – sometimes subconsciously – by the applicant's racial or cultural background). In general, any notes made about the applicant should be capable of being justified by facts, not feelings. So long as the interviewer focuses on the requirements of the job and the extent to which the applicant's background matches these, rather than on personal opinions and impressions of the applicant, they will not go far wrong.

Retention of interview notes   5.21

Once the recruitment process is complete, there will be no longer be any good reason to retain the successful candidate's interview notes since the purpose of these will be purely to assist the employer to select the most suitable candidate for the job. The notes should therefore not be carried over into the person's permanent personnel file as it is unlikely that they can serve any further useful or legitimate purpose.

Carrying Out Checks on Job Applicants   5.22

Considerable time, effort and expense is usually involved in the process of recruitment. It is therefore entirely legitimate for the employer, prior to committing to an offer of employment, to seek to check that the information supplied by the preferred job applicant is accurate and complete and to obtain references from previous employers. It would be simplistic and foolish to assume that all job applicants always told the whole truth about their qualifications, skills and experience during the process of recruitment. Often an applicant will present information in the most favourable light, perhaps giving undue emphasis to a particular aspect of their experience, playing down a weakness or gap in their skills or even implying that a qualification has been obtained when it has not. Whilst a well-structured, thorough interview should bring these issues to light (provided good, probing questions are asked), it is nevertheless advisable to carry out certain routine checks, at least on the applicant selected as the preferred new recruit. Whilst some organisations choose to seek references on *all* job applicants, even prior to interview, this is time-consuming and arguably unnecessary.

As stated at **5.11** above, the employer should include a statement on all company application forms informing prospective job applicants of any checks that they routinely make in order to verify the information provided by the applicant. This information should be repeated at the interview, ie the candidate should be made fully aware of the types of checks that the employer intends to carry out (with the applicant's consent – see below), what information will be verified and how the checks will be carried out (including information about any external sources that will be used to carry out the checks). The employer should also inform job applicants if the

successful candidate will be required to undergo a pre-employment medical examination as a condition of employment (see **CHAPTER 7**).

The Code of Practice sets out the general principle that verification should not go
beyond the checking of information that is sought or supplied during the recruitment process, but can include:

- references;

- confirmation of qualifications; and

- confirmation of financial information, if relevant.

More detailed checks, such as vetting an individual's background and personal
circumstances, or vetting of their family members, would be permitted under the
DPA 1998 and the Code of Practice only where the job was one in which special
circumstances or risks applied, for example jobs involving supervision of children
or certain jobs in government. Even then, the Code recommends that vetting of
this nature should only be carried out where:

- they are proportionate to the specific risks faced by the employer;

- they would be likely to reveal information that would be directly relevant
  to the decision as to whether or not to employ the individual;

- there is no alternative less intrusive way of carrying out the necessary checks
  on the individual; or

- it is certain that the external source to be used for vetting is a reliable
  source.

If it is deemed appropriate and necessary to carry out checks on the applicant's
family members (for example in the case of recruitment of police officers or
prison officers), the employer should bear in mind the rights of the individuals in
question to be informed that information about them will be sought and the purposes for which it will be used.

Obtaining consent for carrying out checks   5.23

The Code of Practice is quite explicit in recommending that the employer should
always obtain a job applicant's signed consent before seeking to conduct any checks
involving the release of information from a third party. This is line with the general
principle of openness and transparency that underpins the *DPA 1998* and the Code
of Practice. Employers should not be tempted to conduct 'secret' enquiries into a
job applicant's background, however useful they think such enquiries might prove
to be. The job applicant has a right to know what the employer's intentions are in
respect of any and all checks, before the checks are instigated.

The job applicant's consent for the necessary checks can be obtained either by
including an appropriate statement on the application form for the applicant to

sign, although a better route would be to use a specially designed form which the applicant could be asked to sign during the course of the interview. Such a form could read:

> I hereby authorise [the company] to take up references from any or all of my previous employers and (after any offer of employment has been confirmed in writing) from my present employer. In addition, I hereby authorise [the company] to carry out checks on my qualifications as [the company] deems appropriate.

The form should, of course be signed and dated by the job applicant.

The *DPA 1998, section 56* provides that it is unlawful to make it a condition of employment that a job applicant must, in connection with recruitment, provide the employer with a record obtained elsewhere by virtue of the individual's subject access rights. This means that employers are not permitted to force job applicants to use their subject access rights under the Act to gain access to information held by other organisations, for example information about criminal convictions held on file. There are exceptions to this provision where the imposition of the requirement to provide a record is required by law or is justified as being in the public interest.

What to do if checks reveal discrepancies   5.24

Rather controversially, the Code of Practice recommends that, where any of the checks carried out on the job applicant produce inconsistencies or discrepancies, the employer should not assume automatically that the applicant has supplied incorrect or deliberately misleading information, but instead should give the applicant the opportunity to 'make representations', ie provide an explanation for the discrepancy between the information he or she has provided and the information revealed as a result of the check. This may be done either by writing to the applicant or by asking them to come in for a second interview.

An obvious problem with this recommendation is that the information obtained from a third party may have been given in confidence, for example in a job reference. If this is the case, the employer may nevertheless be able to address the matter satisfactorily, for example by holding a further interview and asking the job applicant questions pertinent to the area of the discrepancy without disclosing the exact content or source of the reference.

Where, on the other hand, straightforward factual information has been supplied, for example a statement from a university or college that the applicant failed to obtain a particular qualification (in circumstances where the applicant had previously intimated to the employer that they had gained the qualification in question), then the employer would normally be able to put the statement directly to the applicant and give them the opportunity to provide an explanation. This is because the information would not be confidential. No organisation is, after all, infallible and it could happen that the university or college had made a mistake in supplying the information, for example on account of a mix-up of identities. The employer should therefore remain open-minded when carrying out checks and should not be too quick to pass judgement on an applicant about whom negative information is received, but instead should explore the issue further and take a reasoned decision as to where the truth lies. When dealing with such issues, the employer should bear in mind the fourth data protection principle, ie the duty on the employer to ensure personal data are accurate and, where necessary, kept up to date.

References   5.25

A reference that contains factual information about a job applicant's past work experience and performance can usually be viewed as a sound predictor of their future performance in a similar role. It can therefore be very useful for employers to obtain references from the successful job applicant's previous employers, if the previous employers are willing to provide them. Indeed, it is sound practice to make any job offer conditional upon the receipt of references that are satisfactory to the employer. This allows the employer, in the event that one or more of the successful candidate's references prove to be unsatisfactory, to withdraw the job offer without being in breach of contract.

It should be borne in mind that, apart from in the financial services industry, employers are under no legal duty to provide job references. Many employers have a policy of not providing references, or else of providing only the bare minimum of factual information, ie confirmation of the dates of the person's employment and their job title.

It is advisable for each employer to draw up a policy on giving references on behalf of ex-employees and to ensure this policy is properly communicated to all those who might reasonably expect to receive reference requests. The policy should state who in the organisation is authorised to give references, distinguish between references given on behalf of the employer ('corporate references') and personal references and lay down any restrictions on what should be written in a corporate reference. Often it is appropriate to prohibit line managers or others from providing corporate references, but instead require all requests for references to be passed to the HR manager. In this way, consistency in approach will be practised and the organisation protected to a considerable degree against the likelihood of spurious claims arising from allegedly unfair or inaccurate references. Alternatively, it could be made clear in the policy that if a line manager wishes to provide a reference for an ex-employee, they may do so only in a personal capacity, ie not on company-headed notepaper and not stating the manager's job title.

Part 2 of the Employment Practices Data Protection Code (Employment Records) recommends that employers should not provide confidential references about an employee unless they are sure that this is the employee's wish. It is therefore advisable for a company policy to make it clear that references will be provided only if it is known that this is in line with the employee's wishes. To facilitate adherence to the policy, it would be good practice for employers to establish, at the time an employee leaves their employment, whether or not they wish references to be provided in respect of future job applications to other employers and to record the employee's wishes on file. Alternatively, if there is any doubt at the time a reference request is received, the employer should endeavour to contact the ex-employee to check whether he or she is content for them to provide a reference.

Although employers are, as a general rule, not obliged to provide a reference for an employee who has left their employment, court and tribunal precedents indicate that if they do so, they are under a duty of care to ensure that the information they provide in the reference is factual, accurate and not misleading.

As stated earlier, employers should ensure that all applicants are clearly informed at an early stage that obtaining references will form part of the recruitment process.

References – how to handle subject access requests 5.26

The question of whether and to what extent an individual has the right of access to a job reference provided in confidence about them under the *DPA 1998* is somewhat complex and often misunderstood.

There is an exemption under the Act applicable to individuals' access to job references about them in respect of the organisation that supplied the reference. No exemption exists, however, once the reference is in the hands of the organisation to which it has been provided. In the event of the transfer of an employee from one part of an organisation to another in circumstances where the employee's 'new' department has sought and received a reference from the department where the employee originally worked, no exemption from the right of access would arise. This means that employers would be obliged under the Act to treat requests for access to internal references in the same way as access requests in relation to any other personal information, ie disclosure would normally be required.

Although a job applicant about whom confidential references have been obtained and placed in a structured recruitment file would, potentially, have the right of access to those references, a further issue is that the reference, if disclosed, would be likely to reveal the identity of a third party, namely the author of the reference. The *DPA 1998, section 7(4)–(6)* specifies that an employer is not obliged to comply with a subject access request in circumstances where doing so would reveal information relating to a third party who could be identified from the information disclosed. This exclusion includes information identifying the third party as the source (ie the author) of the information sought by the applicant. Because disclosing a reference would reveal the identity of the person who provided it and thus represent a possible breach of the duty of confidence owed to that person, this falls squarely within these provisions. The Act also states, however, that this exclusion 'does not excuse the data controller (ie the employer) from communicating so much of the information sought by the request as can be communicated without disclosing the identity of the other individual concerned, whether by the omission of names or other identifying particulars or otherwise'.

The employer should therefore consider whether it is possible to:

- photocopy the reference in such a way as to remove the name of the employer and the name of the person who signed the reference from the copy, and provide the copy to the applicant;

- seek the consent of the author of the reference for it to be disclosed to the applicant;

- consider whether it is reasonable in all the circumstances to comply with the job applicant's subject access request without the consent of the author of the reference (for example if the company in which the applicant was previously employed no longer exists and the location of the author is not known).

Clearly if the author of the reference expressly and with good reason refuses to give their consent to the disclosure of the reference to the applicant, and if it is not possible to disclose the reference without also disclosing their identity, then the reference should not be disclosed. The employer should make a file note to this effect, recording clearly the fact that they attempted to obtain consent. This would be especially important if contact with the author of the reference was made by telephone. Refusal to consent should not, however, be assumed, and the employer should take reasonable steps to try to secure the necessary consent.

Part 2 of the Employment Practices Data Protection Code (Employment Records) points out, however, that releasing a reference following a subject access request might not in reality be a breach of the duty of confidence owed to the third party. Often a reference will contain only factual information about an individual such as the dates of their previous employment or the number of days absence they have had. Since this information will already be known to the individual who is the subject of the reference, there will be nothing contentious or confidential in the reference and, arguably, no proper reason to refuse to disclose it.

The Code of Practice goes on to express the view that references should normally be disclosed to the employee unless the author of the reference provides some compelling reason as to why it should be edited or not released.

Checks on qualifications   5.27

Where it is necessary for an employee to hold a particular qualification in order to be able to perform the job effectively, the employer should always check that the successful job applicant's qualifications have actually been obtained. This can most readily be done by requesting sight of the original of the appropriate certificates and retaining a copy of these on file. Ideally, this check should be done before any job offer is made. If not, the offer letter should state that the production of documentary evidence about the applicant's qualifications is a pre-condition for employment.

If the employer wishes to verify further that the applicant has the requisite qualifications for the job by writing to the university or college where the qualification was obtained, this should be done only with the employee's express consent. Some universities and colleges may in any event require a signed approval form from the individual before they will release confirmation of their qualifications to a third party.

Checks on applicants' right to work in the UK   5.28

Under the *Asylum and Immigration Act 1996*, it is a criminal offence for an employer to recruit someone who:

- has not been granted leave to enter or remain in the UK; or

- does not have permission to work in the UK.

Employers therefore have duty under the *DPA 1998* to check that anyone who is subject to immigration control and whom they wish employ has the right to work in the UK. The Act does not apply to the employment of British citizens; Commonwealth citizens with the right of abode in the UK; and citizens of any country in the European Economic Area.

To fulfil their duty under the *Asylum and Immigration Act 1996*, employers must take the following steps to check whether the applicant has the right to work in the UK:

- require the job applicant to produce an original document indicating that he or she has the right to work in the UK;

- check that the document appears to relate to the job applicant; and

- either retain the document itself or keep a copy of it for the duration of the person's employment and for six months after termination of employment.

This type of check must be carried out satisfactorily before the applicant is permitted to start work. Employers are not, however, expected to be experts in this area, nor to check the authenticity of any document that a particular job applicant produces, unless there is clear evidence to suggest that the employment of that particular individual would be illegal. Employers who employ overseas nationals in circumstances where it is clear that the they knew that that the person did not have permission to work in the UK can be prosecuted.

Employers should take care when approaching the matter of a job applicant's right to work in the UK that they do not engage in practices that could amount to race discrimination. The *Race Relations Act 1976* requires employers not to treat any job applicant unfavourably on the grounds of nationality. Reconciling the requirements of the *Race Relations Act 1976* with the requirements of the *Asylum and Immigration Act 1996* can be a challenge. Help is at hand in the form of a Code of Practice on the avoidance of race discrimination in recruitment, available at: www.ind.homeoffice.gov.uk/default.asp?pageid=1366. The main recommendation of this Code of Practice is that employers, in carrying out checks of job applicants' right to work in the UK, should require *all* applicants (and not only those who are known or believed to be of foreign nationality) to produce documentary evidence of their right to work in the UK. The Code also lists the types of document that are valid for the purpose of verifying the applicant's right to work in the UK.

One effective way of dealing with this matter sensibly is to include a statement within all letters sent out inviting job applicants to interview to the effect that the employer will require documentary evidence of the right to work in the UK. This can be conveniently combined with a request to bring proof of qualifications to the interview. It is advisable also to inform applicants that it is the company's policy to make such a request, and that all job applicants are required to comply. At the interview itself, the interviewer can request sight of the relevant documents, and make copies for the company's retention.

Checks on criminal records   5.29

Employers may apply to the Criminal Records Bureau (CRB) for information about a job applicant's previous convictions. Such applications must be made in association with the job applicant and must be in relation to a specific post. Applications will be accepted only where the employer is registered with the CRB.

There are three types of certificate, although at the time of writing only the first two are available:

- A criminal records certificate (CRC), which is issued jointly to the individual and a registered employer and includes information on both spent and unspent convictions. This is known as a standard disclosure and the certificate is available in relation to recruitment into posts that are exempt from the provisions of the *Rehabilitation of Offenders Act 1974*.

- An enhanced criminal records certificate (ECRC), which is available jointly to the individual and a registered employer and which includes more detailed information than the CRC. This is known as an enhanced disclosure and the certificate would be appropriate where, for example, the work involved unsupervised contact with children or vulnerable adults.

- A criminal conviction certificate (CCC) which will in future be available to individual applicants and will show unspent convictions only. This is known as a basic disclosure. Once these are available employers will be able to ask job applicants to produce a CCC if they wish at an appropriate point in the recruitment process.

All information about individuals obtained from the CRB will fall into the category of sensitive data and must be treated accordingly.

The Data Protection Code of Practice in Recruitment and Selection states that employers should not force job applicants to use their subject access rights to obtain records (including those from the CRB) by making it a condition of their employment. Once the Criminal Records Bureau becomes fully functional, ie once it begins to issue CCCs, enforced subject access of this kind will become a criminal offence under the *DPA 1998*.

The Code recommends further that employers should:

- not routinely ask all short-listed applicants to obtain a disclosure from the CRB;

- review whether it is necessary to request a disclosure from the CRB in relation to each individual post, bearing in mind the third data protection principle (ie that information must be adequate, relevant and *not excessive* in relation to the purpose for which it is processed); and

- keep any information obtained from the CRB confidential and not share it with other employers.

Employees' Rights in Relation to Automated Decisions in Recruitment **5.30**

The *DPA 1998, section 12* contains specific provisions relating to certain forms of decision-making carried out solely by automated means. Examples include circumstances in which the automated decision-making process evaluates matters such as job applicants' work performance, creditworthiness, reliability or conduct.

Job applicants' rights in this case are to be informed that a decision about them has been taken on the basis of an automated decision-taking process, and to challenge the automated decision if, as a result of it, they have been rejected for employment or treated significantly differently from other applicants. The applicant's challenge must be made in writing within 21 days of the employer informing him or her of the automated decision. The applicant would have the right to request an explanation of the logic involved in the decision, and to ask for the decision to be reconsidered or retaken on a different basis, ie not solely on the basis of the automatic processing. The employer is obliged to provide a response within 21 days. These rights only apply, however, where the employer's decision has been taken *solely* by automated means and not in circumstances where the rejection of a particular job applicant was as a result of a range of factors, at least some of which involved human intervention or analysis.

These provisions mean that job applicants can, in certain circumstances, challenge decisions about their suitability for a job made on the basis of psychometric testing carried out and analysed by means of a computer-based software.

The Code of Practice recommends that employers should be certain that any psychometric testing that they employ for the purpose of short-listing or final selection is done only by people who are qualified to apply and assess the particular test. This is, in any event, common sense and essential good practice. The Code points out that this recommendation is consistent with the third data protection principle which requires employers to ensure that personal data are adequate in relation to the purpose for which they are used.

In light of these provisions, employers should:

- ensure that any psychometric tests to be used have been fully validated;

- review whether any tests used within the organisation measure factors that are relevant to the post in question;

- ensure that any psychometric tests to be used are applied and assessed only by people who have been fully trained in their use;

- set up a system that ensures job applicants are informed up-front if an automated system is to be used as the sole basis of short-listing and how they can challenge any decision made in this way that results in their rejection;

- keep the results of any automated testing under regular review to ensure the tests achieve the outcomes that the employer seeks and that they treat applicants fairly;

- put a system in place to deal with any challenges raised by job applicants following the results of any testing conducted by automated means; and

- refrain from using automated testing as the sole means of short-listing.

Deciding for how long Recruitment Records should be Retained   5.31

There is no time period prescribed in the *DPA 1998* or the Code of Practice in relation to the retention of recruitment records. Employers are therefore free to decide what time period is appropriate for their business needs. Employers should, however, bear the fifth data protection principle in mind – that records should not be kept for longer than is necessary in relation to the purpose for which they were created.

The time limit for a job applicant to bring a claim of discrimination to an employment tribunal is three months after the alleged act of discrimination (usually the date the rejection letter was received). Employers should therefore keep recruitment records for between four and six months (which allows a safety window), after which they should be destroyed. Clearly, however, if a claim for discrimination is lodged with the employment tribunal, then the employer would be justified in retaining the files of the claimant and possibly those of the other short-listed candidates for a longer period, ie until the discrimination claim had been settled. This would be in order to be able to prove to the tribunal's satisfaction that the applicant claiming discrimination was not in fact treated less favourably than other applicants.

The Code of Practice also recommends that employers should:

- assess who in the organisation retains recruitment records;

- establish a policy on a suitable retention period for recruitment records based on clear business needs;

- adhere to that policy unless there are special reasons to retain a particular record for a longer period, for example if there is an ongoing legal claim against the employer from a particular job applicant;

- destroy information obtained as a result of any vetting exercise as soon as possible, and in any event within six months, although the Code suggests a record of the result of vetting or verification may be retained, ie a simple record of whether the result was satisfactory or unsatisfactory;

- destroy information about an individual's criminal convictions once these have been verified through the CRB, unless there are exceptional circumstances that justify retaining the information in respect of the successful applicant (ie it is necessary to retain the information for a purpose relevant to the ongoing employment relationship);

- advise unsuccessful applicants if the employer intends to retain their details on file in respect of future vacancies (rather than assuming that this would be their choice) and give them the option to ask for their details to be removed from the file, if they wish;

- ensure that all information obtained during the course of the recruitment exercise is securely stored, or else destroyed.

In relation to the destruction of information that is no longer relevant and necessary for the employer's legitimate business interests, the Code of Practice recommends shredding manual records and ensuring that electronic files are permanently deleted from the employer's computer system.

Chapter 6
Employee Records

Introduction 6.1

The creation and maintenance of employee records will form the foundation of effective people management in all organisations, whether public or private, large or small. If the records are structured, well-organised and include information that is appropriate and relevant to the employer's needs, they will serve the employer well. If, on the other hand, records are random, unstructured or poorly organised, this will in all likelihood lead to confusion and time-wasting both in relation to subject access requests under the *Data Protection Act 1998* (*DPA 1998* or 'the Act') and in the event of any kind of claim against the employer in an employment tribunal.

Observing the Data Protection Principles in the Maintenance of Employee Records 6.2

The eight data protection principles contained in the Act (see **4.13** to **4.21** above) underpin an employer's duties and obligations under the Act. The Act places responsibilities on all employers to process personal data in a fair and proper way.

The first data protection principle creates the obligation on employers to process personal data 'fairly and lawfully'. This duty is subject to the proviso that personal data must not be processed unless one of a number of conditions is fulfilled. The conditions are that:

- the employee has given his or her consent to the processing; or

- the processing of personal data is necessary for one of the following reasons:

  - for the performance of a contract;

  - in order to ensure compliance with a legal obligation;

  - to protect the vital interests of the employee;

  - for the administration of justice or for the exercise of any public functions;

  - for the purposes of legitimate interests pursued by the employer, for example if the business was about to be transferred.

Further conditions are imposed on the processing of data that is classed as 'sensitive data' under the Act (see **4.6** above).

From the above list, the most likely valid reasons for an employer to process personal data in employment records would be:

- for the purpose of performing a contract, for example the employer may need to hold information about the employee's dependents in order to be able to process any claim for benefit under a contractual private medical insurance scheme;

- in order to ensure compliance with a legal obligation, for example to comply with the duty to process Statutory Maternity Pay for an employee who is pregnant;

- where the employee has given his or her consent to the processing.

It is important, however, to take note of the word 'necessary' used in this part of the Act. Unless the employee's consent has been obtained, the processing of data about them will be fair and lawful only if one of the relevant conditions is *necessary* for the business, and not just because (for example) management would find it helpful or convenient to process personal data.

The second data protection principle requires employers to obtain and use information about individuals only for one or more specified and lawful purposes and not process the information for any purpose that is incompatible with the stated purpose(s). It follows that the employer should firstly be clear as to the (lawful) purpose(s) to be served by the collection and retention of personal information about their employees. Once this is established, the employer must not subsequently use any of the information they hold on file for any purpose that is incompatible with or vastly different from the purpose for which it was collected.

An example of non-compliance in this area would be where the employer carried out monitoring of employees' use of email for the purpose of preventing and detecting unauthorised use of the employer's computer system, and as a result of such monitoring discovered by chance that the employee had disclosed in an email to a company doctor that they had developed an illness. If the employer used that information for any other purpose, for example, to deny the employee a promotion, that would be an unlawful use of the information and would almost certainly amount to a breach of trust and confidence as well.

The third data protection principle states that personal information must be adequate, relevant and not excessive in relation to the purpose or purposes for which it is processed. The employer should therefore review carefully all the information they collect and hold about employees and job applicants and check whether it is:

- sufficient to meet their needs;

- not excessive when viewed in relation to their needs; and

- relevant to the achievement of a legitimate aim.

Any policy or practice as a result of which employees are asked or expected to provide information that is not strictly appropriate, relevant and necessary to the employer's needs should be amended accordingly.

The fourth data protection principle obliges employers to ensure personal data is accurate and kept up to date. This essentially means that the employer should take all reasonable steps to ensure the accuracy of the information they hold, recognising that employees will sometimes neglect to provide up-to-date information to their employer about changes in their circumstances. This topic is dealt with at **6.6** below.

The fifth data protection principle places a duty on employers not to keep personal data for longer than is necessary in relation to the purpose(s) for which it was obtained. Neither the *DPA 1998* nor the Employment Practices Data Protection Code (Employment Records) (see **6.4** below) prescribes any time limitation on the retention of personal data. It is therefore up to each employer to decide for themselves what time periods are appropriate in relation to the needs of their business. This topic is discussed further below at **6.30**)

The sixth data protection principle requires employers to process data in accordance with individuals' rights under the *DPA 1998*. This would include the duty on the employer to ensure that subject access requests are treated properly and in accordance with the provisions of the Act (see **4.23** above).

The seventh data protection principle requires employers to put in place proper measures, eg security measures, to protect personal data against unauthorised or unlawful processing, accidental loss or destruction, or damage. This will include adequate protection for computer systems, eg proper use of passwords and possibly the use of encryption and establishment of firewalls (see **6.8** below).

The eighth data protection principle places the responsibility on employers not to transfer personal data outside the European Economic Area unless the country or territory to which it is transferred has in place an adequate level of protection for individuals' rights and freedoms in relation to the processing of personal data.

Checking up on Records held by Line Managers   6.3

It will be up to each employer to formulate and apply a policy on employment records that sets out what records will be held about employees and other workers, the format in which they will be held and who will be responsible for holding them. Some organisations specify that only the HR department is authorised to hold records about employees, and that no line manager or other person will be entitled to retain separate records.

A blanket ban on the holding of personal records by line managers may, however, be unrealistic. For example, it may fall to a line manager to speak to an employee about a matter of minor misconduct or shortfall in performance, in which case the manager will wish to keep, at the very least, a diary note of the fact that an informal meeting took place, what was discussed, the time and date of the meeting and any outcome. It may be unwieldy or undesirable to expect line managers on every occasion to create a formal record and pass it on to HR department for inclusion in the employee's personal file. This does not mean that this approach should be ruled out, as it would have the obvious advantage of ensuring that all records were held centrally and thus under the control of one department where they could potentially be managed more consistently, efficiently and securely. What it does mean is that each employer should review their needs and devise a policy that suits them, then ensure that the policy is applied consistently throughout the organisation. If, on the other hand, line managers are to retain their own files about employees, the employer should ensure that proper security measures are in place for the files and that line managers fully understand their responsibilities under the Act (see **6 9** below).

The starting point for an employer in relation to the management of employee records would thus be to establish a policy on these matters. At the same time it would be necessary to conduct an exercise to establish what personal information about employees existed other than in the HR department and determine whether the retention of this information was to be allowed to continue or whether the information should be assimilated into one centralised personnel records filing system.

The Code of Practice on Employment Records   6.4

The Employment Practices Data Protection Code, Part 2: Employment Records deals specifically with employment records and provides the Information Commissioner's interpretation and recommendations as to what employers need to do to comply with the Act. The Code, like other Codes of Practice, is not legally binding on employers, but any employer who chooses not to comply with the provisions it contains is likely to find that this fact will act to their detriment in the event of a legal claim against the employer in a court or tribunal. This is because courts and tribunals will take the provisions of statutory codes of practice into account when judging such claims. It is therefore in employers' interests to pay heed to the recommendations and guidance contained in the Code.

The Code of Practice does not in any way prevent an employer from collecting, maintaining or using records about their employees. Its aim is to strike a balance between an employee's right to respect for their private life and the employer's legitimate business needs, including the need to keep records for a number of reasons associated with employment. Adherence to the Code will assist employers to achieve good practice in the maintenance of records as well as helping to ensure compliance with the Act.

The Code of Practice sets down a number of general 'benchmarks' which form the foundation of its recommendations on good practice in the maintenance of employment records. These can be summarised as follows:

- The employer should nominate a senior person within the organisation to hold responsibility for ensuring on an ongoing basis that the employer's policies, procedures and practices comply with the Act. This person should have in place an established mechanism for auditing procedures in order to check that they are being followed in practice and for updating them when necessary.

- The employer should take steps to make sure that line managers who keep personal data about employees are fully conversant with their duties and responsibilities under the Act (see **6.9** below).

- Steps should also be taken to ensure all employees are made aware that they may be held personally criminally liable if they knowingly or recklessly disclose personal information without the authority to do so. In this context, the employer should amend any disciplinary procedures to include any breach of data protection legislation as a disciplinary offence.

- Consultation with trade unions or workers' representatives should be carried out over the design and implementation of any and all employment procedures and practices that involve the processing of personal data about employees. Although there is, at present, no legal requirement to consult in this context, it is considered good practice to do so and consultation is likely to lead to better employee relations.

- The employer should conduct an exercise to establish what personal information about employees exists within the organisation, where information is held and who is responsible for it.

- The employer should identify and remove any information held about employees which is unnecessary or irrelevant to the employment relationship, or excessive when viewed against the purpose for which it was collected. An example given in the Code of Practice of information that is unlikely to be necessary is the collection of facts about employees' personal lives outside of work. Such information, the Code suggests, should not be processed other than in circumstances where it is necessary for legal reasons, for example to ensure compliance with the maximum working hours provisions in the *Working Time Regulations 1998 (SI 1998 No 1833)*. The employer should therefore critically review all the data they hold about individuals and determine whether any of it should be deleted or not collected in the first place. Although this could amount to a substantial piece of work the first time it is done, it should not prove too unwieldy if it is carried out on a regular basis.

- Before any sensitive data about employees is collected, the employer should review whether one of the conditions for processing sensitive data has been satisfied (see **4.7** above).

These general benchmarks are supplemented by further benchmarks in relation to issues such as security of records, references, sickness and accident records, equal opportunities monitoring (see **CHAPTER 8**), discipline, grievance and dismissal records, access requests, etc.

Collecting and Keeping Employee Records   6.5

As part of their policy on employment records, each employer will have to decide what information to collect about their employees, in particular new employees and how they intend to ensure the accuracy of the information and keep it up to date.

There is no legal obligation to obtain employees' consent before collecting information about employees, or prospective employees, although if any sensitive data is to be sought, the employer will need to ensure that either one of the conditions for processing sensitive data is satisfied, or that they have obtained the employee's explicit consent (see **6.7** below). Despite the absence of a duty to obtain employees' consent before a record about them is set up, the employer is under a duty to inform the employee that the record exists.

The following checklist may assist employers to set up and manage their personnel records:

- The employer should, as a matter of routine, inform all new staff what records about them are to be held, the source(s) of any information held about them, the purpose for which the records are to be held, how the information will be used and who it will be disclosed to. This may be done in a number of different ways, for example by distributing a fact sheet, directing the employee to the company's intranet (and requiring them to click confirmation that they have read and understood the information provided) or simply including the information as part of a face-to-face induction programme.

- The employer should also make sure that they fully inform all staff, including new employees, of their rights under the Act, including their right to request access to all data held about them (see **6.14** below). For existing staff, reminders should be issued at pre-defined intervals.

- It will be important to ensure that the employer collects information about employees only when the information is necessary for the achievement of a particular business aim, and that the information gathered is relevant to the achievement of that aim. The employer can assist this process by reviewing any forms or other means used within the organisation to gather data about employees and critically evaluate whether the questions asked produce information that the employer actually needs for a legitimate purpose. If any of the forms in use contain questions that might produce information that is irrelevant or excessive when considered in light of the employer's business needs, they should be amended.

Keeping records up to date   6.6

Under the fourth data protection principle, employers are obliged to ensure personal records are accurate and kept up to date. The most effective way of achieving this is for the employer to provide each employee, on an annual basis, with a copy of all the personal information held about them that may be subject to change, and ask them to check the data for accuracy and notify any changes that are needed to bring the information up to date.

An alternative to providing a copy of the information for this purpose would be to make access to the data available online, provided the employer's computer system is set up to allow this and provided the employee has ready access to a computer. The employer would have to take steps to ensure the security of personal data put online for this purpose, ie to put measures in place that would effectively prevent employees from accessing the personal data of others.

If neither of these two options is possible or practicable, the employer will have to devise an alternative system for ensuring that their personal records are kept up to date, as leaving this matter to chance will be likely to lead to a breach of the fourth data protection principle. It may be possible for computer systems to be set to flag up certain items held on file at pre-defined intervals either for the individual to check or so that a nominated person (for example an HR officer) can speak to individuals (perhaps by telephone) to double-check whether certain data held on their file is still accurate.

Another course of action that will help to ensure accuracy in employment records is to incorporate an audit trail into computerised personnel systems. In this way, a record of anyone who has created, altered or deleted a record and the date and time that the record was amended will be maintained automatically. This would enable the employer to trace the source of all changes made to data and potentially detect any errors or inaccuracies.

Dealing with sensitive data 6.7

The *DPA 1998, section 2* sets out a list of personal information which is to be regarded as 'sensitive data'. The list includes the following features of an individual:

- racial or ethnic origin;

- political opinions;

- religious beliefs or other similar beliefs;

- membership of a trade union;

- physical or mental health or condition;

- sexual life;

- the commission or alleged omission of any offence; and

- anything related to any proceedings for an offence committed or alleged to have been committed.

The *DPA 1998, Schedule 3* sets out a series of conditions, at least one of which must be met before an employer can lawfully process sensitive data about an individual. The conditions that are potentially relevant to data protection in employment are:

- where processing is necessary in order for the employer to comply with a legal obligation in connection with employment;

- where the information has been made public as a result of steps taken by the employee;

- where processing is necessary in connection with any legal proceedings, including the defence of a legal claim against the employer;

- where processing is necessary for the exercise of any functions conferred under an enactment or any functions of the Crown, a Minister of the Crown or a government department;

- where processing is necessary for medical purposes and is undertaken by a health professional or someone with an equivalent duty of confidentiality (see **CHAPTER 7**);

- where processing of information about individuals' racial or ethnic origin, religious beliefs or physical or mental health is for the purpose of carrying out equal opportunities monitoring (see **CHAPTER 8**); and

- if the employee has given their explicit consent to the processing of sensitive data about them.

This topic is explored more fully at **4.6** *et seq* above.

Security of Employment Records   6.8

It is a legal requirement under the *DPA 1998* for the employer to protect both manual and computer-based employment records from unauthorised access, tampering and disclosure. This is because the seventh data protection principle obliges all employers to take appropriate technical and organisational measures against unauthorised or unlawful processing of personal data.

There is a limited number of exceptions to the non–disclosure principle, for example if there is a legal requirement to make the disclosure. These are explained at **4.12** above. In the event of a legal obligation to disclose personal data, the employer will still be under a duty to inform the employee that the disclosure has been made. The only exception to this will be if informing the employee of the disclosure would be likely to prejudice the prevention or detection of a crime.

Where an employer chooses to use an outside company or agency to process their data (for example by outsourcing the payroll function), there is a duty to ensure that the company or agency selected to fulfil this function has provided sufficient guarantees in respect of security measures and to check that these measures are consistently observed.

Recruitment and training of staff who have access to employment records
6.9

In order to meet its obligation under the seventh data protection principle, the employer will need to put a number of measures in place, the first of which will be to ensure that all staff who have access to employees' records as part of their jobs are reliable and competent.

It may be prudent therefore, when recruiting new staff into jobs that involve access to employment records, to conduct careful reference checks on shortlisted applicants plus a check to establish whether the individual selected for employment has any relevant past criminal convictions. The subject of carrying out checks in recruitment and selection is dealt with fully at **5.22** above.

Once recruited, the new employee will need full training in order to make sure they understand their responsibilities and duties under the Act, including the duty to keep personal data confidential, not to obtain it unlawfully, nor to disclose it to any unauthorised person. The training should also make staff aware that they can be held personally criminally liable for any breaches of the Act. A further sensible precaution to ensure security is to place confidentiality and security clauses into the employment contracts of all new staff whose jobs will take them into contact with confidential data.

It may also be advisable to inform employees who use computers in the course of their work that, under the *Computer Misuse Act 1990*, it is a criminal offence to secure unauthorised access to a computer system or to computer material in certain circumstances, or to modify the contents of a computer system without authority. 'Unauthorised modification' of computer material includes deliberate erasure or corruption of programmes or data, modifying or destroying a system file or another user's file or the addition of any programme or data to the computer's contents. It is also an offence under the *Computer Misuse Act 1990* to spread a computer virus. Although this Act applies mainly to unauthorised access to computers from external sources, it has potential application internally as well.

'Unauthorised access' for the purposes of the Act is defined as:

> 'access of any kind by a person to any programme or data held on a computer when such a person is not him or herself entitled to control access to the programme or the data and does not have consent from any person who is so entitled.'

Measures to ensure the security of employment records
6.10

In relation to the physical security of employment records, employers should undertake the following steps:

- Decide who in the organisation needs to have access to personal data held about employees and who is to have the authority to amend the data, then draw up specific guidelines to ensure that these employees understand their duties and responsibilities with regard to the confidentiality of personal data. Access to personal data should essentially be based on the needs of the employee's job, not on the seniority of the employee. Thus, direct access to employee records should not automatically be granted to managers, just because they are managers. The employer should review the needs of each person's job, make objective decisions as to who should have direct access and, if necessary, withdraw the automatic right of access to employee records from anyone for whom it is not strictly necessary. An alternative to granting line managers direct access to data about their staff is to make the data available via the HR department.

- Spell out the particular responsibilities of all employees who have access to personal data clearly and specifically, in particular those employed in the organisation's HR department or IT department.

- Design and implement a rigorous system of employee passwords (see **6.13** below).

- Ensure cabinets that contain manual records have secure locks and that a system is in place requiring them to be kept locked at all times except when in use. Keys should be held securely only by a limited number of authorised people. The aim should be to ensure that staff access employment records only when they have a legitimate business reason for doing so.

- Consult IT specialists with regard to computer security measures. It may also be useful to use the audit trail capabilities of the computer system to track who accesses and amends employment records. The audit trail can be used to follow up on any unusual pattern, for example an instance of an employee accessing someone's file noticeably more frequently than others for no obvious reason.

- Put in place rules about taking employment records outside the organisation, eg on laptop computers, and make sure this is rigorously controlled. If the employer prefers to institute a rule that bans the removal of personal data from the workplace, it may be helpful to disconnect the external disk drives from all workplace personal computers in order to physically prevent the information being transferred to laptops.

- If it is permitted for certain employees to load employee records on to laptops (which is not recommended), put in place strict rules for the security of the laptops, for example by imposing a rule that they must not be left in parked vehicles and not left unattended in the home whilst switched on.

- If information about employees has to be communicated by email, institute a system for ensuring permanent deletion of the emails from the relevant computers – and from servers – once the matter requiring communication of the data has been dealt with.

Rules and procedures on confidentiality   **6.11**

It is strongly advisable for employers to devise and implement clear procedures and rules governing the use of all confidential information, including data held about their employees. A company procedure on confidentiality should establish basic guidelines for employees and identify any prohibited practices so that a framework is established within which all employees can work. There should be internal controls to limit access to confidential information and to prevent the disclosure of sensitive data. The introduction and implementation of such a procedure will minimise the risks to the employer of breaches of confidentiality whilst at the same time educating employees about their individual responsibilities. This will be particularly important for employees who have access to personal data as part of their jobs. The particular responsibilities of such employees, for example those employed in the HR department or IT department, will have to be spelled out unambiguously. The rules and procedures should be made applicable to all staff, including managers, irrespective of their seniority.

Rules and procedures governing confidentiality have a number of key advantages. They:

- will clarify what information is to be treated as confidential;

- will help employees to understand their obligations;

- can define employees' key responsibilities with regard to confidential information and specify rules as to how key information should be kept confidential (eg by keeping passwords secret, etc);

- will reduce the risk of a breach of confidentiality occurring; and

- will allow the employer to enforce the rules on confidential information in the event of a breach by an employee.

Rules should cover issues such as:

- the avoidance of email or fax as methods of sending confidential or personal information;

- the encryption of confidential information which is to be transmitted by email;

- a ban on information being transmitted by email to and from employees' homes;

- the protection of computer data when the computer is logged on, ie a rule that workstations should not be left unattended; and

- the choosing, changing and non-disclosure of passwords.

Another measure that the employer should consider in light of the duty to ensure the security of employment records is to include an express confidentiality clause in the contracts of employment of all staff who have access to confidential or personal information. The precise wording of a confidentiality clause will depend on the nature of the employer's business and the employee's position. At the very least, however, the following issues should be covered:

- the type of information that is to be regarded as confidential;

- rules on confidentiality applicable to the employee during their employment;

- rules on keeping information confidential that will apply after the termination of the employee's employment.

A sample confidentiality clause might read as follows:

> 'You must not at any time, other than in the proper performance of your duties, access, disclose or misuse any information that is confidential. This duty applies to you throughout your employment and following the termination of your employment. Confidential information includes any information of the Company or any of its workers, customers, suppliers or agents which the Company treats as confidential and which is not part of your own general skill and knowledge. In particular you must not disclose any information held by the Company about any of its employees or other workers to which you may have access as part of your job. Such information is to be regarded as confidential whether it is recorded in paper format, on microfiche, on computer or on disk or tape.'

Taking disciplinary action against staff who breach the employer's rules on confidentiality or security   6.12

Employers should ensure that their disciplinary procedures link in with any rules on confidentiality and that they reflect the importance of treating employment records as confidential. Disciplinary rules and procedures should make it clear that any breach of confidentiality, for example the unauthorised disclosure of personal information or careless handling of personal data, is to be regarded as a disciplinary offence which may, depending on the level of seriousness, lead to a warning or to dismissal.

One example of a case in which an employee was (fairly) dismissed for unlawful access to information held on computer was the case of *Denco Ltd v Joinson EAT [1991] ICR 172*. The employee had authority to gain access to certain files held on his employer's computer system, but was debarred from accessing other parts of the computer system. However, having learned the password for access to another part of the computer system from his daughter who worked for the same firm, he deliberately used it to gain access knowing that he was not entitled to see the sensitive information that was held there. When his activities were discovered, he was summarily dismissed, even though his motive for accessing the data was one of curiosity and not malice. The EAT held that the dismissal was fair in all the circumstances and accepted that conduct involving deliberate access to computer data without authority amounted to gross misconduct justifying summary dismissal. The EAT also commented, however, that employers should take appropriate steps to make it clear to employees that any unauthorised access to information held on computer will be regarded as gross misconduct.

It is therefore very important for employers to have clear policies governing who is, and who is not, authorised to gain access to computer data or to modify the contents of files.

Using passwords to protect employment records   6.13

One of the simplest and cheapest methods of ensuring the protection of personal data is for the employer to implement a rigorous system of employee passwords. Rules should be devised for employees governing the choosing of a password and for the regular changing of passwords. There should also be a clear written rule forbidding the disclosure of passwords to any unauthorised person, and this rule should be consistently enforced.

Specifically, the employer should enforce rules that:

- passwords must not be disclosed to any person unless written authority is first obtained from the employee's line manager;

- passwords must be changed at least every [two weeks, four weeks, six weeks] and more often if necessary;

- passwords chosen must not be obvious, for example the name of a partner, house, dog or favourite hobby, etc;

- any unauthorised disclosure of a password will be regarded as a disciplinary offence, rendering the employee liable to disciplinary action.

A model clause governing the use of passwords could read as follows:

'Passwords must be kept confidential at all times and should not be disclosed to anyone else unless prior written authority to do so is obtained from the relevant line manager. The line manager should be notified immediately if there is a suspicion that an employee is using a colleague's password. As a further precaution, employees should change their passwords regularly and no less frequently than once a month. Passwords should not be words or phrases that could be guessed by another person.'

Policies on Handling Access Requests   6.14

The *DPA 1998* gives employees important rights of access to any personal information held about them by their employer. The Act expressly gives individuals the right to submit a written 'subject access request' to their employer, with which the employer must comply within 40 calendar days. Requests for access may be made in respect of manual files, microfiche records, audio or video tapes, computer files and email correspondence that contains information about the individual. The individual making the subject access request is not obliged under the Act to give any reason for seeking the information.

As a result of these provisions, employees have the right to see documents such as:

- performance reviews or appraisals;

- sickness records;

- warnings or minutes of disciplinary interviews;

- training records;

- statements about pay;

- emails or word-processed documents of which they are the subject; and

- expressions of opinion or intention about (for example) promotion prospects.

Employees may also request access to information generated by computer systems involving in automated decision making on matters such as performance and conduct.

It is a sound idea for all employers to devise a policy on the handling of subject access requests. The matters that should be incorporated into such a policy would include:

- who in the organisation is to be responsible for ensuring subject access requests are dealt with competently and promptly;

- a system for verifying the identity of anyone requesting access to their personal files, ie to ensure that personal information is disclosed only to the person who is its subject;

- to whom employees should submit subject access requests and the format in which they should make the request – guidelines should be provided, for example requesting employees to specify as precisely as possible the information to which they are seeking access;

- whether or not the employer will charge a fee for access (up to £10 per access request may be charged) or whether the £10 fee would be applied only in certain defined circumstances, for example an employer might grant one free access to each employee each year, but charge a fee for any and all further access requests during the same year; and

- a checklist that details the locations where personal data is held.

There are some limited exemptions to the general duty on employers to comply with a subject access request. These include circumstances where the information held relates to:

- management planning or forecasting;

- negotiations with employees;

- the price of a company's shares;

- the prevention or detection of crime or the apprehension or prosecution of offenders;

- the assessment or collection of any tax or duty;

- references; and

- data about another person.

A partial exemption also exists where the provision of a permanent copy of the information requested would require disproportionate effort.

The topic of employee access to their records is discussed more fully in at **4.23** above.

Dealing with Requests to Amend an Employee's File Details 6.15

Under the Act, employees (and others about whom personal data is held) have the right to ask for any inaccuracies in their personal data to be corrected or removed. It is obviously as much in the employer's interests as in the employee's to ensure that the data they hold about staff is accurate and up to date, particularly in light of the fourth data protection principle which expressly requires employers to ensure that the personal data they hold is 'accurate and, where necessary, kept up to date'.

There are three ways in which an employee can seek to have any inaccurate personal data held about them corrected:

- by asking the employer to amend the data;

- by asking the Information Commissioner for an assessment as to whether the processing being carried out by the employer complies with the Act, in which case the Commissioner will decide whether or not to investigate the matter; and

- by applying to a court for an order requiring the employer to correct the inaccuracies or destroy the data.

Although employees have no specific legal right under the Act to demand that their employer rectifies any inaccuracies in the personal data held about them, the requirement on employers to ensure personal data is accurate and kept up to date contained in the fourth data protection principle would create the need to accede to an employee's request to alter any information held that was incorrect.

The most likely instance of an employee wishing for their employer to amend or remove data from their file would be where the file showed that they had been accused of misconduct, for example bullying of a colleague. It would be understandable that the employee would prefer not to have any record of the alleged bullying on their file. The employer may, however, have reasonable grounds to believe that the information recorded on the employee's file is accurate, perhaps on the basis of statements provided by another employee. In these circumstances the employer would not be obliged to remove or delete the file note about the alleged bullying, even in circumstances where the matter had not been proved beyond reasonable doubt. The appropriate action in these circumstances would be for the employer to add a note to the employee's file stating clearly that the employee had refuted the allegations of bullying and did not agree with the employer's version of events or with the statement provided by their colleague.

Employees also have a right to put a request in to their employer asking them to stop, or not to begin, processing personal data about them that is likely to cause substantial damage or distress either to them personally or to another person in circumstances where the damage or distress would be unwarranted. This right is very limited, however, and subject to a range of exceptions, for example where processing is necessary to comply with a legal obligation or required for the performance of a contract. An example of this right in practice could be where an employee did not want their new home telephone number recorded on account of a previous problem with nuisance calls.

To exercise this right, the employee must give their employer written notice asking them to stop the processing that they believe is likely to cause damage or distress, stating a reasonable timescale for the employer to comply with the request. The employer must respond in writing within 21 days, stating either that they will comply with the employee's request or that the request is unjustified and giving the reasons why this view has been taken.

If an employer unreasonably fails to comply with a notice of this kind, the employee can apply to the courts for an order for the employer to stop the processing.

Where an employee has suffered any damage or distress, whether as a result of the recording of information that is inaccurate, the continued processing of information that was likely to cause damage or distress following a request to stop, or as a result of any other breach of the Act, he or she can seek compensation through the courts.

Records of Appraisals, Grievances and Disciplinary Proceedings   6.16

Where performance reviews or appraisals are carried out, whether on a regular or ad hoc basis, the employer will wish to keep records of the review itself and any agreed outcomes such as targets for improvement. Similarly, there will be a need to retain records of any disciplinary action taken against employees and details of any grievances raised.

Performance reviews and appraisals 6.17

Many employers conduct regular performance reviews or annual appraisals in respect of some or all of their employees. Typically this will involve carrying out a review of the employee's job performance over a defined period of time and appraising their future training needs and career development. Appraisal is usually a two-headed process of looking backwards over the past year to analyse past job performance, and looking forwards into the future with a view to improving future job performance. The overall objective of an effective appraisal scheme will be to help each employee to maximise their job performance for the benefit of both the employee and the organisation.

The employee should gain from appraisal a clear understanding of how well they have carried out their job over the past year; a full awareness of where they stand at present; and an insight into what training, development and career opportunities might be available or planned for the coming year. All of this will require records to be kept. Typically, the record might contain a list of the features of the employee's job with the employee being given a 'rating' against each feature, a summary of training and development needs and agreed plans or new goals and targets for the following year.

As is the case with other types of employment records, the formulation of a record following an appraisal interview should be an open, two-way process between the employee and manager. With openness and transparency being part of the philosophy of the *DPA 1998*, there can be no 'secret reporting' about an employee. The record created following appraisal should not contain any information that is not already known to the employee and should be a fair summary of points that have been discussed at an appraisal interview. If there has been disagreement over a key issue, this fact should also be recorded in order to provide a fair balance.

The right of access under the Act includes access to data that involves the expression of opinions about the employee, for example, the opinion of an employee's line manager that the employee is, or is not, suitable for promotion into a supervisory post.

Grievances 6.18

The handling of grievances raised by employees will similarly involve the processing of personal data about the employee who has raised the grievance, and may possibly include data about another employee, for example if the grievance is about the conduct of a colleague or manager. There will need to be a proper record of the grievance itself (usually written by the employee at the start of the process), a record of any meetings held to try to resolve the grievance and a record of the outcome.

Disciplinary proceedings   6.19

Whenever any form of disciplinary action is taken against an employee, whether formal or informal, it will be important for the employer to keep a full record.

Informal disciplinary action   6.20

Even if the matter has been handled informally, the employee's manager should, at the very least, record:

- the nature of the problem and the fact that it was brought to the employee's attention;

- the time and date when the manager spoke to the employee; and

- whether there was any outcome, for example the record could simply state that the matter was dealt with informally and there was no outcome, or that an informal oral warning was given.

A copy of the record created by the manager should be given to the employee in order to promote the principle of transparency inherent in the Act. There will be no need for the employee to sign the record, although the employer should record the fact that a copy was given to the employee.

Many managers may not see the need to create a record each time they have words with an employee about unsatisfactory conduct or performance. However, unless a record is kept, the manager will not be in a position to take the matter forward in the event of further misconduct or a failure to improve. Not keeping a record will allow the employee to challenge or deny that they were ever told of the problem at a later stage, and create the risk that any disciplinary action subsequently taken against the employee will not constitute a fair procedure. Furthermore, if the matter escalates and the employee is dismissed, the absence of full records as to how the employer handled the matter will make it virtually impossible for the employer to succeed in defending a claim of unfair dismissal taken against them at an employment tribunal.

Formal disciplinary action   6.21

If the outcome of the disciplinary proceedings is that the employee receives a formal warning, the warning should state:

- the nature and seriousness of the employee's misconduct;

- the improvement required, or a clear statement that there must be no further instance of misconduct;

- the timescale for improvement;

- the period of time the warning will remain 'live' on the employee's file and what will happen to the warning once it expires (see **6.28** below);

- what will happen if there is no improvement, ie further disciplinary action or dismissal;

- the employee's right to appeal against the warning, how they should appeal and the timescale within which the appeal must be raised.

The warning, together with a record of the disciplinary interview, should be given to the employee and copies of the relevant documents placed in their file.

Security of disciplinary records   6.22

It will, of course, be essential to keep records relating to disciplinary proceedings secure and make sure that they are made available only to those who need access to them as part of their jobs. If the employee has elected to involve a trade union representative or colleague, for example as a companion at a disciplinary interview, the employer should not automatically make the records available to this person but instead should first check with the employee whether that is his or her wish.

Employees' rights of access to disciplinary records   6.23

Employees have the right of access to all data held about them in connection with disciplinary proceedings. This will include the right of access to:

- any notes made by the employer as part of an investigation into their conduct;

- interview notes or minutes of meetings held in connection with the matter under review;

- copies of any warnings and any other associated documentation placed on the employee's file;

- the expression of any opinion about the employee, for example whether the line manager believes that the employee was, or was not, guilty of a particular offence; and

- information indicating the employer's intentions in respect of the employee.

It is important to recognise that employees have the right of access to such information under the *DPA 1998* even if the disclosure of some of the information might impact on the disciplinary investigation or on prospective disciplinary proceedings. The only exception to the employee's right of access to documents containing information about disciplinary proceedings would be if the information was associated with a criminal investigation and disclosing it to the employee would prejudice that investigation.

The rights of employees under the Act make it essential for the employer to be completely open with the employee throughout any disciplinary investigation and subsequent proceedings. Nothing should be placed on the record that the employee has not already been made fully aware of as a result of face-to-face communication.

Disciplinary investigations   6.24

Unless the facts of an employee's misconduct are undisputed, it will be essential for the employer to carry out a fair and thorough investigation into the alleged misconduct before any decision is made on whether to impose a disciplinary sanction on the employee. Unless and until all the facts relevant to the case are established, the manager dealing with the employee will not be in a position to judge whether the employee's behaviour potentially amounts to misconduct sufficient to justify disciplinary action. Furthermore, if an employee is dismissed without a proper investigation having first been carried out, this will almost certainly have the effect of rendering the dismissal unfair under the *Employment Rights Act 1996, section 98*. The information gathered through the investigation should of course be presented to the employee so that he or she has the opportunity to make representations before any decision is taken as to whether formal disciplinary action is appropriate. This should be done at a properly set up disciplinary interview.

It is important to bear in mind that information to be used as evidence to support disciplinary proceedings against an employee must not be gathered by deception. Equally, the person conducting the investigation should not mislead those from whom they seek information in respect of why the information is required and how it will be used.

Whenever an investigation into an incident of alleged misconduct has been carried out, a record will need to be made of the investigation itself and the conclusions drawn from it. It will be important for the record to be accurate, to distinguish between what is known as fact and what is stated as opinion, and to contain sufficient detail to support any conclusions that are drawn from it.

Witness statements   6.25

Where, as part of the investigation, witness statements have been taken from other employees, the employer should seek those employees' consent to the disclosure of the statements to the employee accused of misconduct in order to provide the accused employee with a full and fair opportunity to answer the allegations against them.

If, however, the employee providing the witness statement has a sound reason for not wishing their identity to be disclosed (for example if they have reasonable grounds to fear retaliation from the accused employee), the employer should respect their wishes. Disclosing the witness statement in these circumstances could lead to a breach of confidence and a violation of the data protection rights of the employee who provided the witness statement. In such a case, the employer may, however, be able to disclose the content of the statement without revealing the individual's identity or edit the statement in such a way that the individual's identity is not disclosed. The employer should take a reasoned decision on whether it is reasonable to disclose witness statements in these circumstances, by balancing the witness's right to privacy against the accused employee's right to know the allegations made against them and their source. Further information about disclosing data that would reveal information about third parties is provided at **4.31** above.

Accessing information for incompatible purposes   6.26

The second data protection principle states that employers must not process personal data in any manner that is incompatible with the purpose or purposes for which the data was originally obtained. When conducting disciplinary investigations, therefore, the employer must not access or use information held about employees for the purpose of the investigation if the original reason for collecting the data was something completely different. It would, for example, be a breach of the *DPA 1998* to access and read an employee's emails in order to ascertain whether the employee had made any remarks relevant to the issue under review unless:

- a policy is in place allowing interception of emails to be carried out for this purpose;

- employees have been properly informed about the employer's policy of interception; and

- the purpose of the interception is one of those defined as permissible in the *Telecommunications (Lawful Business Practice) (Interception of Communications) Regulations 2000 (SI 2000 No 2699)*.

If the above conditions are not all met, the employer's only recourse would be to obtain the employee's express consent before proceeding to read their emails as part of the disciplinary investigation. Furthermore, reading an employee's emails without lawful authority to do so would represent a breach of Article 8 of the *Human Rights Act 1998* (the right to respect for private and family life, home and correspondence) unless the intrusion into the employee's privacy could be justified as proportionate in light of the seriousness of the matter under investigation. An example of circumstances that may justify this course of action could be where an employee had been accused of sending emails to a colleague that contained sexually or racially offensive material. In this case it would be proportionate for the employer to read the employee's emails in order to take the necessary steps to protect the other employee from unlawful harassment.

Even if the employer has a clear policy in place allowing for the interception of employees' communications in certain defined circumstances, there is still a requirement under the Act for data processing to be fair. If, following a disciplinary investigation, the employee is dismissed, the employer may later have to demonstrate to an employment tribunal that the dismissal was carried out fairly and reasonably. Even though the interception of the employee's emails for the purpose of the investigation might have been *lawful*, this does not necessarily make such interception *fair and reasonable* in relation to the dismissal process. Unless the employee had been informed beforehand that his or her email messages might be intercepted for the purpose of investigating allegations of misconduct, it would be necessary for the employer to obtain their express consent before proceeding to intercept any emails. This is because interception without consent as a means of gathering evidence against the employee would create a serious risk that an employment tribunal could find a subsequent dismissal unfair on procedural grounds on the basis that such a course of action was unreasonable. Once again, openness and transparency form the key to compliance with the relevant legislation.

Records of allegations that are unsubstantiated   6.27

Part 2 of the Employment Practices Data Protection Code (Employment Records) states that, as a general principle, records of allegations made about employees that have been investigated and found to be without substance should not be retained following the conclusion of the investigation. The Code goes on to point out that there may be exceptions to this general principle, for example if the employee was accused of harassment, bullying or abuse, in which case the employer may wish to keep a limited record of the allegations for their own protection. In this case, the record should show:

- the fact allegations were made and by whom they were made;

- the nature of the allegations;

- the key points that emerged from the investigation;

- what, if anything, was established as fact; and

- the fact that, following an investigation, the allegations were found to be unsubstantiated.

Spent disciplinary warnings   6.28

The employer should devise and implement a clear procedure on the time periods for which warnings are to remain 'live', and on what is to happen to them when they lapse.

There is no time period laid down in law as to how long disciplinary warnings should remain active on employees' files. It is therefore up to each employer to make their own policy decision on this matter, and to communicate the policy to employees as part of the organisation's overall disciplinary procedure. An employee who receives a warning should also be specifically informed at the time the warning is given how long it will remain 'live' on their file, ie the time period after which the warning will no longer be taken into account. At that point, it must be made clear what will happen to the lapsed warning, for example whether it will:

- be physically removed from the employee's file and destroyed;

- be removed from the employee's file, but a record kept elsewhere of the fact the warning was given, the date it was given, the date it expired and the type of warning (eg first written warning); or

- remain on the employee's file even though it will no longer be taken into account in determining any future disciplinary penalty.

Whilst there would be little point in retaining warnings on file that related to conduct that took place many years earlier, there may be good reason for an employer to want to retain a record of the fact that a warning was given to a particular employee, particularly if the conduct that gave rise to the warning was of a fairly serious nature, or if the same employee had received several warnings over a period of time, indicating a pattern. The employer may legitimately wish to retain some flexibility in their procedures in regard to this matter. Whilst this is acceptable, the employer should always tell the employee, at the time a warning is issued, when it will lapse and what will be done with it at that time.

Another task for the employer in relation to disciplinary warnings is to put in place a reliable system for ensuring that, where their policy provides for the removal or deletion of warnings, this actually takes place on the set dates. A simple diary system may be sufficient for this purpose, given that the number of warnings should not (hopefully!) be too large.

Records of termination of employment   6.29

The employer should keep accurate records of the circumstances leading to employees' termination of employment. A clear distinction should be drawn in the records between a resignation and a dismissal. Furthermore, where an employee is dismissed, the employer should ensure that there is a clear and accurate record of the reason for the dismissal, and that this is consistent with what the employee was told about the reason for their termination. In any event, employees who have one year's service or more have the right under the *Employment Rights Act 1996, section 92* to request a written statement giving particulars of the reason for their dismissal. In the event of such a request, the employer must respond within 14 days. It is sound practice, however, to adopt a policy of providing all employees with a written statement outlining the reason for their dismissal, regardless of length of service and whether or not a request is made.

The reason given should always be the true reason, because if at a later date a claim for unfair dismissal is brought to an employment tribunal, the statement can be used in evidence. At a tribunal hearing for unfair dismissal, the onus is on the employer to show the reason for dismissal, and that it was one of the potentially fair reasons. Thus the written statement giving the reason for the employee's dismissal could support the employer's case, or, if no adequate or potentially fair reason had been provided, considerably weaken the case.

Retention of Records

There is no provision in the *DPA 1998* imposing a time limit on the retention of employment records. However, the fifth data protection principle provides that personal data must 'not be kept for longer than is necessary' taking into account the purpose for which the data was collected in the first place. Thus, it is up to each employer to decide how long to retain employment records, including the files of those whose employment has come to an end. This decision should be based on business needs, taking into account any separate statutory requirements, for example the law relating to the retention of income tax records. Decisions should, of course, be made objectively, and records should not be maintained 'just in case' they might be needed at some future point in time.

Proper policy decisions should therefore be made and adhered to as to the specific retention periods for different types of records, for example the retention of leavers' files (see **6.31** below) or recruitment files (see **5.31** above). Once such policy decisions have been made, they should of course be consistently adhered to and the employer should have in place a system to ensure the regular clearing out of records. This may involve manually 'weeding' out paper-based files on a regular basis (for example once every six months) whilst for computerised records it may be possible to set the computer to flag up information that is due for deletion, or delete it automatically.

Part 2 of the Employment Practices Data Protection Code states that employers should:

- establish retention times for employment records on the basis of their genuine business needs;

- adopt a risk analysis approach to retention, ie consider whether there would be any realistic risk to the business or to the employees concerned if employment records were deleted or destroyed after a set period of time;

- base any decision to retain employment records on the principle of proportionality;

- treat different records individually or in logical groupings rather than automatically retaining all the information about employees just because there is a need to retain some of it; and

- anonymise information where possible, for example if the employer wishes to hold data for the purpose of reviewing the average length of employment of various groups of staff.

The removal of records should be dealt with carefully and thoroughly so that they are properly destroyed, either by being shredded (in the case of paper records) or permanently deleted from the employer's system and from any servers (in the case of computer records). Furthermore, the employer should not sell on their computers unless they can be confident that all employment records have been fully removed.

Leavers' files **6.31**

When employees leave their employment, the employer may legitimately wish to retain their file details for a limited period of time. This will be in case the ex-employee chooses to bring any kind of claim against the employer in an employment tribunal, for example a claim for unfair dismissal. The time limit for most claims to employment tribunals is three calendar months, although in the case of claims for equal pay and for redundancy payments it is six months. The employer would therefore be justified in retaining leavers' records for up to six months. In certain industries, there may be justification for retaining leavers' files for longer periods, for example in the case of employees who worked with hazardous substances.

After this period of time, there may be still be sound reasons why the employer may wish to retain a record of the fact that the person was employed, although it will be neither appropriate nor necessary to retain a complete file record of everything that occurred during the person's employment. Different elements of the person's employment record should be treated differently rather than an all-or-nothing approach being adopted. Specific records should be retained only if there is a realistic likelihood that the information may be needed in the future.

An appropriate compromise may be to destroy most of the existing data, but create a new centralised filing system for leavers. Such a system could be set up to record:

- the person's name;

- their address, in case of the need for contact in the future, for example in relation to a reference request;

- some means of ensuring correct identification to guard against the possibility of confusion between two or more leavers with the same name, for example a company reference number or date of birth;

- the dates when the person was employed;

- their job title or designation and department;

- the reasons why their employment ended, for example whether they resigned or were dismissed, and if the latter, the reason for dismissal; and

- space for any comments.

If the employer elects to write any specific comments about the person in the file, they may wish to bear in mind that these comments could be read by the employee at a future date following a subject access request. Nevertheless, this approach should allow employers to retain limited records on leavers without imposing an undue burden on them in relation to their obligations under the Act.

Chapter 7
Health Records

HR Issues Relating to Health Records

Introduction 7.1

Information about workers' health held in the context of employment is an issue that must be treated with care and respect, taking into account the duty of confidentiality owed by employers to their employees in respect of such information. Data about an individual's physical or mental health are regarded as 'sensitive data' under the *Data Protection Act 1998* (*DPA 1998* or 'the Act') and must be treated accordingly. Although the Act does not prevent employers from collecting or using health information about employees, its use must be justified by one of a list of sensitive data conditions. Employers, especially those in the public sector, must also be mindful of the rights contained in Article 8 of the *Human Rights Act 1998*, namely the right to respect for private and family life.

What health records may legitimately be held? 7.2

Information concerning employee's health may consist of a wide range of data, for example:

- information about current or past illnesses revealed during pre-employment medical screening (see **7.17** below);

- information relating to an individual's disability, including how the particular condition affects the employee (see **7.14** below);

- information on an employee's state of health provided by an employee's GP (with the employee's consent) following a request for a medical report submitted by the employer;

- the results of eye tests carried out in respect of employees who work regularly with display screen equipment;

- the results of drugs or alcohol testing carried out on employees for safety reasons and held in a personnel file.

Sensitive data   7.3

As soon as an employer collects information about an employee's physical or mental health or condition, they will be processing 'sensitive data' under the Act. In order for this to be lawful, the employer must be sure that the collection and use of the data satisfies one of the sensitive data conditions set down in the Act.

Conditions for the processing of health information   7.4

The conditions that are potentially relevant to the collection of health records in employment are listed below.

- **Where processing is necessary in order for the employer to comply with a legal obligation in connection with employment.**

  Such a legal obligation may arise as a result of statute or common law, ie decisions of courts and tribunals which interpret the law. There are many legal obligations on employers that may require the processing of sensitive data, for example:

  - health and safety legislation;

  - anti-discrimination legislation, including the duty to make reasonable adjustments under the *Disability Discrimination Act 1995*;

  - the duty under the *Social Security Contributions and Benefits Act 1992* to process Statutory Sick Pay for employees who are absent from work due to sickness;

  - unfair dismissal rights contained in the *Employment Rights Act 1996.*

  This list is, of course, not exhaustive.

  The condition would apply whether the legal duty in question related to the individual about whom the sensitive data was held, or to another employee. For example, it may be necessary to record details of a particular employee's physical condition or mental illness in order to protect that person from injury in the workplace, or in order to be able to ensure the safety of others to whom the employer owes a duty of care.

- **Where processing is necessary to protect the vital interests of the employee or another person in circumstances where the employee cannot give consent.**

  This condition is likely to be satisfied only in serious medical emergencies where the health or safety of the employee or another person is at serious risk, thus justifying the disclosure of health information.

- **Where the information has been made public as a result of steps taken by the employee.**

  An example of this could be where an employee has disclosed to a local newspaper that they are suffering from a particular illness in the context (for example) of fund-raising to support research into the illness.

- **Where processing is necessary in connection with any legal proceedings, including the defence of a legal claim against the employer, or necessary for the purpose of obtaining legal advice.**

  This means that if an employee or job applicant has brought a complaint against their employer to court or tribunal, it would be legitimate for the employer to retain details of the employee's health in order to facilitate the employer's defence against the claim. An example could be the retention of an employee's health record in order to defend a claim of disability discrimination brought to tribunal by the employee.

- **Where processing is necessary for medical purposes and is undertaken by a health professional or someone with an equivalent duty of confidentiality.**

  This condition would apply where there is a necessary medical purpose and where health information about employees was held by a company doctor, nurse or similar health professional. It would not be applicable when information on employees' health was held by HR professionals or line managers.

- **Where processing of information about individuals' physical or mental health is for the purpose of carrying out equal opportunities monitoring.**

  If the sole purpose of retaining health data is to promote and maintain equality of treatment, and provided the information is necessary in order to achieve this purpose, it will be lawful to hold the data (see **CHAPTER 8** for details of equal opportunities monitoring).

One common thread in most of the above conditions is that it must be *necessary* for the employer to hold the sensitive data in order to fulfil the condition. This means that it is not, for example, open to employers to retain sensitive data about individuals in circumstances where the reason for doing so is convenience or 'just in case' a particular situation might arise.

Gaining employees' consent to the collection and use of health information 7.5

If none of the other conditions for processing sensitive data applies, the only course of action open to an employer who thinks they need to collect and hold information about their employees' health is to obtain individual employees' consent to the processing of sensitive data. However, according to the Information Commissioner's advice, consent to the processing of sensitive data must be 'explicit', and 'freely given'.

Furthermore, the EU Data Protection Directive states of consent:

' ... freely given specific and informed indication of his wishes by which the data subject signifies his agreement to personal data relating to him being processed.'

As far as 'freely given' is concerned, it is difficult to imagine there being no adverse consequences to an employee except where the requirement is to sign up to something voluntary. This point is well made in the Employment Practices Data Protection Code, which, in the context of consent, distinguishes between an existing employee and a job applicant. If, for example, the employer is a transport undertaking and there is a 'no drugs and alcohol' policy enforced by testing, job applicants should be made aware of this as part of their recruitment, ideally early on in the process. This will give the applicant the free choice to accept a job in the knowledge of the drug and alcohol testing that is a condition of that job or to decline because of the condition. An existing employee, on the other hand, may have no realistic choice but to agree to drugs testing if the employer introduced such a policy following consultation.

The issue of consent is explained more fully at **4.8** above.

Who should have access to health records?   7.6

The Employment Practices Data Protection Code, Part 2: Employment Records (which at the time of writing is in draft form) emphasises that the assessment of health issues, including judgements about an individual's fitness to work, should normally be left to suitably qualified medical personnel, for example an occupational doctor or nurse, or a specialist in a particular condition. In the same way that the income tax and National Insurance implications of a particular expenses payment are best left to the experts in payroll, so too should interpretations of medical information be left to experts. It follows that medical information should only be given to those who can interpret it, and employees' health information should not be widely available. Since line managers and HR professionals are unlikely to be medically qualified, they should not have access to details about an employee's medical condition, nor become involved in the interpretation of medical testing. Instead their access to health information about employees should be restricted to whether or not employees are fit to perform their jobs and whether there are legitimate reasons for employees' absences from work.

Another recommendation in the draft Code of Practice is that employees should be informed:

* when information about their health is collected;

* the nature and extent of the health information held about them;

* the reasons for which health information is held; and

* who will have access to the information and in what circumstances.

These points reflect some of the general principles inherent in the *DPA 1998* that data collection and use should be open and transparent.

Where health information is held on employees' personnel files, it will be very important for the employer to ensure a high level of security and confidentiality in respect of these records. It may be advisable to keep information on employees' health separately (see **7.7** below), for example on a separate computer database that is subject to extra-rigorous security controls. Access should then be restricted to those who both have the knowledge to understand the data and the need to know.

The Employment Practices Data Protection Code – Part 4: Information about Workers' Health 7.7

The fourth part of the Employment Practices Data Protection Code that is produced by the Information Commissioner is entitled 'Information About Worker's Health'. It is supported by supplementary guidance and a shortened code for small businesses. The main code is itself in three sections: a description of the code, information about workers' health and recommendations for good practice.

The Code looks at five areas of employee's health:

- general considerations;
- occupational health schemes;
- medical examination and testing;
- drug and alcohol testing; and
- genetic testing.

The Code sets out a number of core principles:

- **It will be intrusive and may be highly intrusive to obtain information about workers' health.**

  This is a simple statement of fact but it acts as a reminder that even for those routinely dealing with personal data and health records, obtaining information about an employee's health will be far from routine for the employee. It follows that any decision on gathering of employees' health data should be taken at the highest level within an organisation. Local managers must not be able to gather health data from employees without consultation with the appropriate central function.

- **Workers have legitimate expectations that they can keep their personal health information private and that employers will respect this privacy.**

  All employees will expect their employer to protect their personal data. In the case of health data, which is much more 'personal' than, for example, an employee's address, employees will expect a greater level of privacy and confidentiality. It should be borne in mind that the eighth Article of the European Convention on Human Rights creates a right of individuals to respect for their private and family life.

Employees' health records should not be kept physically as part of their personnel files. Ideally a separate filing system should be used so that only health professionals (with their own ethics standards) are able to access the data. There should be a policy on the handling of employees' health records which should identify the different types of health information that may be held within the organisation possibly assigning different levels of confidentiality to the different types. The organisation should:

–   Identify the destination (keeper) of each type so that any data can be quickly and efficiently delivered to their proper destination.

–   Publish the policy throughout the organisation so everyone knows what to do with any medical data they accidentally receive.

This will also promote amongst employees the organisation's good understanding of employees' concerns about confidentiality of health records.

● **If employers wish to collect and hold information on their workers' health, they should be clear about the purpose and satisfied that this is justified by real benefits that will be delivered.**

The third core principle encourages employers to undertake an impact assessment before gathering and using health information about employees. The supplementary guidance to the Code recommends four elements that should be considered in the impact assessment before judging whether processing health data is justified:

–   the purposes (see **7.9** below);

–   adverse impact (see **7.10** below);

–   alternatives; and

–   obligations.

● **One of the sensitive data conditions must be satisfied (see 7.4 above).**

Impact assessments   7.8

Employers should always consider carefully whether they actually need to collect and hold health information about their employees, and what level of detail is necessary to protect their business interests. If justification for processing health data exists, the employer should still aim to keep the collection and retention of such data to a minimum.

The draft Employment Practices Data Protection Code Part 4: Information about Workers' Health recommends that employers should conduct an impact assessment to establish whether there is justification for holding information about their employees' health.

Through the impact assessment, the employer can establish what benefits would be gained from processing information about their employees' health, and whether those benefits are sufficient to justify the inevitable adverse impact on employees.

The Code explains that an impact assessment involves:

- identifying the purpose(s) for which health information would be collected and held and the likely benefits (see **7.9** below);

- identifying any likely adverse impact on employees of collecting and holding the information (see **7.10** below);

- considering whether there are less intrusive ways of achieving the employer's objectives (see **7.11** below);

- taking into account the obligations that arise out of the collection and holding of health information; and

- deciding whether or not collecting and holding health information is justified (see **7.12** below).

The purpose of an impact assessment   7.9

The purpose or purposes for which employees' health data are being gathered and used must be assessed in terms of the risks that the purposes address. Many of the risks to the organisation will relate to health and safety issues in respect of its employees, other workers and the general public. The employer will need to consider whether the medical data being collected will address these risks.

Many employers collect information about their workers' health without thinking through why they do so, or what legitimate purpose the information serves. An impact assessment should, as a starting point, identify clearly the purposes for which the employer requires different types and levels of health information about their employees. An 'all-or-nothing' approach will be inappropriate in this context because there will be different risks applicable to different groups of workers. For example, if the employer employs drivers, the need for a high standard of health, fitness and alertness will be greater for the drivers than the fitness threshold required for those doing routine desk-based jobs. The impact assessment should therefore:

- identify the purposes for which health information on different groups of workers will be genuinely necessary;

- specify the type of information that will be necessary to meet the stated purpose(s); and

- clarify that the collection and use of health information will actually be relevant and appropriate to the stated purposes.

Some of the legitimate business purposes for which an employer may wish to hold health data about their employees might be:

- to ensure safety in the workplace;

- to be able to process properly the payment of sick pay, including Statutory Sick Pay;

- to establish employees' entitlement to health related benefits, for example membership of a health insurance scheme operated by the employer;

- to prevent discrimination against an employee who has a disability;

- to identify when it is necessary to make reasonable adjustments for an employee who has a disability;

- to encourage and maximise attendance and thus reduce costs; and

- to be able to offer support to employees who develop health problems.

The key to compliance with the Act is to be certain that the information collected and retained on employees' files is actually appropriate and relevant to the purpose in question, and not excessive when viewed against the purpose.

Adverse impact   7.10

The collection and use of information about an employee's health will inevitably have an adverse impact on that employee, as it will represent an intrusion into their privacy. It has been accepted in law that the right to respect for privacy (under Article 8 of the *Human Rights Act 1998*) extends into the workplace (see **9.38** below). Employees will therefore have legitimate expectations that their personal health information will remain private. Some employees may also resent the idea of being asked to disclose personal health information, or find the prospect of medical testing during employment embarrassing or demeaning.

The supplementary guidance to the Code of Practice encourages a very wide view, embracing:

- the possible effect on employees' families;

- the likelihood of those without a business need to know seeing medical data;

- the possible impact on the relationship of mutual trust and confidence between employee and employer; and

- to what extend the gathering of the data may be oppressive or demeaning.

In conducting an impact assessment, the employer should seek to identify:

- the likely extent of the adverse impact, ie the consequences for employees of the collection and retention of health information about them;

- the degree of intrusiveness that the employer's health policies and practices will actually create;

- whether information about employees' health is to be disclosed to anyone other than qualified medical practitioners, eg to HR staff or IT workers involved in maintaining employees' files, thus causing potential discomfort amongst employees;

- whether the trust and confidence in the employment relationship could be threatened by the collection of health information; and

- whether the collection of health information could be embarrassing or demeaning for employees.

Minimising the intrusion into employees' privacy   7.11

Assuming that the employer has established that there is a genuine business need to collect certain information about their employees' health, they should then seek to establish what steps can be taken to ensure the minimum degree of intrusiveness. The employer should take steps to minimise the intrusion into employees' privacy by:

- taking all reasonable steps to minimise exposure to hazardous substances in the workplace, in order to remove or reduce the need for medical testing;

- ensuring that their practices of collecting and using health information about employees are not any more intrusive than is absolutely necessary to meet the employer's stated business objectives, for example using medical questionnaires would be less intrusive than conducting a physical health check;

- targeting medical testing, for example drugs screening, only at employees who work in safety-critical jobs or following an incident or accident, rather than testing everyone;

- restricting the numbers of staff who have access to health information about employees to medically qualified staff only;

- designing medical testing to reveal the minimum amount of health information that is required for the purpose for which the testing was undertaken; and

- devising systems and procedures that allow employees to communicate confidentially with any occupational health professionals, ie so that staff know that certain types of communications will not be monitored.

Justification for processing health information   7.12

The key purposes of carrying out an impact assessment will be so that the employer can decide whether there is justification for them to collect information about their employees' health, and if so how much information needs to be collected and the purposes for which it will be used. It should not be assumed that there is a business need for collecting and/or retaining detailed health records on all staff, but instead the employer should adopt an open-minded approach and examine:

- what the purposes of collecting and holding health information would be;

- whether the type of information the employer proposes to collect and hold would actually achieve those purposes;

- whether the collection and use of health information would produce benefits for the business that outweighed the adverse impact to employees;

- whether there are any alternatives to the methods proposed to collect health information that would be less intrusive to employees (see **7.11** above); and

- whether there has been a full process of consultation with trade unions, with employee representatives or with employees directly prior to the introduction of any new policy on medical screening.

Impact assessments need not be formal and lengthy processes and may be a simple mental assessment. However, whenever the balance is in favour of processing health records, it is strongly advisable to write down the assessment. Clearly this will be particularly important in the more intrusive cases.

Sickness and absence records

7.13

The Employment Practices Data Protection Code, Part 2: Employment Records recommends that employers should keep sickness records separately from absence records. Sickness records will provide information about employees' health, for example the reason why a particular employee was absent from work at a particular time, or information about a particular employee's illness and its effects on him or her. Such records will, as stated above, be classed as sensitive data under the *DPA 1998*. Absence records (or attendance records), on the other hand, will show only the dates of employees' absences and the fact they were attributable to sickness (or injury) without giving any information on the specific medical condition or injury that caused them.

The Code of Practice also suggests that the employer should use absence records (rather than sickness records) whenever possible. For example if a line manager wished to review information about the overall patterns of absence or lengths of absences of a group of employees, the absence record should be sufficient. In contrast, if the line manager needed to review an individual's record in order to investigate frequent or persistent short-term absences, or a single long-term absence, it may be justifiable for the manager to be granted access to the individual's sickness record. Managing attendance is a key line management responsibility and line managers will need certain information at certain times if they are to ensure the efficient running of their departments. If information about an employee's health or sickness is necessary for the manager to carry out their managerial role, then its disclosure for that purpose will be potentially justifiable, depending of course on the circumstances of the individual case.

Information contained in sickness records should generally not be disclosed to non-medical personnel unless one of the sensitive data conditions is satisfied (see **7.4** above).

The fourth data protection principle in the *DPA 1998* requires that data are held only as long as is necessary. This principle is no different in the case of health records. Where an organisation has carried out medical examinations or testing, they should retain for audit purposes only records about the administration of the medical examinations or testing (dates, numbers involved, etc) and not the medical information obtained.

The Access to Medical Reports Act 1988   7.14

Sometimes an employer may wish to seek information from an employee's GP or consultant about a particular health issue affecting the employee's ability to perform their job. In this case the *Access to Medical Reports Act 1988* will apply.

Under the *Access to Medical Reports Act 1988,* employers are not allowed to apply to an employee's GP for a medical report unless they have first obtained the employee's written consent. Employees have the statutory right to refuse such consent under the Act and the employer must respect this right.

The employer should proceed as follows if the organisation wishes to obtain a medical report about an employee from the employee's GP or specialist:

- notify the employee in writing that the employer wishes to apply to the employee's doctor for a medical report;

- inform the employee of his or her right to withhold consent for the application to be made;

- inform the employee of his or her rights under the *Access to Medical Reports Act 1988*;

- obtain the employee's written consent for the application to be made; and

- inform the doctor to whom any request for a medical report is sent if the employee has stated his or her intention to seek access to the report before it is forwarded to the employer.

If an employer has a valid reason for requesting an employee's consent to apply to their GP for a medical report, the employer should seek only that information which is relevant and necessary from the GP. Employees should not be asked to consent to the disclosure of their entire health record, as this would be excessive and unnecessarily intrusive. Instead the employer should devise specific and relevant questions to pose to the GP and ensure that the information requested is relevant to the employee's ability to perform the job for which they are employed.

A summary of employees' rights under the *Access to Medical Reports Act 1988* are:

- to refuse to give consent for the employer to contact their GP for a report;

- to gain access to any medical report prepared about them by their GP or consultant and to be given or allowed to take a copy of the report;

- to ask the doctor to amend the report, if it is inaccurate or misleading in any way; and

- to refuse to allow the report, once prepared, to be passed to the employer.

The *Access to Medical Reports Act 1988* does not normally apply to medical reports prepared by occupational doctors. This is because this Act's provisions cover only reports 'relating to the physical or mental health of the individual prepared by a medical practitioner who is or has been responsible for the clinical care of the individual'. For this reason, it is often more convenient for employers to use occupational doctors to provide advice on employees' general health and fitness to work.

Employees and job applicants who have a disability   7.15

The *Disability Discrimination Act 1995* (*DDA 1995*) currently applies to organisations that employ 15 or more staff (although the threshold of 15 is to be removed in October 2004). The *DDA 1995* defines a disabled person as someone who 'has a physical or mental impairment which has a substantial and long-term adverse effect on his ability to carry out normal day-to-day activities'. 'Long-term' in this context means 12 months or more. The *DDA 1995* thus covers:

- a range of physical illnesses, conditions and injuries;

- any clinically recognised mental illness or condition including many stress-related illnesses;

- progressive conditions such as multiple sclerosis, cancer and AIDS;

- recurring conditions, even during periods of remission, provided the condition is likely to recur;

- conditions that fluctuate between minor and substantial; and

- past disabilities.

It is important to recognise that someone who is disabled does not necessarily have poor health, as the disability may have occurred as a result of an injury, or may be the result of a condition the individual was born with, for example a hearing impairment. Nevertheless, as can be seen from the above list, physical and mental illnesses may constitute disabilities for the purposes of the *DDA 1995*, depending on how long the particular illness has lasted (or is likely to last) and whether its effect on the individual's day-to-day life is 'substantial'.

Apart from the duty in the *DDA 1995* not to treat an employee or job applicant unfavourably on grounds related to a disability, there is also an important duty on employers to make reasonable adjustments to their working arrangements, working practices and premises in order to accommodate the needs of the particular disabled person. A failure to meet this duty will render employers liable to claims of disability discrimination unless the employer can objectively justify not making the adjustments.

If an employer is to be in a position to fulfil its obligation under the *DDA 1995* to make reasonable adjustments for an employee or job applicant with a disability, it will be necessary for them to collect and retain data about the individual's condition and its effects on his or her ability to perform his or her job. The collection of such data will be justified under the provision in the *DPA 1998* that allows employers to process sensitive data if it is necessary to do so in order to comply with a legal obligation (see **7.4** above).

Clearly, the disabled person will have a more in-depth knowledge of his or her condition, its effects and what measures would be likely to help him or her at work than any HR practitioner or line manager. It follows that the employer should initiate open discussions with the disabled employee (or job applicant) as to what adjustments would help them, and adopt a supportive approach.

Some examples of adjustments that employers may wish to consider in relation to an employee who has had frequent or extensive sickness absences on account of a condition that amounts to a disability could be to:

- allow the disabled employee to take more time off work than would normally be acceptable;

- look into the possibility of alternative employment that the employee could do;

- alter the employee's job duties, or allocate some of the duties to another employee if, as a result of a disability, the employee cannot carry out those duties or has difficulty carrying them out;

- adjust working hours, for example to fit in with the employee's need to attend weekly medical appointments, or by providing additional or longer rest breaks if the employee's illness causes them to tire easily;

- allow an employee who is beginning to recover from an illness to work part-time or work partly from home for a temporary period in order to ease them back into full-time employment.

Further examples of reasonable adjustments that employers should consider are to be found in **8.14**.

Medical screening 7.16

In order to promote safe and healthy working, an employer may wish to conduct medical screening on their existing employees and also on job applicants to whom it is intended to make an offer of employment. As with any fair and lawful data gathering, employees will need to know about how their health information will be used and who will have access to it both inside and outside the organisation. Generally, when individuals give information to a health professional, they expect that the information will remain confidential and not be passed to others.

Medical examinations during employment 7.17

It is common for employers to exercise the right (through clauses written into employees' contracts of employment) to require their employees to undergo a medical examination with a company-nominated doctor either on a regular basis (for example every three years) or at the employer's request. Although the *DPA 1998* does not cover the issue of whether medical examinations or medical testing is legitimate or desirable, the Act does come into play whenever the results of a medical examination are recorded, including the retention of samples that can be tracked back to an individual employee. Similarly, Part 4 of the Employment Practices Data Protection Code does not address how those examining and testing employees should conduct themselves. Medical examinations and testing should, however, be carried out by suitably qualified health professionals who will be bound by their own professional codes of conduct especially in their responsibility to the employee for a duty of confidentiality.

Employees' consent to undergo medical examinations with a company-nominated doctor should therefore cover not only the medical screening itself, but also the production of a medical report and the subsequent recording of the information. This approach can be advantageous for employers since a company doctor will have more thorough knowledge than the employee's GP of the employer's business requirements and whether or not the particular employee's job involves any specific physical or psychological demands that might require the employee to have a higher than normal level of health or fitness. The issue of employee consent is explained further at **4.8** above.

Where it is the employer's policy to require employees to undergo medical screening with an occupational doctor, they should:

- ensure the employer's policy on medical screening and any associated rules and standards are clearly communicated to all staff;

- set out the circumstances in which medical examinations or testing may be required, for example whether the rules apply to all staff, or only to staff in certain jobs, and whether testing is conducted on a routine basis or whenever the employer deems it appropriate;

- ensure the policy states the nature of the testing, for example whether it is general health check or whether it also designed to detect specific conditions or exposure to defined substances or drugs use (see **7.19** below);

- explain fully the consequences for employees of refusing to agree to be tested, and the consequences if a test proves positive or negative;

- inform employees how information obtained through testing will be used and to whom it may be disclosed;

- be sure that samples of blood, urine, etc, provided by employees are not tested for any condition or substance unless the employee concerned has given their free and explicit consent to the particular type of test;

- refrain from using or recording any information that comes to light by chance during medical testing, for example if a routine medical examination revealed that an employee was pregnant, this fact should not be recorded or used by the employer in any way; and

- destroy all medical data as soon as there is no further need to keep it.

The employee will be entitled to a copy of any reported findings from an examination or test. It is therefore advisable whenever samples are taken that pairs are taken in order to provide a sample for the employee.

Part 4 of the Employment Practices Code on Workers' Health suggests that employers should conduct medical examinations on existing employees only on a voluntary basis, or where they are satisfied that testing is a necessary and justified measure to:

- ensure health and safety in the workplace;

- determine employees' fitness for continued employment;

- establish employees' entitlement to health related benefits, for example payment of sick pay; and

- prevent discrimination against an employee who has a disability.

Part 4 of the Code is, at the time of writing, in draft form and may therefore be subject to changes before it is finally published.

Pre-employment medical screening   7.18

Many employers require all new recruits to undergo a pre-employment medical examination prior to confirming their appointment. This is generally legitimate in order to ensure that the person is sufficiently fit and healthy to perform the job in question and possibly to determine whether he or she will be eligible to join any pension or health insurance scheme operated by the employer. The draft Employment Practices Data Protection Code on Workers' Health suggests, however, that employers should:

- carry out medical screening only on the person whom they intend to appoint (and not on other shortlisted candidates);

- identify and record the specific business purpose(s) for which the medical examination is being carried out;

- ensure that the medical examination covers only those aspects of the employee's health and fitness that are relevant to his or her ability to perform the job into which he or she is being appointed;

- consider whether there is a less intrusive way of meeting their business objectives, the most obvious example being to use a medical questionnaire (see **7.19** below) rather than requiring the candidate to undergo a medical examination; and

- inform all job applicants at an early stage during the recruitment process that the successful applicant will be required to undergo a medical examination or complete a medical questionnaire and that any offer of employment will be conditional on the results of these being satisfactory to the employer.

Using medical questionnaires   7.19

Asking employees or job applicants to complete a medical questionnaire will be considerably less intrusive than requiring them to undergo a medical examination. This approach should therefore be used whenever possible as an alternative to a medical examination, or as a first stage in order to establish whether a full medical examination is necessary.

Employers who use medical questionnaires should review them in order to make sure that they ask only for information that the employer needs for a stated legitimate purpose. Information that is not relevant and necessary should not be requested.

The best way forward for an employer that wishes to use medical questionnaires to collect health information about their employees or job applicants would be to have the questionnaire designed (or at the very least reviewed and edited) by an occupational doctor. The information provided by employees or job applicants on the questionnaire should also be interpreted only by qualified medical practitioners, and not (for example) by an HR officer.

Drugs and alcohol testing   7.20

Before contemplating introducing a policy of drugs and/or alcohol testing, the employer should be quite certain that there are legitimate grounds for implementing such a policy. The retention of results, including samples, following a drugs or alcohol test will fall squarely under the *DPA 1998* and will of course also have considerable implications under Article 8 of the *Human Rights Act 1998* (the right to respect for private life).

One underlying principle is that the purpose of any drugs and/or alcohol screening programme in employment should be about assessing the competence of an employee to perform a specific job, and not a way of controlling off-duty behaviour, if the employee's work is unlikely to be affected. Employers should therefore (wherever possible) seek to use tests that are designed to identify impairment at work rather than more general tests that identify the use of (illegal) substances in an employee's private life.

For employers who already have a drugs/alcohol screening programme in place, it may be advisable to review it in order to ascertain whether its application in its present form is justified. If the employer conducts drugs/alcohol testing without having a proper business reason to do so, it is likely that any resultant dismissal on account of a positive test result would be found unfair by an employment tribunal.

Drugs or alcohol testing and the retention of results will be particularly intrusive for employees. The purpose for carrying out the testing must therefore be proportionate in light of the employer's real business needs. Urine analysis, for example, will reveal not only the presence of certain illegal drugs in the employee's body, but may also bring to light the existence of other medical conditions.

Normally, the only grounds that will justify drugs/alcohol testing at work will be for the purpose of ensuring safety. Thus routine testing should be limited to employees whose jobs are safety-critical, for example those who work with heavy machinery, employees whose jobs involve intense concentration or those who have responsibility for the care of others (for example drivers). Otherwise, the only justification for testing an employee whose job did not fall into the safety-critical category would be if there were reasonable grounds to suspect that the employee was under the influence of drugs or alcohol whilst at work, and that this state of affairs was likely to have a negative impact on safety. Even then, the employer would be obliged to consider whether a less intrusive test could be used to determine whether the employee was impaired, for example by using a test that measured speed of reaction.

A measured approach to policy formulation should always be taken, bearing in mind the need for proportionality. This means that the employer should think carefully whether the testing and methods proposed are appropriate, relevant and necessary in relation to the purpose for which testing is proposed.

It is important to bear in mind that under the *DPA 1998*, random drugs or alcohol screening of all employees in the business will not be justified on the grounds that some of the employees perform safety-critical roles. It will not be valid to argue that everyone (for example administrative staff who perform desk-based jobs) should be subjected to random testing in order to promote fairness and consistency. This argument cannot be sustained because it does not make sense to treat everyone in the same way when the circumstances of employees' jobs are completely different. Blanket policies on testing should therefore be avoided.

Equally, it will not normally be justifiable to conduct drugs or alcohol screening on an employee for performance-related or conduct reasons, unless there is also a safety issue at stake.

If an employer has established (ideally through an impact assessment – see **7.7** above) that drugs and/or alcohol screening is necessary and appropriate in order to ensure health and safety, there will be certain important steps that they will have to take to ensure their practices remain within the law:

- consult employees or their representatives before deciding to introduce a drugs or alcohol screening programme;

- consult qualified experts before finalising the type of testing to be used;

- institute clear guidelines informing employees of the purpose of the drugs or alcohol screening programme and what the tests are designed to detect;

- ensure drugs testing is carried out and interpreted only by qualified and competent professionals who can provide guarantees that they will meet appropriate standards of quality, integrity, confidentiality and security;

- adopt a policy of testing only for substances that are likely to impact on health and safety at work and a level of exposure that is likely to cause impairment;

- seek, where possible, to use tests that detect only recent exposure to the substances being tested for;

- aim to use the least intrusive method possible to achieve the stated business purpose;

- minimise the amount of personal data that is collected during drugs or alcohol testing; and

- review whether it is possible to use tests of cognitive ability instead of drugs or alcohol testing, for example a test that measures hand–eye coordination and response times.

It will be important also for the employer to communicate clearly to all employees who are subjected to drugs or alcohol testing what will happen if they fail a test. Other company procedures will have to be amended, where appropriate, to make reference to this, for example the employer's disciplinary procedure will have to make it clear if an employee who tests positive will be subjected to disciplinary action or dismissed (see **7.22** below).

Finally, of course, the consent of employees will be required before any drugs screening can be lawfully carried out. This can be obtained by incorporating both the drugs/alcohol screening policy and the requirement to undergo screening into employees' contracts of employment. Otherwise any drugs or alcohol screening programme would have to be conducted on a purely voluntary basis. Consent should, of course, include the employee's permission for the employer to process any data that are obtained as a result of the drugs or alcohol test.

Selecting employees for testing   7.21

Where drugs or alcohol screening is conducted on a random basis, it will be important to ensure that the methods used to select employees for screening are truly random, and include everyone within the group of staff for whom testing is considered necessary (for example managers should not be excluded solely on the basis that they are considered too 'senior'). If testing is to be conducted on a 'with cause' basis only, employees should be clearly informed of the criteria that will be used to trigger a test, usually an incident or accident or possibly where the employee's behaviour is observed to be unusual or erratic.

Dismissal following a positive test result 7.22

Where an employer has a drugs and/or alcohol screening programme in place, the employer will have to decide what action to take in the event that an employee fails a test. Two different approaches are possible:

- implementing a programme of rehabilitation and support for the employee if the employee agrees; or

- disciplinary action up to and including dismissal.

Dismissal for testing positive may be fair provided that all of the following conditions are met:

- there is a contractual right to carry out drugs or alcohol screening;

- there were reasonable grounds for requiring the employee to submit to a test, ie either as a result of a screening programme implemented for safety-related reasons or because the employee has shown signs of impairment whilst at work;

- health or safety may be put at risk or there is likely to be substantial damage to the employer's reputation; and

- the employer's rules provide for dismissal on account of a positive test result, including where the drugs have been taken outside of working time.

Dismissal may also be fair where the employer has a contractual right and a proper reason to require employees to undergo drugs or alcohol screening and the employee has refused to submit to a test without good reason.

The fairness of any dismissal will depend on all the circumstances of the individual case and in particular whether the employer has handled the matter in a reasonable way. One case that dealt with dismissal on account of a positive test result was *O'Flynn v Airlinks the Airport Coach Co Ltd [2002] EAT 0269/01*. In this case, the employee worked as a customer care assistant, but her job occasionally involved assisting drivers to manoeuvre coaches and serving hot drinks on moving coaches. The employer had introduced an alcohol and drugs policy and random screening, details of which had been well communicated to all staff. The policy ruled that employees were prohibited from having drugs or alcohol in their systems whilst at work, and that a positive drugs test would lead to disciplinary action and possibly dismissal. Some five months after the introduction of the policy, the employee was selected for a random drugs test, and admitted to having taken drugs in her own time. The test proved positive for cannabis. The employee was consequently dismissed following a disciplinary interview. She claimed unfair dismissal.

151

The EAT upheld the employment tribunal's decision that the dismissal was fair. Although the case occurred prior to the implementation of the *Human Rights Act 1998*, the EAT elected to consider the effect Article 8 of the European convention on Human Rights (the right to respect for private life) might have had on the decision. They found that the drugs screening policy infringed the employee's right to a private life to the extent that it meant that certain drugs could not be taken in her own time without jeopardising her employment, and because it required her to provide a urine sample if she was randomly selected for screening. Nevertheless, the EAT held that the policy and the testing were necessary and appropriate for reasons of public safety, and that the employee's dismissal following the positive test result and her admission that she had taken drugs was not disproportionate in light of the safety issues at stake.

Genetic testing 7.23

Genetic testing should generally not be used by employers. Genetic testing is still under development and cannot normally predict reliably if an individual will in fact develop a particular disease or condition during his or her working life, nor (if the person does develop the condition), how severely it will affect the individual. Because of this, it would be inappropriate to base employment decisions on such testing. Genetic testing would, in any event, be extremely intrusive and would normally not therefore be justifiable in the employment context.

The only exception to this general principle would be in a situation where factors in the workplace were known to pose particular risks to those with particular genetic variations. In this case, genetic testing might be justified in order to alert the employer (and any employee who is vulnerable) to the possibility that an individual might be at risk. This would only be valid, however, if the type of test used was likely to be reliable in detecting the genetic condition in question, and even if this was the case, the link between a particular hazard in the workplace and the individual's susceptibility to it would be unlikely to represent a certainty.

The draft version of Part 4 of the Employment Practices Data Protection Code (on Workers' Health) suggests that:

- genetic testing should be used only as a last resort if there is no other way of minimising particular risks to health inherent in the workplace;

- genetic testing should not be used to try to predict an employee's future general health;

- genetic testing should be contemplated only if there is scientific evidence that the particular test is valid for the purpose for which it is to be used;

- where the potential risk of a particular condition developing is to the employee rather than to other staff, genetic testing should be done purely on a voluntary basis;

- employers should communicate the results of any genetic test directly to the employee concerned and ensure professional advice is available to him or her; and

- employees should not be required to disclose the results of previous genetic testing they have undertaken, eg to a potential new employer.

Payroll Issues Relating to Health Records 7.24

The occasions when the payroll department will need to know about an employee's ill health will be limited to the payment of statutory and/or contractual sick pay. For this it is only necessary to know whether the employee is or is not fit for work under the contract. The payroll department should not, therefore, collect or process any personal data about individual employees' state of health or ill health.

Employees will often provide a medical certificate from their general practitioner, which will state that the employee is unable to work for a given period and also why the employee cannot do so. This latter information is unnecessary and excessive for payroll department's requirements. It is thus contrary to the third data protection principle (the duty to ensure data is adequate, relevant and not excessive in relation to its stated purpose) for them to process this data. However, it is very difficult to stop employees providing this level of detailed information.

Where the employer employs health professionals, perhaps as part of an occupational health care scheme, they will be accustomed to receiving details of employees' illnesses. The health professionals can separate health information from information about an employee's fitness to work and forward to payroll and other parts of the organisation the simple 'yes/no' information as to an employee's fitness for work.

Health data should not be retained on employees' files within the payroll department. Where the data are required for industrial injuries or monitoring an employee's health, separate filing systems with appropriately restricted access should be used (see **7.13** above).

There is one other occasion when payroll may need to know something about an employee's health: when he or she is leaving the organisation. This could be because the employee is retiring on grounds of ill health or because of his or her lack of capability to work the notice period arising from ill health. Whichever of these is the reason, the only information that payroll requires is that the employment has been terminated due to ill health. The nature of the illness is immaterial and should not be provided to payroll.

Payroll will need to know about the death of an employee as this ends the employee's liability to National Insurance contributions. The death must be recorded on the Form P45 and all parts of the form must be sent to the Tax Office. Since the *DPA 1998* is concerned with the personal data of living individuals, information about dead persons is beyond the scope of the Act. It is good practice, however, to continue to afford data protection to the deceased employee's personal data especially in the time soon after the death. A code for dealing with deaths in service should include statements on how the data protection principles will be applied and for how long the data will be treated as private and confidential.

Chapter 8
Equality and Equal
Opportunities Monitoring

Introduction   8.1

Any employer who wants their business to succeed will place the promotion of equal opportunities high up on their management agenda priority listing. Taking steps to promote equality of opportunity amongst all staff and ensure the workplace is free from all forms of discrimination will help the organisation to retain and motivate their staff and create a working environment in which employees feel comfortable. Employees who feel comfortable, ie reassured that they will be treated with respect and not become the victims of any unfavourable treatment, including harassment, will be enabled to perform to the best of their abilities. The promotion of equal opportunities in the workplace will be particularly important so as to ensure that people from minority groups are treated fairly and equally in every respect, both during the process of recruitment and once employed.

An employer who devises and implements clear policies on equal opportunities and the prohibition of all forms of harassment will thus go a long way to combating unfairness, prejudice and harassment and help to create an environment of mutual trust and respect in which workers can exercise their talents fully to the benefit of the employer.

Equal Opportunities Monitoring   8.2

In order to ensure equal opportunities in the workplace, many employers conduct monitoring. Monitoring may be done in relation to the numbers and composition (in terms of gender, racial or ethnic origin, religion or belief, age and disability) of:

- successful and unsuccessful job applicants;

- staff who receive training;

- employees who have been promoted;

- employees who benefit or suffer detriment as a result of performance assessment;

- staff who are the subject of disciplinary action;

- staff who raise grievances; and

- employees who leave the company (possibly divided into those who resign and those who are dismissed).

The key purposes of monitoring will be to:

- analyse the reasons for any differences in treatment of different 'groups' of staff and ensure these reasons are not linked directly or indirectly to gender or race;

- audit the processes of recruitment to ensure that the composition of the numbers of staff being shortlisted and selected (for example in terms of racial group) is proportionate to that of the total number of people applying for posts;

- check that there is no disparate impact on different groups of staff as a result of the organisation's policies and procedures, for example the ways in which grievance and disciplinary procedures are applied;

- discover whether there any barriers to equality of opportunity in appraisal, training and promotion;

- identify areas where change is needed; and

- take action to deal with any inequalities discovered as a result of monitoring.

The investigation and record keeping associated with monitoring is naturally controversial as it requires employers to seek to obtain personal information about individuals and to distinguish between individuals based on this information. Some people may object to being asked questions about, for example, their religion or belief, on the basis that the question represents an intrusion into their private lives. It should be borne in mind, however, that it is the motive for which information is sought and kept and the purpose to which the information is put that are important. Nowadays there is a wide acceptance that the information and record keeping required for equal opportunities monitoring represents a valid and useful tool for identifying and tackling discrimination and promoting equal opportunities.

In the public sector, monitoring in respect of the racial origin of job applicants and employees is compulsory (see **8.13** below).

Responsibility for equal opportunities monitoring 8.3

As part of the process of equal opportunities monitoring, the employer should nominate a senior person within the organisation to be responsible for planning, designing and carrying out monitoring, and for ensuring that the record keeping associated with monitoring complies with the *Data Protection Act 1998* (*DPA 1998* or 'the Act').

The person appointed to hold such responsibility should, ideally, be someone who has the authority to challenge and change any procedures or practices that are found to have a discriminatory impact.

Equal opportunities monitoring and the DPA 1998

8.4

Information gathered about individuals' gender, racial or ethnic origin, religion or belief, age, sexual orientation (possibly) and disability will constitute personal data under the *DPA 1998*. Information obtained as a result of equal opportunities monitoring must therefore be treated in accordance with the provisions of the Act and the Employment Practices Data Protection Code.

Some of this information will constitute 'sensitive data' and thus require special treatment (see **8.5** below). The employer is required to abide by all the data protection principles when processing such data and will also, for example, have to:

- inform staff how and why their data will be used;
- inform staff to whom the data will be disclosed; and
- ensure the security of the data.

When data gathered for monitoring purposes constitutes sensitive data

8.5

Some of the information that will be required to conduct monitoring is regarded under the *DPA 1998* as sensitive data, in particular, information about individuals':

- racial or ethic origin;
- religious beliefs or other beliefs of a similar nature;
- physical or mental health or condition; and
- trade union membership.

When it is lawful to process sensitive data in relation to monitoring

8.6

As a general principle, the *DPA 1998* states that employers may not process sensitive data about an individual unless either the person has consented to processing, or one of a limited number of conditions is fulfilled.

DPA 1998, Schedule 3 contains a list of the conditions that may justify the processing of sensitive data, but in relation to the types of sensitive data listed above, the only conditions likely to be relevant would be:

- where processing is necessary in order for the employer to comply with a legal obligation in connection with employment;
- where processing is necessary in connection with any legal proceedings, including the defence of a legal claim against the employer; and

- where processing of information about individuals' racial or ethnic origin, religious beliefs or other similar beliefs, or physical or mental health is for the purpose of carrying out equal opportunities monitoring with a view to promoting and maintaining equality of treatment, and the information is necessary in order to achieve this purpose. The Act adds another condition relevant to this provision which is that the processing must be carried out with appropriate safeguards in place to ensure the rights and freedoms of the individuals.

The processing of information about gender or age does not constitute sensitive data under the Act and employers are therefore free to conduct monitoring on these features without any particular restraints or conditions.

Obtaining consent   8.7

If employers wish to monitor their staff in respect of features other than those necessary for equal opportunities monitoring, and if the information they wish to collect is not necessary to comply with a legal obligation in connection with employment or for conducting any legal proceedings, they will essentially have to obtain the consent of their employees to the processing.

Under data protection principles, consent to the processing of sensitive data must be 'explicit', and 'freely given'. 'Explicit' in this context means that the employee must have signed a document indicating his or her agreement, having first been clearly informed how the information will be used. 'Freely given' is described as giving the employee a genuine choice as to whether or not to consent to the processing, and operating a policy of not subjecting anyone who declines to give their consent to any detriment. Part 2 of the Employment Practices Data Protection Code (on Employment Records) points out that the extent to which individuals' consent can be relied on in the context of employment is limited on account of this requirement for consent to be freely given.

Despite the fact that it may not always be a sound prospect for an employer to rely on consent as a means of justification for the processing of sensitive data about their employees, it is nevertheless a sensible precaution for an employer as a matter of course to seek employees' (and job applicants') consent to the collection and use of sensitive data about them.

Consent from job applicants for the employer to process information about them, including sensitive data, can be obtained during the process of recruitment either by including an appropriate statement on the application form for the applicant to sign, or by using a specially designed form which the applicant is asked to sign, for example at the time of a recruitment interview (see **5.23** above for further information about obtaining consent from job applicants).

Obtaining consent from existing employees, for example where an employer decides to commence equal opportunities monitoring for the first time, could be obtained by placing an appropriately worded clause on the equal opportunities monitoring form for each employee to sign when they complete the form. The form should also explain clearly the purpose for which the data will be used.

The employer should, in any event, always assess whether there is justification for seeking any sensitive data from employees or job applicants, and explain properly why the information is being requested and how it will be used. It should also be a part of the monitoring policy that any employee who declines to provide the information requested by the employer is not penalised in any way (unless the information is needed for legal reasons – see **8.8** below).

An alternative way forward, which would avoid the need for consent altogether, would be to conduct monitoring of existing employees in an anonymised way, ie by asking employees to complete an equal opportunities monitoring form without disclosing their identity. This approach may not, however, be altogether satisfactory as there would be no method of checking whether the individuals who chose to supply the information had supplied it fully and accurately. There might also be a substantial proportion of the workforce who would choose not to return the form at all.

Nevertheless, Part 1 of the Employment Practices Data Protection Code (Recruitment and Selection) suggests that, even though equal opportunities monitoring is a legitimate reason to collect information about applicants' racial or ethnic origin, the processes used to conduct such monitoring should, if possible, be based on anonymous or aggregated information.

Where the processing of sensitive data is necessary in order to comply with a legal obligation 8.8

One of the conditions that justifies the processing of sensitive data is if the data is necessary in order for the employer to comply with a legal obligation in connection with employment. Such a legal obligation may arise as a result of statute or common law, ie decisions of courts and tribunals which interpret the law. The scope of this condition is fairly wide in the context of employment. For example, it would be relevant to public sector organisations who are obliged by law to conduct monitoring in respect of their employees' racial and ethnic origins (see **8.13** below) and, from October 2004, monitoring in respect of disability (see **8.14** below). It is important to note, however, that, in order to fulfil this condition, processing must be *necessary* to comply with a legal obligation and not merely convenient or desirable from the employer's point of view.

The following is a list of possible legal obligations that could potentially justify the processing of sensitive data that might be used also for monitoring purposes:

- Information about a worker's health or disability may be necessary to comply with the provisions of the *Disability Discrimination Act 1995* (see **8.14** below), in particular the duty to make reasonable adjustments. The employer may wish also to monitor equality of opportunity by checking (for example) whether staff with disabilities are promoted or transferred at the same rate as non-disabled people.

- Information about health or disability will also be necessary to allow the employer to process Statutory Sick Pay and possibly Statutory Maternity Pay. The employer may also wish to conduct monitoring in relation to the sickness records of various groups of staff, for example men and women, people from different racial groups, etc in order to ensure equality of treatment.

- Information about employees' health may be necessary for the employer to fulfil their duties under the *Health and Safety at Work Act 1974*, ie so that the employer can take the appropriate and necessary steps to ensure the health, safety and welfare of all their employees at work.

- Information about trade union membership will be necessary to enable the employer to deduct members' subscriptions from their pay at source.

- Information about an employee's previous criminal convictions may be necessary in relation to certain sensitive posts in order to ensure the safety of, for example, children or vulnerable adults (see **5.16** above for further information). Certain public sector bodies may also have specific statutory duties imposed on them in relation to the qualifications or background of their employees.

- Information about individuals' racial and ethnic origins, religion or belief, sexual orientation and disability, all of which are governed by anti-discrimination legislation, may be processed because of the duty placed on every employer not to discriminate on any of the prohibited grounds against job applicants or employees.

- Information about employees' racial and ethnic origin is required for public authority employers to fulfil their duties under the *Race Relations (Amendment) Act 2000* and the *Race Relations Act 1976 (Statutory Duties) Order 2001 (SI 2001 No 3458)*. The Order imposed a duty on public sector employers to carry out regular monitoring of the racial balance of their employees and all applicants for employment, training and promotion (see **8.13** below for further information).

- Information about job applicants' nationality may be necessary at the time of recruitment in order for the employer to avoid being in breach of the *Asylum and Immigration Act 1996* (by employing someone who does not have the right to work in the UK). Although nationality is not, in itself, regarded as sensitive data, it is often inextricably linked with individuals' racial origins. This subject is explored more fully at **5.28** above).

Where the processing of sensitive data is necessary in connection with legal proceedings   8.9

The *DPA 1998* states that an employer may process sensitive data if such processing is necessary in connection with any legal proceedings, including the defence of a legal claim against the employer. This means that if an employee has brought a complaint against his or her employer to an employment tribunal, alleging for example that they have been subjected to race discrimination in the course of their employment, it would be legitimate for the employer to process information relating to the race or ethnic origin of that employee, and possibly the race or ethnic origin of other employees. This would be in order to facilitate the employer's defence against the claim, ie to prove to the tribunal's satisfaction that the employee alleging race discrimination had not in fact been treated less favourably than other employees in similar circumstances. Alternatively, if the employee had in fact been treated less favourably than another employee (for example if they had been unsuccessful in an application for a promotion), the employer would be entitled to produce sufficient evidence to persuade the tribunal that the reasons for the employer's actions (ie their selection of one employee in favour of another for promotion) had nothing to do with the respective racial groups of the respective employees.

Monitoring of job applicants and employees   8.10

Although there is no positive duty on employers to monitor their staff in terms of equality of opportunity (except in the public sector where there is a duty to monitor staff and job applicants by reference to their racial groups – see **8.13** below). Nevertheless monitoring is recognised as an appropriate tool for employers to use to ensure equality of opportunity within the organisation and to eliminate any discriminatory practices.

Monitoring for the purposes of promoting equal opportunities may be conducted on both job applicants and existing employees. Monitoring will essentially have three stages:

- gathering information about job applicants or employees;

- analysing and interpreting the information; and

- defining a programme of action to remedy any inequalities that have been identified.

Where monitoring is carried out, the employer will be under a duty to ensure the security of the personal data gathered. This is in line with the seventh data protection principle, namely that employers should put in place measures to protect personal data against unauthorised or unlawful processing, accidental loss or destruction, or damage. In order to achieve this goal, the employer should:

- limit the number of staff who have access to personal information obtained as a result of equal opportunities monitoring (and also other forms of monitoring);

- ensure staff who have access to personal data, and in particular sensitive data, have been fully trained so as to ensure that they understand their duties and obligations under the *DPA 1998* including the data protection principles; and

- refrain from using personal information collected for the purposes of equal opportunities monitoring for any other purpose.

Job applicants   8.11

It is considered good practice for organisations to carry out monitoring of job applications in order to promote equality of opportunity as between people of different racial groups and both sexes and protect against any inequalities that may otherwise creep into the recruitment process.

One of the key principles in the Employment Practices Data Protection Code is that information should not be collected and retained about individuals unless it is necessary for a legitimate business purpose. Whilst monitoring of racial origin, gender, disability, age and possibly religion may be justified as part of the recruitment process to ensure equality of opportunity and the avoidance of discrimination, once the recruitment exercise is complete, the further retention of data relating to unsuccessful candidates is unlikely to be justifiable. Instead, the employer should devise a system for retaining anonymised data on the numbers of candidates who applied for each post and the number shortlisted, together with their 'categories' eg gender, family status, racial origin, age and whether or not they are disabled. In this way, the data is no longer 'personal data' for the purposes of the *DPA 1998*, but will still allow the employer to conduct a meaningful review of the figures.

Anonymised data will be sufficient to allow the employer to draw the necessary conclusions, ie whether the number of shortlisted applicants and successful applicants in each category (ie sex, racial group, etc) are proportionate to that category's numbers in the organisation, and within the community as a whole. The names of the individuals (or other identifying features such as serial numbers that can then be tracked back to an individual) will no longer be necessary for this purpose.

Existing employees   8.12

Before embarking on a process of monitoring existing employees, the employer should review the advice available from the various equality bodies, namely the Commission for Racial Equality (CRE), the Equal Opportunities Commission (EOC) and the Disability Rights Commission (DRC). The respective web sites are:

- www.cre.gov.uk;
- www.eoc.org.uk; and
- www.drc.gov.uk.

The Code of Practice on Employment Records suggests that employers will need to take specific advice about the forms, procedures and ethnic grouping categories to be used in any monitoring exercise. A further recommendation is that the range of choices of ethnic origin should not be limited to the extent that those completing the form are obliged to make a choice that does not properly reflect their ethnic origin.

Where an employee declines to complete a monitoring questionnaire, the employer should:

- keep a record of the fact that the employee did not complete the form; and

- (if the employer elects to assign an employee to categories on behalf of the employee) note that the categorisations have been made by the employer and not the employee, and that the categorisations are therefore based on assumption and not fact.

Public sector employers' duty to monitor in respect of racial groups   8.13

The *Race Relations Act 1976* prohibits discrimination on grounds of colour, race, nationality, ethnic origins and national origins. This Act applies throughout the process of recruitment, during employment, at termination of employment and post-employment (for example in respect of any reference provided to an ex-employee).

The *Race Relations (Amendment) Act 2000* imposed a general duty on all public authorities to take positive measures to eliminate unlawful racial discrimination and promote equality of opportunity and good relations as between persons of different racial groups. The *Race Relations Act 1976 (Statutory Duties) Order 2001 (SI 2001 No 3458)* obliged public sector organisations to prepare and publish a race equality scheme, ie a plan as to how they intend to achieve racial equality in their employment practices and to ensure the training of all staff on racial equality. The Order also imposed a duty on public sector employers to carry out regular monitoring of the racial balance of their employees and all applicants for employment, training and promotion.

Where a public sector employer has 150 or more full-time staff (or the equivalent, taking into account the hours worked by part-time staff), there are further duties on public sector employers to collect information relating to the racial groups of staff who:

- receive training;

- benefit or suffer detriment as a result of performance assessment procedures;

- are involved in grievance procedures;

- are the subject of disciplinary procedures; and

- cease employment.

The law requires the results of this monitoring to be published annually.

The imposition of this public duty means that public sector organisations can rely on the existence of the legal duty as a justification for retaining records associated with equal opportunities monitoring in respect of the racial groups of their employees and job applicants. As stated in **8.7** above, however, if the employer wishes also to monitor in respect of other features, for example religion or disability, employees' explicit consent will be required since the information being sought constitutes sensitive data under the *DPA 1998*.

Disability   8.14

Under the *Disability Discrimination Act 1995* (*DDA 1995*), organisations that employ 15 or more staff are obliged:

- not to treat a job applicant, employee or ex-employee unfavourably on grounds related to that person's disability, unless the particular treatment can be justified; and

- to make reasonable adjustments to their working arrangements, working practices and premises in order to accommodate the needs of the particular disabled person.

The threshold of 15 is, however, to be removed on 1 October 2004 when the *Disability Discrimination Act 1995 (Amendment) Regulations 2003* (SI 2003 No 1673) are implemented.

A disabled person is defined in the Act as someone who 'has a physical or mental impairment which has a substantial and long-term adverse effect on his ability to carry out normal day-to-day activities'. 'Long-term' in this context means 12 months or more. To qualify as a disabled person, the impairment must have a substantial adverse effect on one of the following:

- mobility;

- manual dexterity;

- physical coordination;

- continence;

- the ability to lift, carry or otherwise move everyday objects;

- speech, hearing or eyesight;

- memory or ability to concentrate, learn or understand; or

- the perception of the risk of physical danger.

Someone with a severe disfigurement will also be classed as disabled under the Act.

The *DDA 1995* is thus very wide in scope and covers:

- a range of physical illnesses, conditions and injuries;

- any clinically recognised mental illness or condition including many stress related illnesses;

- progressive conditions such as multiple sclerosis, cancer and AIDS, which are covered as soon as the condition is diagnosed, provided there are some effects on the person's normal day-to-day activities at that point in time and these effects are likely to become substantial;

- recurring conditions, even during periods of remission, provided the condition is likely to recur;

- conditions that fluctuate between minor and substantial; and

- past disabilities.

The *DDA 1995* protects all workers and also job applicants. Like the other anti-discrimination statutes, it does not require an employee to have any minimum period of service in order to be eligible to bring a complaint to an employment tribunal. It places considerable responsibility on employers to be positive in their attitude to the employment of people with disabilities and to do whatever they reasonably can to accommodate their needs.

Apart from outlawing discrimination on grounds related to an individual's disability, the *DDA 1995* imposes a duty on employers to make reasonable adjustments to the working environment, working arrangements and working conditions in order to accommodate the needs of disabled workers and job applicants. Failure to meet this duty will render employers liable to claims of disability discrimination unless the employer can objectively justify not making the adjustments.

There is, however, no general duty to make adjustments, but instead the duty arises when an employee becomes disabled or a someone with a disability applies for a job. Some examples of adjustments to working practices could be to:

- transfer the employee to a different job in circumstances where the employee is no longer able to perform their own job, bearing in mind that this could only be done lawfully with the employee's express agreement (an enforced transfer would be in breach of the employee's contract);

- alter the employee's job duties, or allocate some of the duties to another employee if, as a result of a disability, the employee cannot carry out those duties or has difficulty carrying them out;

- adjust how the job is done, for example by arranging for an employee with a mobility impairment to have work brought to their work station rather than requiring the person to walk to other parts of the building);

- adjust working hours, for example to fit in with the employee's need to attend weekly medical appointments, or by providing additional or longer rest breaks if the employee's condition causes them to tire easily;

- move an employee who uses a wheelchair to a different place of work, for example locate them somewhere more readily accessible;

- allow an employee whose disability means they cannot drive to work partly from home;

- acquire or modify equipment to assist a disabled person to perform their job;

- adjust procedural requirements, for example by condoning more frequent periods of absence from work than would normally be acceptable, or adjusting sickness absence procedures so that disability related absences are discounted;

- modify instructions or manuals, for example by providing them on cassette tape, or in Braille;

- provide additional supervision or coaching, for example to assist an employee with learning difficulties to grasp the key principles of a new method of working;

- adjust selection tests for job applicants, for example by using a different method of testing for a candidate with dyslexia so that they are given the opportunity to compete for the job on a level playing field;

- modify premises, for example by installing a ramp, widening a doorway or moving furniture for a wheelchair user or relocating door handles or shelves for someone who has difficulty reaching.

The duty to make adjustments is subject to the word 'reasonable' and it will therefore not be necessary for an employer to make adjustments where, for example:

- making the adjustment would incur excessive cost in relation to the employer's size and resources;

- making the adjustment would be impracticable or would cause major disruption to the employer's business;

- the adjustment would not help the employee or would be unacceptable to them; or

- making the adjustment would contravene health and safety law, or fire regulations.

As a result of the duties imposed under the *DDA 1995*, and in order to promote good practice generally, many employers conduct monitoring in respect of job applicants and employees with disabilities. Furthermore, as stated earlier, it will be necessary for an employer to collect and retain data about a disabled employee's condition and its effects if they are to be in a position to fulfil their obligation under the *DDA 1995* to make reasonable adjustments for that person.

The type of monitoring that may be undertaken could, for example, include tracking how many people with disabilities are being promoted within the organisation, and to what levels of seniority. This type of monitoring will require data to be kept on specific individuals in relation to promotions, and it will not be possible to hold the data anonymously. Employees would therefore have the right to be informed of the type of monitoring that was taking place and how their personal data was used as part of the monitoring process.

The collection and retention of data about an individual's state of health and about their disability should be the subject of open discussion between the employer and the disabled person. Disability should not be regarded as a taboo subject in the field of employment and in any event, it will arguably be necessary for the employer to raise the question of how the person's disability affects them in order to be able to determine what types of adjustments would assist them to perform the job. The disabled person will obviously have a more in-depth knowledge of what measures would be likely to help facilitate effective working and help them to overcome any disadvantage that their disability would otherwise cause. Thus the provision in the *DPA 1998, Schedule 3* that allows employers to process sensitive data if it is necessary to do so in order to comply with a legal obligation will be satisfied.

There is no duty in the *DDA 1995* on a job applicant or employee to reveal a disability, unless asked. The onus therefore lies with the employer to raise the issue, ask appropriate questions and make an appropriate record in order to establish what adjustments might reasonably be required to for them to fulfil the duties imposed under the *DDA 1995*.

Changes to the *DDA 1995* are, at the time of writing, in the pipeline. The Government has proposed under a new Disability Discrimination Bill that there will be a duty on all public sector bodies to take positive steps to eliminate unlawful disability discrimination and promote the employment of people with disabilities. There may also be a statutory duty to monitor employees and job applicants in respect of disability. It is thought that these duties will be similar in structure to the statutory duties imposed in respect of race by the *Race Relations (Amendment) Act 2000* and the *Race Relations Act 1976 (Statutory Duties) Order 2001 (SI 2001 No 3458)*. At the time of writing, the precise date of implementation of this Bill is not known.

Recommendations of the Employment Practices Data Protection Code of Practice, Part 2: Employment Records in relation to equal opportunities monitoring 8.15

The Information Commissioner published a Code of Practice in 2003, Part 2 of which provides guidance on how employers can comply with the *DPA 1998* in the context of employment records. The full name of the Code is the Employment Practices Data Protection Code, Part 2: Employment Records. The Code contains a section on equal opportunities monitoring. One key recommendation contained in this section of the Code is that information gathered for the purpose of monitoring should be kept to a minimum.

The Code of Practice is not legally binding, but represents the Information Commissioner's recommendations as to how employers should fulfil their legal requirements under the *DPA 1998* in relation to the collection and use of personal information relating to job applicants and employees. Even though there is no legal duty to follow the Code's recommendations, a court or tribunal can, in the event of a legal challenge against the employer, take the provisions of the Code into account. This means that if there is evidence that the employer has declined or failed to comply with the provisions of the Code, the chances of a court or tribunal making a finding against them will be substantially increased.

Part 2 of the Code expressly recommends that, in relation to equal opportunities monitoring, employers should:

- make sure that the processing of information about employees' racial and ethnic origin, religion or disability satisfies one of the conditions for processing sensitive data (see **8.6** above);

- collect information that identifies individual employees only where it is necessary in order to conduct meaningful equal opportunities monitoring;

- keep information relevant to monitoring in anonymised form if possible;

- ensure that the questions on monitoring forms are designed so that they will collect information that is accurate and not excessive; and

- refrain from collecting unnecessarily detailed information about employees, for example about their nationality or linguistic group.

Dealing with Equal Pay Questionnaires   8.16

In April 2003, a procedure was introduced to allow employees to serve a questionnaire on their employer requesting information about their pay in comparison to someone of the opposite sex doing similar work. This was introduced through the *Equal Pay (Questions and Replies) Order 2003 (SI 2003 No 722)* made under the *Employment Act 2002*. The key aim of the questionnaire procedure is to speed up the resolution of equal pay disputes by allowing the potential claimant to gain useful information at an early stage. An employee may use this procedure either before commencing equal pay proceedings in an employment tribunal (for example to allow a decision to be made on whether or not such a claim would have any merit), or after such proceedings have already been instigated.

Similar procedures are in place in respect of complaints under the *Sex Discrimination Act 1975* and the *Race Relations Act 1976* allowing employees to question their employer about alleged discriminatory treatment on grounds of sex or race respectively.

The *Equal Pay Act 1970 (EPA 1970)* covers equality of treatment in pay and contractual terms as between men and women – where a man and a woman are doing like work, work rated as equivalent (in a job evaluation scheme) or work of equal value. Although men and women are equally protected under the *EPA 1970*, in practice most claims are brought by women.

How to answer an employee's questions without breaching the DPA 1998   8.17

Because the type of information that an individual may seek under the equal pay questionnaire procedure usually involves personal data relating to another employee, or several other employees, the *DPA 1998* is a relevant feature of this process. This compels employers to balance their duties under the Act against the rights of the employee under the statutory procedure to request information about the employer's pay practices in order that they can satisfy themselves that they are not being subjected to sex discrimination.

Legal effect of the equal pay questionnaire   8.18

As stated at **8.16** above, an employee who is bringing, or considering bringing, an equal pay claim against his or her employer can elect to serve an equal pay questionnaire on the employer. There is, however, no statutory obligation on the employer to respond to an equal pay questionnaire served upon them, but because the replies given (or lack of them) are admissible in evidence, a failure to reply can be taken into account by an employment tribunal if an equal pay claim is taken forward. Essentially, the employer will place themselves at a disadvantage if, at a subsequent tribunal claim for equal pay, the evidence shows that they declined without good reason to answer the employee's questions, provided incomplete answers, or gave answers that were equivocal, evasive or untrue. This would be likely to lead the tribunal into drawing inferences that were unfavourable to the employer. It is therefore in employers' interests to ensure they provide a carefully worded and detailed response to the employee's questions. The time limit for doing so is eight weeks.

The purpose of the equal pay questionnaire   8.19

The key purpose of the equal pay questionnaire is to assist employees who believe that their level of pay is unjustifiably less than a comparator of the opposite sex who is performing similar work to obtain relevant information. The information, if provided, will enable the employee to establish whether or not they are receiving equal pay, and if not, the reasons for any differences or discrepancies. The provision of clear information from the employer may, arguably, satisfy the employee that he or she is not being treated unfairly in respect of pay and benefits, and thus stop a claim for equal pay going forward to a tribunal.

The equal pay questionnaire form   8.20

The form (which is available in a pre-printed version) includes factual questions to establish whether the employee is receiving less pay than a named comparator, and if so, why. The named comparator(s) must be someone whom the employee believes is performing like work or work of equal value. The questionnaire includes:

- space for the employee to identify a comparator (or more than one comparator), ie the employee(s) of the opposite sex whom the employee believes are engaged on like work or work of equal value;

- space for the employee to state why he or she believes they are not receiving equal pay in relation to the named comparator(s);

- a question asking the employer whether they agree that the named comparator(s) is engaged on like work or work of equal value;

- questions to establish whether the employee is in fact receiving less pay than the named comparator(s) and if so, why.

The form also includes space for the employee to add their own questions, which allows individuals to tailor the form to their own specific situation. Questions may, for example, be asked about how pay is determined, how skills and experience are reflected in the employer's pay system, any job grading scheme in operation and specific information about the named comparator's pay and benefits package.

Data protection issues associated with equal pay questionnaires
8.21

Whenever an equal pay questionnaire is served on an employer, there will inevitably be data protection and confidentiality issues to take into account. Information as to details of employees' pay will constitute personal data for the purposes of the *DPA 1998*, although pay does not fall into the category of 'sensitive data'.

One of the most obvious problems for the employer is that it may be viewed as inappropriate to disclose to the employee who has served the questionnaire how much another employee is earning, what benefits package they have under their contract of employment or how they were assessed under a recent appraisal review that was linked to a pay rise.

One key point to bear in mind, however is that there is nothing in the Act that expressly prevents the disclosure of employees' salaries for the purpose of responding to an equal pay questionnaire. Pay is not classed as 'sensitive data' and hence not subject to the restrictive provisions in place to protect such data (see **8.5** above). Furthermore, the *DPA 1998, section 35* states that personal data will be 'exempt from the non-disclosure provisions where the disclosure is necessary for the purpose of, or in connection with, any legal proceedings (including prospective legal proceedings). Where an employee has served an equal pay questionnaire on his or her employer, this will indicate that either legal proceedings under the *Equal Pay Act 1970* have been instigated, or that the employee is thinking about commencing such proceedings, thus falling squarely within the meaning of *section 35*.

In any event, there is nothing to stop an employer who is concerned about the disclosure of pay information from consulting the named comparator in relation to the proposed disclosure of his or her pay to the employee who has served the questionnaire. The employer can explain to the employee that it is necessary in the interests of justice for them to disclose details of their pay and benefits package to the person who has served the questionnaire. It may be that an employee will have no objection to the potential disclosure of this information to a colleague, and even if they do object, they may understand why it is necessary in the interests of justice for the employer to make the disclosure. Permitting an employee to refuse to consent to the disclosure of the requisite information could cause considerable disgruntlement to the employee who served the equal pay questionnaire, thus increasing the chances that a claim for equal pay will be taken to an employment tribunal. Given the statutory force of the equal pay questionnaire procedure, a tribunal may not regard the employee's unwillingness to agree to the disclosure as a legitimate reason for the employer to decline to disclose the information.

Arguably, therefore, the disclosure of an employee's pay in response to the serving of an equal pay questionnaire is necessary if justice is to be achieved, unless of course the employee's questions are obviously frivolous or misconceived, in which case the employer would be justified in refusing to disclose the information requested on those grounds.

Providing generalised information   8.22

Concerns over confidentiality and data protection will not, however genuine, excuse the employer from providing a response to the employee who has submitted an equal pay questionnaire. It is likely that in many cases information can be readily provided about a number of items that do not constitute personal data under the Act, for example information about:

- the employer's general pay structures and how pay is determined;

- any job evaluation scheme in place within the organisation;

- how skills and experience are reflected in the pay system or job evaluation scheme;

- pay grades or bandings;

- the minimum and maximum pay for each grade or band;

- the average salary of a group of employees who are performing the same work as the employee who submitted the questionnaire;

- criteria that the employer uses to determine individual pay rises;

- the fact that another employee is, or is not, receiving a higher rate of pay than the person submitting the questionnaire (without disclosing the actual amount of the employee's pay);

- how the employee's own salary and recent pay rises have been determined;

- the reasons why the employee's pay is set at its current level; and

- whether the employer has an equal opportunities policy in place and what the policy says in relation to pay.

Disclosing the types of information listed above will not compromise the anonymity or confidence of individual employees. Furthermore, if the employee has named several comparators, rather than just one, the employer may be able to disclose an average of their salaries, thus avoiding any possibility of a breach of confidence.

The employer can also, if appropriate, give an explanation of any significant differences between the job duties of the person serving the questionnaire and those of their chosen comparator, ie any factors that justify a difference in pay.

In general, the employer should provide as much information as they reasonably can in response to an employee's equal pay questionnaire, in particular where the data can be anonymised thus allowing meaningful information to be disclosed whilst also preserving the confidentiality of other employees' pay and benefits packages.

Court orders in relation to the disclosure of information   8.23

It is worth bearing in mind that, even where an employer has refused to disclose information on the grounds that it is confidential, an employee who pursues a claim through an employment tribunal can ask the tribunal to order the employer to disclose the relevant information for the purpose of dealing with the claim. The tribunal will order disclosure if they believe that it is in the interests of justice to do so. The *DPA 1998, section 35* states that personal data will be 'exempt from the non-disclosure provisions where the disclosure is required by or under any enactment, by any rule of law or by the order of a court'.

Further information about equal pay questionnaires is available in the Equal Opportunities Commission's Code of Practice on Equal Pay, available from www.eoc.org.uk.

Chapter 9
Employee Monitoring

Introduction 9.1

Monitoring the activities of people at work is an important but sensitive issue. Clearly no reasonable employer would wish to intrude unnecessarily into employees' private lives, nor alienate their staff. Nevertheless, it can be argued that a degree of monitoring of employees at work is a business necessity for many employers in order to protect their interests, together with those of their staff and their clients. The main aim should be to strike a reasonable balance between the need to monitor as judged against employees' rights in contract, including the mutual duty of trust and confidence, and the right to privacy under the *Human Rights Act 1998* (*HRA 1998*). Essentially, monitoring should be carried out only where it is necessary and relevant to the business, and where the legitimate business needs of the employer outweigh the inevitable intrusion into employees' private lives.

Before deciding what type of monitoring to carry out and how the monitoring is to be targeted, the employer may wish to consider the legal issues relating to restrictions on employee monitoring and weigh these up against the legal risks of not monitoring. Arguably, most employees will be capable of understanding the need for a reasonable degree of monitoring, provided that managers clearly explain the employer's position and the reasons why monitoring is necessary for the organisation.

The key objective of this chapter is to explore the data protection implications of monitoring employees at work, in particular with regard to monitoring employees' use of the telephone, email and the internet. Equal opportunities monitoring is dealt with in **CHAPTER 8**.

What is Employee Monitoring? 9.2

The Data Protection Code of Practice on Monitoring at Work (see **9.10** below) defines monitoring as any activity that is designed to 'collect information about workers by keeping them under some form of observation, normally with a view to checking their performance or conduct'.

The *Data Protection Act 1998* (*DPA 1998* or 'the Act') and the Code of Practice on Monitoring at Work will be engaged only if a record is kept of the employer's monitoring activities. If, for example, a manager listens in to an employee's tele-phone calls, but does not create any record of the calls nor of the fact they were monitored, then there will be no 'personal data' to protect. By contrast, if the manager was to make a written note of (for example) the employee's name and a summary of the content of the calls, then a record will have been created, thus potentially giving rise to issues under the Act and the Code of Practice (depend-ing on how the written record is subsequently retained).

Whose records are protected? 9.3

Employers will need to consider records they hold about:

- their current employees, including temporary and part-time employees;
- agency staff;
- casual workers;
- contract staff;
- apprentices;
- students who work for the organisation;
- anyone on a work experience placement with the organisation;
- past employees, so long as the record identifies the ex-employee;
- job applicants (whether successful or unsuccessful);
- their customers and clients;
- suppliers; and
- anyone else where the record identifies an individual.

The purpose of monitoring 9.4

There may be many different reasons why an employer may legitimately decide to monitor the activities of their employees. The main purposes of monitoring are likely to be to (the points below are not in any particular order):

- obtain information about employees' efficiency and productivity;
- ensure quality of the employer's product or service;
- check whether there is any evidence of malpractice on the part of workers generally, or by a particular worker;
- protect the employer against legal liability, for example in the event of inap-propriate use or serious misuse of email or the internet;
- record information as part of employees' training;
- maintain records in case of a customer complaint;

- ensure security measures are effective; and

- ensure that safety policies and procedures are being implemented properly in order to protect employees working in a hazardous environment.

The Data Protection Code of Practice on Monitoring at Work (see **9.10** below) recommends that employers should not be tempted to monitor their workers just because one of their customers or clients has imposed a condition requiring them to carry out such monitoring. Instead, the employer should carry out an impact assessment (see **9.11** below) to review whether monitoring is justifiable in the circumstances. The Code points out that a condition of business imposed by a customer cannot override the employer's responsibilities under the Act.

The potential benefits of monitoring 9.5

Monitoring should be carried out only where the employer is clear about the purpose(s) of the monitoring, and where they have clearly established that the type of monitoring that is proposed will bring tangible benefits to the organisation. Benefits could include:

- a reduction in the likelihood that employees will misuse the employer's computer and telephone systems;

- protection against legal action that might be taken by employees against the employer on account of any alleged breach of their employment rights; and

- an increase in quality, efficiency and productivity.

Responsibility for monitoring 9.6

It is important for all employers to identify who within their organisation will be responsible for employee monitoring, and for ensuring that employment policies and procedures on monitoring comply with legislation, including the *DPA 1998*.

The person appointed to hold such responsibility should, ideally, be a senior manager who has sufficient authority to challenge any practices that might risk being in breach of legislation or associated Codes of Practice and make decisions about data protection compliance. In a large organisation, a senior HR manager would be an ideal candidate for such responsibility, whilst in a small business it may be appropriate for the owner or managing director to hold responsibility.

The senior manager should be responsible for ensuring policies and procedures are regularly checked, in particular against the *DPA 1998* and the Data Protection Code of Practice on Monitoring at Work. The manager should also be made accountable for ensuring that policies and procedures are put into practice by all staff, and especially by those whose jobs take them into contact with personal data held about employees. Particular examples include line managers and supervisors, and HR or IT staff who may be involved in the processes of monitoring, and who may consequently gain access to a range of information about other staff in the course of their work.

Someone who is newly appointed to the role that involves responsibility for monitoring may wish to review:

- what personal data about employees exists within the organisation and where and by whom it is held;

- the type of information produced by monitoring and whether it is genuinely appropriate to the needs of the organisation;

- whether any information obtained through monitoring is unnecessary and whether the employer should consequently refrain from collecting it (or discard it);

- whether it is necessary or appropriate for individuals other than HR staff to hold personal data about staff, especially information gleaned from monitoring;

- whether any sensitive data is likely to be obtained as a result of monitoring, and if so whether one of the conditions for the processing of sensitive data is satisfied;

- whether clear data protection guidelines have been devised and communicated to all staff involved in monitoring;

- whether newly recruited staff are properly informed of the employer's data protection rules and guidelines during induction;

- whether those who have access to personal data are aware of their legal responsibilities under the *DPA 1998* and that they may be held personally liable for any breach of the Act.

Different Forms of Monitoring   9.7

Monitoring can take many forms and can include:

- the interception of employees' telephone calls, voicemails or email messages, where a record is subsequently created;

- checking logs of telephone numbers called by employees, whether individually or by group;

- using automated software to collect information about the types of emails employees are sending or receiving;

- creating a log of the internet sites visited by employees, whether by individual or as a group;

- CCTV or audio surveillance;

- videoing workers outside the workplace;

- installing devices into company vehicles to track the location of the vehicle;

- supervisory observation;

- checking up on employees through credit reference agencies or the Criminal Records Bureau; and

- gathering information through point-of-sale terminals in order to check the efficiency of individuals who are employed as check-out operators, for example in a supermarket.

Covert Monitoring 9.8

Covert monitoring should not normally be undertaken within the workplace. 'Covert monitoring' is defined in the Data Protection Code of Practice on Monitoring at Work as 'monitoring carried out in a manner calculated to ensure those subject to it are unaware that it is taking place'. The only exception to the general principle that covert monitoring should not be carried out in employment would be in circumstances where there were proper grounds for suspecting an employee of criminal activity or equivalent malpractice (for example a suspected serious breach of safety rules), and it was reasonable to conclude that informing the employee that they were to be monitored would prejudice prevention or detection of the malpractice. If in doubt about whether to instigate covert monitoring, the employer should consider whether the criminal activity of which the employee is suspected is one that would be sufficiently serious to justify involving the police (although the decision as to whether to involve the police will, of course, be a separate decision that management will be entitled to make for themselves). If the answer to that question is 'yes', then covert monitoring may be justified, depending on all the circumstances.

The Code of Practice on Monitoring at Work suggests that the employer should take steps to limit the number of staff involved in any covert monitoring and set down very clear rules restricting the access to and disclosure of any personal information obtained as a result.

Further guidelines recommend that, in circumstances where covert monitoring is justified, the employer should take steps to ensure that any incidental information gathered about the employee that has nothing to do with their suspected wrongdoing is disregarded and subsequently deleted from the employee's file.

Dealing with Information Obtained from Monitoring 9.9

Information gained as a result of monitoring must be treated in accordance with the provisions of the Act and the Data Protection Code of Practice on Monitoring at Work. The Code suggests that, where information gathered as a result of monitoring might have an adverse impact on an employee, the information should be presented to the employee to allow them to comment on it and make representations. This should be done before any decision is taken as to whether there are grounds for disciplinary action against the employee. It is noted in the Code that equipment and systems sometimes malfunction, resulting in the possibility of inaccurate or misleading information being produced. There is the further possibility of information being misinterpreted. Employees should always be given a full and fair opportunity to comment on, challenge or explain the results of any monitoring exercise whenever the results may be detrimental to them.

The Data Protection Code of Practice on Monitoring   9.10

The Employment Practices Data Protection Code of Practice on Monitoring at Work was published by the Information Commissioner in June 2003. It is available at www.dataprotection.gov.uk. The Code represents the Information Commissioner's interpretation of how the *DPA 1998* should be implemented with regard to monitoring the activities of employees at work. Useful Supplementary Guidance accompanies the Code. The Code does not prevent monitoring of employees at work, but rather sets out to regulate when and how monitoring is carried out.

The Code, like other Codes of Practice, is not legally binding on employers, but a failure to follow its recommendations can be used in evidence against an employer in the event of a court or tribunal claim. It is therefore in employers' interests to follow the Code, which in any event is a useful source of information and guidance.

In general, information will be covered by the Act and the Code of Practice if an individual can be identified (whether by name or by other means, for example a reference number). The *DPA 1998* covers:

- information held manually, whether (for example) in a structured filing system, a reference card system or in a supervisor's notebook;

- information held on computer; and

- information contained in the body of an email.

Where, however, information is held about a group of people in such a way that individuals are not named or otherwise identifiable, the information will not constitute personal data, and hence will not be covered by either the Act or the Code of Practice.

Impact assessments   9.11

One of the key recommendations of the Data Protection Code of Practice is that employers should carry out an impact assessment in order to decide whether monitoring is appropriate for their business, and determine how any monitoring should be carried out. Through the impact assessment, the employer should review the likely effect of monitoring on the privacy and other rights of employees, and establish whether or not any adverse impact of monitoring on employees is justifiable when balanced against the needs of the employer (see **9.13** below). Impact assessments should be conducted to establish justification for monitoring in a general sense and also to review whether or not monitoring in specific circumstances would be justifiable (see **9.15** below).

The Code explains that an impact assessment involves:

- identifying the purpose(s) of any proposed monitoring and its likely benefits;

- identifying any likely adverse impact on employees of monitoring, for example the inevitable intrusion into employees' private lives that monitoring will cause (see **9.13** below);

- considering alternatives to monitoring or different ways in which monitoring might be carried out (see **9.17** below);

- taking into account the obligations that arise out of monitoring; and

- deciding whether or not monitoring is justified (see **9.15** below).

The benefits of carrying out an impact assessment   9.12

There may, in any event, be considerable benefits for the employer in conducting a written impact assessment with regard to employee monitoring, for example:

- conducting an impact assessment in an open and transparent manner will create trust between management and staff and hence enhance employee relations generally;

- the results of the assessment will help employees to understand why certain forms of monitoring are necessary for the organisation;

- the assessment should assist employees' general understanding of data protection issues and the parameters of workplace privacy;

- the measured and targeted approach required to conduct an impact assessment will ultimately save the employer time and resources; and

- if at any time legal action is taken against the employer in relation to workplace monitoring, the fact that the employer has conducted an impact assessment will place them in a much stronger position to defend the action.

Adverse impact   9.13

Monitoring at work will inevitably have some adverse impact on employees. The Data Protection Code of Practice on Monitoring at Work suggests that an impact assessment should be carried out in relation to proposed monitoring (see **9.10** above) and that one of the purposes of this will be for the employer to identify the likely extent of any adverse impact that monitoring would create for employees (or for others, for example customers or suppliers).

The first and most obvious general adverse consequence of monitoring will be the inevitable intrusion into employees' private lives that monitoring will cause. It has been accepted in law that the right to respect for privacy (under *Article 8* of the *HRA 1998*) extends into the workplace (see **9.38** below). Some employees may resent the very idea of monitoring in principle, whilst others may fear its effects or suspect management of underhand dealings. Excessive monitoring, or monitoring without proper cause, could also be perceived as a breach of the employer's duty of trust and confidence towards their employees and, in a worst scenario, could lead to an employee resigning and complaining to an employment tribunal that their treatment amounted to unfair constructive dismissal.

These concerns can, to a great extent, be resolved, or at least minimised, by regular open two-way communication between management and staff and by making all monitoring policies and procedures transparent and ensuring they are well regulated. Arguably, most employees will be capable of understanding the need for a reasonable degree of monitoring, provided that managers clearly explain the employer's position and the reasons why monitoring is necessary for the organisation.

Minimising the intrusion into employees' privacy   9.14

The employer should take steps to minimise the intrusion into employee's privacy by:

- providing a transparent system of monitoring and a procedure that allows employees to be aware when monitoring that might affect them is being carried out;

- ensuring that the type of monitoring carried out is not any more intrusive than is absolutely necessary to meet the employer's stated business objectives;

- restrict the numbers of staff involved in monitoring so as to limit the disclosure of any sensitive information about an individual that may come to light as a result of monitoring;

- avoid opening and reading emails whenever possible, especially those that are obviously personal or private, unless there is a clearly identifiable reason why it is necessary to examine the content of the email in question;

- devise systems and procedures that allow employees to communicate confidentially with certain professionals, ie so that staff know that certain types of communications will not be monitored. Examples would include employee communications with an occupational health practitioner, a counsellor whose services are provided by the employer, and a trade union representative.

Justification for monitoring 9.15

One of the key purposes of carrying out an impact assessment (see **9.10** above) will be so that the employer can determine whether or not any form of monitoring is justified. It should not be assumed that there is a business case for monitoring, but instead the employer should adopt an open-minded approach and examine:

- what the purposes of monitoring would be;

- whether the type of monitoring proposed might reasonably achieve those purposes;

- whether the results of the monitoring would produce benefits for the business that outweighed any adverse impact caused to employees;

- whether there is any alternative to monitoring that would be less intrusive to employees (see **9.17** below);

- whether the proposed systems of monitoring are fair towards staff in a general sense; and

- whether there has been a full process of consultation with trade unions, with employee representatives or with employees directly.

Assessing what type of monitoring is appropriate for the business 9.16

The Data Protection Code of Practice on Monitoring at Work makes it clear that proportionality is the key to compliance with the *DPA 1998,* ie the employer must design systems of monitoring that are linked to specific business needs and balance those needs against the reasonable rights of employees to be granted respect for their private lives and correspondence.

Employers who decide that it is prudent to carry out monitoring on their employees' use of the telephone, email and the internet will have to decide as a preliminary, but very important, issue whether monitoring should consist of:

- occasional spot-checks on the telephone numbers, email addresses and internet sites that are being accessed by employees generally, without pin-pointing which employees are responsible for accessing specific numbers and sites; or

- specific checks on individual employees' use of the communications network by reviewing each person's access to telephone numbers, email addresses and internet sites individually. Often this would be done following the identification of a problem as a result of a general spot check, or following a complaint about a particular employee's activities; or

- interception of employees' telephone calls and email messages, ie listening to the calls and reading the email messages.

The important thing is to understand that, whenever a record is created of the communications that have been monitored, the provisions of the Act and the Data Protection Code of Practice on Monitoring at Work will be engaged. For example, where the employer records a telephone conversation, or creates a file on a particular employee's email and internet activities, the record would then be subject to the provisions of the Act and the Code and the data protection principles would have to be observed.

One key message inherent in the Code is that, if there is a less intrusive method for an employer to establish facts that they need to know, then they should pursue that less intrusive method (see **9.17** below). The only exception would be where the employer had reasonable grounds to suspect that an employee had been involved in criminal activity such as accessing child pornography on the internet, or serious misconduct, for example harassing another employee by email, or acting in breach of safety rules.

Alternatives to monitoring 9.17

The Code of Practice and its accompanying supplementary guidance stress that employers should consider alternatives to monitoring and cites as examples new methods of supervision or further training. The underlying message is that if there is an alternative, less intrusive, way of dealing with a particular situation, then monitoring should not be undertaken. Another suggestion is that employers should restrict monitoring, either by:

- targeting monitoring only at employees who work in jobs which pose a particularly high risk to the employer, rather than monitoring everyone;

- monitoring only workers about whom complaints have been made, or about whom there are reasonable grounds to suspect misconduct;

- conducting spot-checks rather than continuous monitoring;

- adopting a policy of analysing email traffic rather than monitoring the content of messages, or reviewing whether traffic records can be used to narrow the scope of content monitoring;

- using technology that prevents misuse (such as web-filtering software) rather than introducing systems designed to detect misuse after the event.

The Implications of Monitoring Employees' Communications 9.18

The Data Protection Code of Practice on Monitoring at Work highlights the threat monitoring can pose to personal privacy and provides guidance on how employers can balance the requirement to protect employees' privacy against the need to pursue legitimate business interests.

In relation to monitoring of employees' email, telephone and internet use, the Code of Practice and supplementary guidance provide a number of suggestions for employers to:

- refrain from reading emails that are clearly personal or private and, if personal use of the email system is banned, consider instead whether sufficient information is available in the subject header or address of a particular email to instigate appropriate action against the employee for breach of the rules;

- provide secure lines of communication for employees so that they can transmit legitimate personal or sensitive information, for example to an occupational health adviser or a trade union official, in the knowledge that it will not be monitored;

- set up a system whereby private emails can be marked 'personal and private' and adopt a policy of not monitoring such emails unless the employee is genuinely suspected of serious wrongdoing;

- review (where a reasonable level of personal use is permitted) whether it is feasible to provide employees with two different passwords or methods of logging on depending on whether their internet access is work-related or personal;

- inform all employees of the extent to which information about their email use and internet access is retained in the employer's system and for how long it is retained;

- consider whether it is sufficient to record the time employees spend accessing the internet rather than monitoring the actual sites visited or the content viewed.

In essence, the Code recommends that emails that are clearly personal or private should not be intercepted, even in organisations that impose a complete ban on personal use of email and the internet. The supplementary guidance to the Code points out that although a ban is an important factor, it is not necessarily an overriding one and the employer would have to be able to justify taking action to read a personal email by weighing up the intrusion into the employee's private life with the employer's need to know the content of the email. Some apparently personal emails may in any event be legitimate work-related messages, for example an email from an employee to an occupational health adviser concerning a personal health matter.

The Inter-relationship between Data Protection Rules and the Lawful Business Practice Regulations 2000   9.19

The *Telecommunications (Lawful Business Practice) (Interception of Communications) Regulations 2000 (SI 2000 No 2699) (LBP Regulations 2000)* make it lawful for an employer to monitor employees' communications provided monitoring is being done for one of the purposes specified in the Regulations. Under the *LBP*

Regulations 2000, interception of employees' communications will be lawful provided it is carried out for one of the purposes listed at **9.25** below, and provided that the employer has taken all reasonable steps to inform employees and the people with whom they communicate that interception might take place. Employers are not required to gain employees' consent to monitoring if the purpose of the monitoring is consistent with one of the purposes approved in the Regulations, although they must ensure that employees are informed in advance of any monitoring that may take place. This contrasts with the general rule that interception without consent is against the law, ie the Regulations specify legitimate exceptions to the principle that consent to interception is required.

The *LBP Regulations 2000* are thus concerned with the question of whether the interception of employees' communications will be lawful, whilst the *DPA 1998* deals with the processing of information about employees. In respect of the information gathered as a result of interception, the Act will kick in whenever personal information about an individual is recorded and held on file, whether manually or on the employer's computer system.

The Data Protection Code of Practice on Monitoring at Work goes much further than the *LBP Regulations 2000* to protect employees from over-intrusive monitoring. Whilst the Regulations are concerned primarily with the purpose of monitoring and ensuring that employees are properly informed of their employer's monitoring policies and practices, the Code of Practice is concerned also with whether any data held on record as a result of monitoring is processed in accordance with the data protection principles.

The impact of the data protection principles on the operation of the LBP Regulations 2000   9.20

When taking steps to adhere to the *LBP Regulations 2000*, employers need also to bear in mind the eight data protection principles that form part of the *DPA 1998*. The first three data protection principles are particularly relevant, namely the duty to process personal data fairly and lawfully (see **9.21** below); the duty to obtain personal data only for one or more specified and lawful purposes (see **9.23** below); and the duty to ensure personal are adequate, relevant and not excessive in relation to the purpose(s) for which they are processed (see **9.24** below).

The impact of the first data protection principle- processing personal data fairly and lawfully   9.21

The first data protection principle contained in the *DPA 1998, Schedule 1* creates the obligation on employers to process personal data 'fairly and lawfully'. Where an employee has consented to monitoring, or if the monitoring is being conducted for one of the purposes authorised by the *LBP Regulations 2000* (see **9.25** below), it will be lawful. Fairness, however, is quite another matter. It is possible for monitoring to be lawful, but unfair. If, for example, an employer was to intercept and keep records of employees' personal emails (as opposed to work related emails) ostensibly for the purpose of investigating or detecting unauthorised use of the system (one of the permitted purposes available in the *LBP Regulations 2000*), this would be lawful, but could be unfair if such monitoring was excessive or carried out without good cause.

The duty under the Act to process personal data fairly and lawfully is subject to the proviso (contained in *Schedule 2* of the Act) that personal data must not be processed unless one of a number of conditions is fulfilled. The conditions are that:

- the employee has given his or her consent to the processing; or

- data processing is necessary for one of the following reasons:

    - for the performance of a contract, for example the processing of employees' wages;

    - in order to ensure compliance with a legal obligation, for example information about an employee's working hours may be necessary in order to comply with the *Working Time Regulations 1998 (SI 1998 No 1833)*;

    - to protect the vital interests of the employee;

    - for the administration of justice or for the exercise of any public functions;

    - for the purposes of legitimate interests pursued by the employer, for example if the business was about to be transferred.

It is important to note the word 'necessary' used in this part of the Act. If the employee's consent has not been obtained, data about that person can be processed only if one of the relevant conditions is necessary for the business, and not just because (for example) management would find it convenient.

This raises the interesting question of whether random monitoring of employees' email and internet use could be viewed as 'necessary' under the banner of 'performance of the contract'. It is highly unlikely that an employer would be able to assert in a general sense that monitoring of all employees' emails on a regular basis was necessary for the performance of employees' contracts. However, it may (arguably) be necessary to monitor an individual employee's emails or internet traffic following a specific complaint about that employee, or where there were reasonable grounds to suspect that the employee had been abusing the system. This acts as a reminder of the general principle inherent in the Act that monitoring of employees' communications should only take place if it is proportionate in light of the employer's legitimate business aims.

Obtaining employees' consent   9.22

On the face of it, it would appear that the most straightforward way of ensuring fairness in data processing is to obtain employees' consent to data processing, for example by including a clause authorising monitoring and recording of employees' communications in all employees' contracts of employment. Whilst obtaining employee consent to the monitoring and recording of data is advisable in a general sense, it is questionable whether this alone will act to protect the employer against a challenge of unfairness under the first data protection principle (the duty to process personal data fairly and lawfully). This is because the Data Protection Code of Practice on Monitoring at Work points out that there are limitations as to how far consent can be relied on in an employment context to justify the processing of personal data generally. This is because consent must be 'freely given' in order for it to be valid under the *DPA 1998*. In an employment relationship, the balance of power is not even and it may be that an employee feels that he or she has no choice but to agree to sign a document giving their consent. The Code stresses that a better way forward for employers is to conduct a proper impact assessment (see **9.11** above), rather than rely on employee consent to authorise monitoring and data recording.

This does not, however, mean that seeking employee consent should be dispensed with. It is still advisable to request each employee's consent to both monitoring and recording, whilst at the same time clearly informing the employee about the purpose for which the data obtained from monitoring will be used, who in the organisation will have access to the data, and any other relevant information. The key to fairness in processing is transparency.

The duty to obtain and process personal data only for specified and lawful purposes 9.23

The second data protection principle (*DPA 1998, Schedule 1*) is the duty to obtain and process personal data only for one or more specified and lawful purposes, and not process it in any manner incompatible with those purposes. This means that employers must specify clearly the purpose(s) for which they intend to obtain and process data about employees. It would be unlawful therefore for an employer to use information obtained from monitoring for any purpose other than that defined as the purpose of the monitoring. This restriction would appear to prevent employers from using information about an employee that is uncovered by chance as a result of monitoring for other purposes.

The duty to ensure that personal data is adequate, relevant and not excessive 9.24

The third data protection principle cited in the *DPA 1998, Schedule 1* imposes a duty on employers to ensure that personal data is adequate, relevant and not excessive in relation to the data's stated purpose or purposes. This means that employers should ensure that any personal information they hold about their employees is created and stored for a proper business purpose, and that, in relation to this purpose, the information is relevant, sufficient, and not excessive.

This could be interpreted as a requirement for employers to use the least intrusive means possible to achieve their business aims, a principle that is put forward also in the Data Protection Code of Practice on Monitoring at Work (see **9.10** above). It may, for example, be excessive or irrelevant in relation to an employer's business to monitor all employees' emails on a routine basis, where spot monitoring, or monitoring of selected employees' correspondence, would suffice to protect the interests of the business.

The circumstances in which it is lawful for an employer to monitor employees' communications under the LBP Regulations 2000   9.25

Under the *LBP Regulations 2000*, it will be lawful for an employer to intercept and record an employee's email correspondence and telephone calls and/or monitor internet use in the circumstances listed at **9.26** to **9.34** below, irrespective of whether or not the employee has given their express consent to the interception. The employee must, however, have been informed that interception may take place (see **9.19** above).

To establish the existence of facts relevant to the business   9.26

It may be justifiable for an employer to intercept and record employees' telephone calls or email messages in circumstances where the business transactions of the organisation are conducted largely by telephone or email. The employer may, for example, legitimately wish to maintain records to provide evidence about the terms of contracts they have entered into or details of other business transactions.

To ascertain compliance with regulatory and self-regulatory practices or procedures that are relevant to the business   9.27

This heading is potentially very wide in scope. Whenever an organisation seeks to monitor in order to achieve compliance with any Regulations, Codes of Practice or Guidance issued by bodies such as the DTI, ACAS, the Equal Opportunities Commission, the Commission for Racial Equality or the Health and Safety Executive (for example), monitoring would be potentially legitimate. Equally, potentially anything issued by any EU-based organisation that had amongst its objectives the publication of Codes of Practice or Standards could give rise to a legitimate decision to monitor employee communications.

To ascertain or demonstrate standards that employees achieve or ought to achieve when using the employer's systems of communication   9.28

This clause allows employers to monitor and record employees' communications for the purpose of ensuring that the organisation's quality standards (for example standards of customer care) are being met, or to demonstrate standards that should be met as part of a training programme. Recording could also be used to identify areas in which there may be a training need for a particular individual or group of employees.

For example if the employer of a group of workers in a call centre had trained those workers to use key words or phrases when dealing with customer queries on a particular topic, it would be legitimate to record a cross-section of calls and use them to identify which employees needed further training or as examples on a training programme for new staff to demonstrate the 'right' and 'wrong' way to handle a telephone call.

In the interests of national security   9.29

Interception may be carried out if its purpose is the interests of national security, but such interceptions can only be carried out by certain specified public officials.

To prevent or detect crime   9.30

It would be lawful for an employer to intercept employee communications for the purpose of detecting fraud, corruption or criminal activity amongst the work-force.

To investigate or detect unauthorised use of the system   9.31

Employers may decide to intercept or monitor their employees' communications in order to establish whether any unauthorised use of the system is taking place. For example, if a company policy stated that email was provided strictly for business use only, then monitoring could be carried out to establish whether any employees were breaching the policy by sending personal emails during working time.

It is important to note, however, that even though monitoring may be conducted for the purpose of detecting unauthorised personal use of the employer's computer system, this does not give the employer carte blanche to read through the content of an employee's personal emails. The supplementary guidance to the Data Protection Code of Practice on Monitoring at Work points out that an employer would have to be able to justify taking action to read a personal email by weighing up the intrusion into the employee's private life with the employer's need to know the content of the email. In many cases it will be enough for the employer to detect from an email's address and subject header that it is a personal email rather than a work-related communication. The employer could then set up a meeting with the employee in order to discuss the matter and establish whether unauthorised use of the system had in fact taken place.

If the company policy is that reasonable personal use of the telephone, email and the internet is permitted, monitoring could be carried out to establish whether, on the whole, employees are confining their personal use of the communications systems to within the bounds of reasonableness. Clearly it would be helpful in these circumstances if the employer provided specific examples of what they regarded as reasonable personal use.

To ensure the effective operation of the system   9.32

It is lawful for an employer to monitor their computer systems for the purpose of checking for potential viruses or other threats to the system, such as hacking.

In addition to the above purposes, monitoring of employee communications, *but not recording*, is permissible under the *LBP Regulations 2000* if it is done for one of the two purposes outlined at **9.33** and **9.34** below.

To determine whether received communications are relevant to the employer's business   9.33

This provision provides employers with authority to check employees' voicemail and email inboxes whilst they are absent from work (for example if they are on holiday or absent on account of sickness) if the purpose of so doing is to identify business communications that need to be dealt with. It is important to note that if interception is done for this purpose, only monitoring is authorised, and not recording of the data monitored. It will be equally important to ensure that employees have been properly informed that communications addressed to them will be opened in their absence.

One further restriction under this heading is that only communications that are received during the employee's absence can be monitored, and not any pre-existing incoming emails, nor previous outgoing emails that are still in the computer system. Monitoring of these outgoing emails would only be permissible if the purpose of such monitoring was compatible with one of the other purposes contained in the *LBP Regulations 2000*, or unless the employee had expressly consented.

The phrase 'relevant to the business' is further defined in the *LBP Regulations 2000, Reg 2(b)* as:

'(i) a communication:

  (aa) by means of which a transaction is entered into in the course of that business; or

  (bb) which otherwise relates to that business; or

(ii) a communication which otherwise takes place in the course of the carrying on of that business.'

It is apparent therefore that any telephone calls or email messages that are personal or private in nature and unrelated to the employer's business will fall outside the scope of the Regulations. This is consistent with the advice given in the Data Protection Code of Practice on Monitoring which is that emails that are clearly personal or private should not be intercepted, even where the employer has imposed a complete ban on personal use of email and the internet. Employers should not therefore be tempted in normal circumstances to open or read any of their employees' incoming or outgoing email messages that are obviously personal.

There may (arguably) be limited exceptions to this principle if, for example, there is evidence to suggest that the employee has been engaging in criminal activity or other malpractice, for example where it is reasonably suspected that the employee has:

- transmitted confidential information by email to an outsider without authorisation;

- forwarded pornographic material as an email attachment to a colleague or outsider; or

- made a defamatory statement about an individual or another organisation in an email.

Provided there were proper grounds (and not, for example, just a vague, whimsical suspicion based on a purely personal view) to believe that an employee's personal telephone messages or email communications were 'relevant to the business' in this way, then interception of those personal messages could potentially be justified. This is in contrast with monitoring of communications that are obviously private and unrelated to the business, which would not conform with the provisions of the *LBP Regulations 2000* and which would risk being in breach of the employee's right to privacy under the *HRA 1998*.

To identify calls being made to anonymous counselling or support helplines   9.34

This category includes the monitoring of calls to confidential or welfare helplines in order to protect or support helpline staff.

The employer must be acting for one of the above specified purposes in order for monitoring and/or recording to be lawful. The *LBP Regulations 2000, Reg 2(b)* states that the interception must be 'solely for the purpose of monitoring or (where appropriate), keeping a record of communications relevant to the [business].' Thus employers are not permitted to use these purposes as a shield for monitoring that is in reality for a different purpose. Monitoring for any other purpose, for example out of curiosity, will be unlawful.

When Monitoring Employees' Communications might Constitute an Unacceptable Invasion of Privacy 9.35

Monitoring employees' private mail, telephone calls or email communications where there was no legitimate business need to do so would in all likelihood be in breach not only of the *LBP Regulations 2000* (unless the employee had given his or her consent to the monitoring) but also of the *HRA 1998*. *Article 8* of the *HRA 1998* (see **9.38** below) is the right to respect for private and family life, home and correspondence and any kind of unnecessary, unjustified or over-intrusive monitoring would be likely to be in breach of this provision.

The starting point for examining whether monitoring is lawful is to understand that any form of monitoring in the workplace will constitute an intrusion into employees' privacy. Monitoring may also undermine employment relationships and damage the mutual trust and confidence that plays a key role in employment. One general principle is that employers should seek to settle on the least intrusive method of monitoring that will meet their legitimate business objectives.

The Data Protection Code of Practice on Monitoring at Work in general requires employers to recognise employee interests and provide real justification for any intrusive monitoring practices (see **9.10** above).

The implications of the Human Rights Act 1998 9.36

The *Human Rights Act 1998* (*HRA 1998* or 'the Act') gives private individuals the right to take legal action against a public authority if they believe that one of their rights, as defined in the Act, has been infringed by that authority. This means that employees of public authorities can take a direct claim against their employer in a court or tribunal (as appropriate) if the employer infringes any of their rights under the Act.

Although the Act does not confer any similar benefit on private sector employees, the Act contains a separate provision which obliges courts and tribunals (as public authorities themselves) to interpret legislation, including employment law, in such a way as is compatible with the rights contained in the European Convention on Human Rights (and by extension the *HRA 1998*). Thus private sector employers are protected, albeit indirectly.

Although the *HRA 1998* confers rights on all citizens, it is possible in law for an individual to agree to waive their rights under the Act. For example, an employee who signs a document signifying their consent to email monitoring conducted by their employer is volunteering to waive their right to privacy in relation to their email correspondence.

The principle of proportionality 9.37

The European Convention on Human Rights contains a standard known as the principle of proportionality. This principle requires a balance to be struck between the rights of individuals as defined in the Act and the general interests of the community at large. In *Soering v United Kingdom [1989] 11 EHRR 439,* the European Court of Human Rights described the principle of proportionality as 'the search for a fair balance between the demands of the general interest of the community and the requirements of protection of the individual's fundamental rights'.

This means that the rights contained in the Convention and in the *HRA 1998* are not absolute rights that can be insisted upon irrespective of everyone and everything else. An individual's rights stand to be balanced proportionally against the interests of the community, ie the rights of others (including the rights of the employer and the rights of the individual's colleagues). This means that individuals' rights can be limited or restricted by their employer provided the employer can show that there is proper justification for such limitations. If, therefore, an employer applies a policy or procedure that is likely to infringe employees' rights to privacy under *Article 8*, this may be justifiable provided the policy or procedure is:

- designed to achieve a legitimate business aim;

- likely to achieve that aim in practice; and

- proportionate to the achievement of that aim.

This demonstrates the importance for the employer of:

- setting out clearly what the aim(s) of any employee monitoring would be;

- examining closely whether the means chosen to carry out the monitoring were likely in practice to assist the achievement of the aim(s); and

- ensuring that any monitoring carried out was not excessive in relation to the achievement of the aim(s).

Article 8 – the right to privacy 9.38

Article 8 of the *HRA 1998*, the right to respect for private and family life, home and correspondence, impacts upon a number of issues in the workplace including:

- CCTV surveillance of employees at work (see **9.44** below);

- searching of employees and their personal property (see **9.48** below);

- medical examinations and questionnaires (see **CHAPTER 7**);

- drugs screening programmes (see **CHAPTER 7**); and

- monitoring of employees' communications. 'Communications' in this context would include employees' telephone calls, voicemail, letters, memos, faxes, email correspondence, internet use and use of pagers and company mobile phones.

The principle of proportionality contained in the Convention (see **9.37** above) will, however, in most cases permit activities such as those listed above provided the employer can show that the monitoring they carry out is designed to achieve a legitimate business aim and is proportionate (ie not excessive) to that aim. However, there will of course be the need to ensure that the data obtained from such activities is handled correctly and in accordance with the *DPA 1998*.

It was established by the European Court of Human Rights in *Halford v United Kingdom [1997] IRLR 471*, that employees at work do in fact have a right to privacy. The *Halford* case concerned a complaint brought by a senior police officer about the interception of her telephone calls at work without her knowledge or consent. The Court held that, where an employee has a reasonable expectation of privacy and is unaware that his or her communications are liable to be intercepted by their employer, it will be unlawful for the employer to carry out interceptions. This case also suggests, however, that the right to privacy can be asserted only where the employee reasonably expects their communications to remain private. If, therefore, an employee has been properly informed that their communications are to be monitored, or has given their consent to monitoring, than an expectation of privacy cannot be argued.

The most important matter for the employer to address before deciding whether to carry out activities which would amount to a breach of the right to respect for privacy (such as monitoring of employee communications) is to ascertain the aim of the particular activity and whether any proposed monitoring is relevant and proportionate to the achievement of that aim.

Monitoring as an intrusion into employees' privacy 9.39

The Data Protection Code of Practice on Monitoring at Work emphasises that workplace monitoring will be an intrusion into employees' privacy and may thus undermine employment relationships and damage the mutual trust and confidence that plays a key role in employment. Employers should therefore seek to settle on the least intrusive method of monitoring that will meet their legitimate business objectives. There are also implications under the *HRA 1998* (see **9.40** below).

Another potential problem that the Code identifies is the risk that confidential, private or otherwise sensitive information may be seen by staff who carry out monitoring in circumstances where they do not need to know it, or have no right to know it. In general, the Code of Practice requires employers to recognise employee interests and provide real justification for any intrusive monitoring practices.

How to reconcile compliance with the Data Protection Code of Practice with the privacy provisions of the HRA 1998   9.40

There are a number of measures an employer can take, and should take, to ensure compliance with the *DPA 1998* whilst at the same time ensuring respect for employees' right to privacy under the *HRA 1998*. The starting point would be to nominate a senior person within the organisation to be responsible for ensuring the organisation's policies, procedures and practices comply with the *DPA 1998*. Other courses of action would include:

- training all line managers and others whose jobs involve handling personal data obtained from monitoring in the operation of the *DPA 1998* and in particular ensuring they understand their responsibility to maintain confidentiality with respect to personal information;

- giving careful consideration to the question as to who in the organisation should carry out monitoring activities;

- keeping to a minimum the number of people who have access to personal information obtained through monitoring;

- requiring employees who have access to personal information in the course of their work to sign confidentiality and security clauses and ensuring these are clearly stated to be contractually binding;

- reviewing on a regular basis what personal information about employees exists within the organisation, how it is held and whether it is still necessary and appropriate for the employer to hold it;

- carrying out regular reviews of whether personal information is out of date and should be destroyed; and

- ensuring all employees are aware of the nature, extent and reasons for any monitoring.

Policies on Monitoring Employees' Communications   9.41

Because of widespread access to email and the internet in today's hi-tech workplaces, and because of the wide range of potential legal liabilities that can be created for employers as a result of misuse of these facilities, it is essential for employers to devise and implement comprehensive policies, procedures, rules and guidance notes for employees who have access to email and the internet in the course of their work. Such policies would normally include a statement outlining the employer's approach to monitoring and a specific procedure explaining what type of monitoring the employer carried out and how it was carried out.

Clearly every employer's needs are different, and there is no one policy or set of rules that will be appropriate for all businesses. In some larger organisations, it may be desirable to have different sets of rules for different groups of employees, depending on the requirements of their jobs and the degree to which they need to use email or the internet in the course of their work. For example employees who, because of the nature of their jobs, have access to confidential information, or who have authority to enter into contracts with suppliers may need to be monitored more closely than those who perform routine work that is not in any way sensitive to the organisation.

In general, an employer may wish to consider introducing some or all of the following:

● a policy governing access to email and the internet, together with security and confidentiality measures that employees must adhere to;

● guidelines on the extent to which employees may use email and the internet for personal or private purposes (if at all);

● (where reasonable personal use is allowed) clear guidance on the extent and type of private use that is permitted;

● rules on how email should be used, the content of emails and email etiquette, for example the type of personal information that may, or may not, be included in emails;

● rules governing how the internet should be used, whether and to what extent surfing is permitted, together with a clear statement on any uses that are prohibited, for example the viewing or downloading of pornography;

● a statement advising employees of alternative methods of communication, for example sending a confidential communication to an occupational doctor by internal post rather than by email;

● a policy on monitoring explaining the purpose(s) for which the organisation conducts monitoring, the extent of the monitoring and the means used to monitor employee communications;

● the ways in which the policies on the use of the employer's communications system are enforced and the penalties that will be imposed on any employee who is found to be in breach of the employer's policy or rules.

The purpose and content of a policy on monitoring **9.42**

Although the *LBP Regulations 2000* authorise the interception of employee communications in a wide range of circumstances relevant to the business, it is nevertheless important to have a clear policy in place regarding any monitoring that takes place in the organisation. It is also necessary to obtain employees' consent to any monitoring that does not fall within the ambit of the *LBP Regulations 2000* (see **9.19** above).

The Data Protection Code of Practice on Monitoring at Work makes it very clear that 'it is a fundamental requirement of data protection law that workers are aware of … monitoring'. The Supplementary Guidance to the Code suggests that the most obvious way to achieve this is to 'establish, document and communicate a policy on the use of electronic communications systems'. The Guidance goes on to state that it is not only the employer's policy that will be important, but the day-to-day practice in the organisation will also be relevant, in particular if the employer does not always impose the policy or any rules consistently.

A policy on monitoring should:

- explain what monitoring activities the employer carries out and the extent of those activities;

- explain the purposes for which monitoring is carried out;

- make it clear that employees' telephone calls, email messages and internet access cannot be regarded as private; and

- nominate a senior person within the organisation whom employees may approach if they have any questions or concerns about monitoring.

Checklist on monitoring 9.43

A checklist for employers considering introducing systems for monitoring employees' communications is as follows:

- Should monitoring be designed primarily to highlight access rates, as a spot check on possible problem areas, or to monitor actual content?

- How will the data obtained as a result of monitoring be held (ie location, format and content of the data)?

- Will it be necessary for individual employees' names to be identified in the records obtained as a result of monitoring (in which case the provisions of the *DPA 1998* will be engaged)?

- Should monitoring be restricted to workers about whom complaints have been made, or about whom there are reasonable grounds to suspect misconduct?

- Should monitoring be targeted only at employees who work in jobs which pose a particularly high risk to the employer?

- In the event of a problem being identified as a result of monitoring (for example if an employee is found to have accessed an inappropriate web site), what will the appropriate procedure be and how will the records be handled?

- What action will be taken against an employee who, as a result of monitoring, is found to have been misusing email or internet access?

- Who within the organisation will have the overall responsibility for carrying out monitoring and for the data protection issues arising from monitoring?

- Who will be given the task of carrying out the monitoring and what type of training (including training in the *DPA 1998*) will be required?

- How will employees be informed about the monitoring carried out by the employer, and the extent and frequency of the monitoring?

- What steps will be taken to ensure that monitoring is carried out fairly and lawfully and only for the purposes defined in the employer's policy?

- What steps will be taken to ensure the confidentiality of the results of monitoring?

- How will the policy be kept under review in the light of the results of monitoring?

Video and Audio Monitoring 9.44

The collection and processing of video images and audio recordings relating to individuals falls under the *DPA 1998* in the same way as information about individuals held on files or on computer. It will rarely be appropriate, however, for an employer to deploy video (CCTV) or audio monitoring within their workplace. Being subjected to video monitoring whilst working would be particularly intrusive for employees and likely to make many feel uncomfortable and inhibited in their work. Such monitoring would also be hard to justify, except in specialised circumstances. By contrast, a policy of CCTV recording in corridors within a building that is open to the public or in a company car park might, for example, be justifiable for reasons related to security or safety.

Employers should not therefore, as a general rule, conduct video or audio monitoring of their staff in the course of their work, unless there are special reasons to do so. Such special reasons might involve work areas where highly valuable items were handled by employees in the course of their work, for example expensive jewellery, or where particular safety risks existed and there had been previous incidents of breaches of safety procedures. Employers should not, however, consider installing cameras or microphones in areas where workers would have a genuine and reasonable expectation of privacy, for example in private offices or toilets.

Any employer that considers that they have special reasons that might justify video or audio monitoring of their employees should, in the first instance, conduct an impact assessment (see **9.11** above). The Data Protection Code of Practice on Monitoring at Work suggests that, when conducting such an impact assessment, the employer should consider the following points:

- whether monitoring, if it is required at all, can be restricted to areas of special risk;

- whether monitoring can be confined to public areas only;

- how subject access requests would be dealt with, in particular bearing in mind the duty to remove any information that identifies a third party from data before allowing disclosure to the person requesting access.

The final point above is a reminder that any video or audio recording in which a person features would be regarded as personal data under the *DPA 1998*. Thus, any person caught on camera or tape would have the right to request access to the video or audio tape.

As with other types of monitoring, the employer must inform employees (and others who may, for example, be caught on camera) what monitoring is taking place, where it is taking place (ie where any cameras or microphones are located), why the employer considers it necessary to monitor in this way and what the cameras or tape recorders are intended to detect. In most circumstances, a prominent notice informing people that CCTV cameras are in operation, why they are being deployed and where they are located will suffice.

CCTV monitoring – Code of Practice   9.45

A Code of Practice on CCTV, published in 2000 under the *DPA 1998*, deals with CCTV surveillance in public areas and aims to set out the measures that must be adopted by CCTV operators in order to ensure compliance with the *DPA 1998*. The Code also provides guidance as to good practice in this area. The Code does not, however, apply to the use of surveillance techniques by employers to monitor their employees, and is thus outside the scope of this book. Instead, employers should refer to the Data Protection Code of Practice on Monitoring at Work (see **9.10** above).

In-vehicle Monitoring   9.46

The *DPA 1998* and the Data Protection Code of Practice on Monitoring at Work will extend to cover in-vehicle monitoring whenever the data obtained from monitoring can be linked to a particular individual, usually the driver of the vehicle. Except when in-vehicle monitoring is required by legislation (for example the installation of a tacograph in a lorry), the employer should conduct an impact assessment (see **9.11** above) before introducing any form of in-vehicle monitoring. The purpose of the impact assessment will be to determine whether the benefits that are likely to be obtained from this type of monitoring justify the intrusion into employees' privacy that will be caused, in particular by the constant tracking of the location of the vehicle.

With respect to in-vehicle monitoring, the Data Protection Code of Practice on Monitoring at Work recommends that employers should:

- formulate and apply a policy that states clearly whether employees may use company vehicles for private purposes, and if so, the extent to which private use is permitted and any conditions or restrictions attached to both business and private use;

- make sure employees have been fully informed of the type and extent of in-vehicle monitoring that will take place and how the information obtained from monitoring will be used;

- obtain express consent from employees prior to conducting any monitoring of the movements of company vehicles during periods when the vehicle may be being used for private purposes;

- consider whether it is possible and/or appropriate to install a monitoring device that can be switched off during periods when the employee is using the vehicle for private purposes.

In the unlikely event that an employer decided that it was appropriate and necessary to carry out monitoring in relation to employees' own vehicles (for example if private vehicles were, by agreement, to be used for business purposes), it would be necessary for the employee to have given their free consent to the installation and use of any monitoring device. Such a course of action should only be contemplated if monitoring is absolutely necessary for business reasons, for example, to establish the extent of business use in order to reimburse the employee the appropriate costs.

Third-party Monitoring 9.47

Third-party monitoring means obtaining information about employees from third-party organisations such as credit reference agencies or the Criminal Records Bureau for use within the business.

As with other types of monitoring, the employer should carry out an impact assessment (see **9.11** above) before deciding whether to undertake any third-party monitoring. This should be done in order that the employer can properly determine whether third-party monitoring is necessary and appropriate for the business, and what the precise objectives would be of such monitoring.

The Data Protection Code of Practice on Monitoring at Work suggests that employers should:

- inform their employees whether any third party source of information is used to carry out checks, the identity of the third-party source, and why the particular type of checking is believed to be necessary and appropriate with respect to the needs of the business;

- inform employees whenever a specific check is to be carried out, unless doing so would be likely to prejudice the prevention or detection of a crime or serious malpractice;

- refrain from monitoring an employee's personal financial circumstances unless there are firm grounds to believe that there would be a significant risk to the business if the employee concerned was experiencing financial difficulties;

- ensure any agency used to provide information about employees is aware of the use to which the employer intends to put the information that is provided to them;

- avoid using a credit reference agency that has been set up to check on customers or potential customers to vet or check up on employees;

- retain only the minimum amount of information provided by third parties about employees, for example record only the fact that a check took place and the overall result and, unless there are compelling reasons to do otherwise, delete the information after no more than six months.

Employee Searches   9.48

The question as to whether an employer should conduct random searches of employees, their personal property, their files or lockers and/or their vehicles should be subjected to the same scrutiny as the prospective monitoring of employee communications. Searching employees will be highly intrusive and will represent a breach of the right to respect for privacy enshrined in *Article 8* of the *HRA 1998* (see **9.38** above). There will therefore have to be strong justification for any policy to conduct searching. It follows that any employer who is considering introducing a random employee search programme should:

- identify the aim of the proposed search programme, for example the aim might be to protect an employer in the retail sector against employee theft;

- establish whether the proposed search programme is necessary for and relevant to the achievement of the stated aim; and

- examine whether the carrying out of personal searches, locker searches or even searches of employees' vehicles is proportionate to the aim (ie not excessive in relation to the employer's need to protect their business interests).

It may, for example, be proportionate to carry out searches in relation to employees whose jobs take them into contact with valuable equipment or materials (such as storekeepers and shop assistants), but excessive to apply the policy of random searching to office-based staff if, because of the nature of their work, they have little or no opportunity to access company equipment or materials.

Conclusion   9.49

In terms of adhering to data protection legislation when monitoring employees, the key to staying within the law whilst at the same time ensuring fairness is to adhere to the data protection principles and aim to strike a reasonable balance between the needs of the business to operate efficiently and lawfully, and the rights of employees to enjoy privacy and to be treated with respect. The level and nature of any monitoring should be proportionate to the employer's stated business needs, or to any specific problem that has been identified, for example an inordinate amount of time being spent by an employee visiting non work-related internet sites. Employees' explicit consent should be obtained before any data about them is collected, stored or used in any way.

Chapter 10
Conclusion

Introduction 10.1

HR and payroll managers may believe data protection issues are impossibly complicated. Whilst it is true that very detailed guidance (such as the guidance provided in this book) needs to be considered and followed, in practice most of the rules amount to little more than commonsense. Employees who believe that their confidential personal information is properly protected will work better and stay longer with their employer than those who believe the business rides roughshod over their rights.

However the data protection officer at any business must not be complacent. Regular checks should take place in areas such as passwords. Often good systems are set up but then employees become sloppy in their habits. Examples include:

- Passwords written on post-it notes left on PCs so all can use them, when the password protection was set up to ensure exactly that did not occur.

- New members of staff giving information to callers over the telephone without checking basic security details first.

- Waste paper or computers not disposed of carefully enough so that others can access and read confidential information contained on the paper or on the PC.

Most readers could come up with many examples themselves along the lines of the above list. The year 2004 has seen a new data protection pragmatism emerging from the Information Commissioner's Office. Richard Thomas, the Commissioner, was formerly with solicitors Clifford Chance and is author of a book on Plain English for Lawyers. Since taking on his role as Commissioner, he has sought to ensure data protection guidance is clear and simple to follow. This will help employers to understand and comply with the law.

Data Protection – the Law 10.2

Twenty years after the UK first introduced data protection legislation, the job of those involved in this area remains difficult. Data protection is one of the few areas of legislation that has broad principles and less than clear rules. Almost certainly, no organisation can be one hundred percent compliant. Nevertheless, businesses do need to take positive steps to ensure that they properly protect all the data that they hold on employees and on customers and suppliers. Many examples of such positive steps are provided in this book.

A good starting point is to look at the Information Commission's Audit Manual and undertake an audit, as is also suggested in the Employment Practices Data Protection Code, published by the Information Commissioner. Employers should look very thoroughly at both the process of application for jobs and the records that are kept once an employee joins the organisation. Some key actions will be to ensure that proper consents from employees are obtained for the various activities that may be undertaken in relation to their data. Activities will range from handling sickness records to putting pictures of employees on the corporate web site, from installing CCTV cameras to monitoring emails, internet access and telephone calls. As a general principle, if the employee knows a particular use will be made of their personal data, then the employer can proceed with it, but the maxim should always be: 'if in doubt, spell it out'. It might be assumed, for example, that every employee would know that their emails might be read whilst they are on holiday so the business can be properly managed in their absence, but this is an area where the Information Commissioner says an employee should always be notified that such surveillance might take place.

It will also be very important for employers to review regularly their data protection procedures. New rules come into force all the time so it can be very useful to send the data protection policy document, employment contract term and privacy notices posted on the corporate web site to lawyers to check on an annual basis. In addition, some organisations will find it useful to run an annual training course on data protection for managers and other employees whose jobs entail handling personal data. This will help to ensure that they fully understand and are up to date with the law in this important area.

Managing data protection is about how the organisation sets up methods to protect personal data about workers. This covers allocating responsibility, establishing what personal data are processed, ensuring employment practices are compliant with the *DPA 1998* and checking whether the organisation needs to notify the Information Commissioner about any data held. These benchmarks appear in all parts of the Employment Practices Data Protection Code as many of them will be relevant to every employer. How far they are applicable and what is needed to achieve them will, of course, vary from employer to employer and depend very much on the size and nature of the organisation and its activities.

Data protection compliance should be seen as an integral part of employment practice. It is important to develop a culture in which respect for private life, data protection, security and confidentiality of personal data are seen as the norm. The Information Commissioner's guidelines on Managing Data Protection should be uppermost in the minds of HR and payroll managers and are outlined at **10.3** below.

The benchmarks 10.3

1. Establish a person within the organisation responsible for ensuring employment practices and procedures comply with the Act and for ensuring that they continue to do so. Put in place a mechanism for checking that procedures are followed in practice.

2. Ensure that business areas and individual line managers that process information about workers understand their own responsibility for data protection compliance and if necessary amend their working practices in the light of this.

3. Assess what personal data about workers are in existence and who is responsible for them.

4. Eliminate the collection of personal data that are irrelevant or excessive to the employment relationship. If sensitive data are collected ensure that a sensitive data condition is satisfied.

5. Ensure that workers are aware of the extent to which they can be criminally liable if they knowingly or recklessly disclose personal data outside their employer's policies and procedures. Make serious breaches of data protection rules a disciplinary offence.

6. Allocate responsibility for checking that the organisation has a valid notification in the register of data controllers that relates to the processing of personal data about workers, unless it is exempt from notification.

7. Consult Trade Unions or other workers' representatives, if any, or workers themselves over the development and implementation of employment practices and procedures that involve the processing of workers' data.

If these steps are taken, then most organisations should be able to achieve compliance with data protection legislation.

Data protection compliance should also be seen as part of wider legal compliance. Some other areas of law will overlap with it. Many employment policies are set up to ensure no sex, race, religious, sexual orientation or disability discrimination takes place. When age discrimination is outlawed in 2006, further changes will be needed. So a regular review of policies is necessary not only because of changes in data protection law, but also on account of changes in other areas of legislation.

There is a close overlap between data protection law and the law of confidentiality. Trade secrets, customer lists, business information and other valuable know-how must be protected and employees trained so they do not discuss confidential business matters with others, nor inadvertently disclose confidential information.

Those bodies within the state sector and thus caught by the *Freedom of Information Act* when it comes into force in 2005 will need to ensure their policies are compliant with that legislation too.

At its best, data protection legislation ensures employees are protected and respected. Their rights to privacy are treated seriously and both the employee and the employer gain. Where instead employers breach the legislation, staff will leave, public damage will be done to a company's business reputation, and a criminal offence will occur with potential fines being imposed and the risk of expensive damages actions being started.

Notification 10.4

It is a legal requirement for data controllers to provide notification to the Information Commission on an annual basis. A fee is payable on first notification and on annual renewal of the notification. As a result of the notification, an entry is placed in the register of data controllers that the Commissioner maintains. This register is open for public inspection. The exceptions to notification are limited to some core business functions and some not-for-profit organisations. One of the core business functions is staff administration, which embraces the HR and payroll functions. Data controllers who are exempt from notification may, however, notify voluntarily.

Because there can be only one entry in the register for each organisation, it is important to establish who in the organisation is responsible for data protection matters and specifically, for making the notification. Notification is a legal requirement and failure to notify when not exempt is a criminal offence. Equally, each legal entity in a group of companies must have its own register entry (unless it is exempt from notification). There cannot be 'group' notification covering a number of associated companies.

HR and payroll will inevitably process sensitive personal data so this will need to be included in the notification (unless staff administration has not been notified or the organisation is exempt). If the register entry is incomplete, it will need to be amended to include the processes of HR and the payroll function. Equally, they may have been treated as being exempt from notification, and if this is the case the register entry should contain a note about exempt processing.

Amendments can be made to the notified particulars whenever they are incorrect or out of date. No additional fee is due for amendments. It is a criminal offence to fail to keep the notification up to date.

Notification includes a statement about the organisation's security measures in respect of personal data. The statement is not, however, published as part of the public register. The employer can draw up the security statement by answering a series of questions that are available in the notification process. Answering 'no' to all the questions is permitted, but will not show that the data controller understands his or her responsibilities for data security under the *DPA 1998*. The result is likely to be that the Information Commissioner's office will query the notification. There is a question on the security standard BS7799, but this is not a requirement of the Act. Certified compliance to BS7799 is an extensive task and would be disproportionate for almost all small and medium-sized enterprises.

The questions form a checklist for considering the security measures the employer has or needs to have in place. As well as considering practical matters such as passwords on computer systems and locks on filing cabinets, the employer must also consider a range of organisational issues, for example the implementation of a security or data protection policy that is endorsed at the highest level and known, understood and applied by all staff. There may be further, more specific policies for the human resources and payroll functions, which can be established by using the organisational policy as a foundation and developing it for the high incidence of personal data that is inevitably held in HR and payroll.

Employers may find it useful to use the online notification process on the Information Commissioner's web site as they can build the purposes from the templates and print out the document ready for submission. A decision will need to be taken as to whether to notify processing that is exempt from notification. Online notification is not yet possible but the web site provides the facility to create the notification forms on-screen which can then be printed, signed and sent through the post. This is probably the shortest route to notification.

One further very important point to remember is that an exemption to notify is not an exemption from the requirements of the *DPA 1998*.

Human Resources   10.5

The overall responsibility for ensuring compliance with data protection legislation will usually fall to a senior HR director or manager. Nevertheless, line managers and staff alike will have to be aware of their responsibilities and duties under the Act if the employer is to achieve full compliance. It will be up to HR, however, to make sure that all staff, and in particular those whose jobs take them into contact with personal data held about employees, fully understand their responsibilities under the *DPA 1998* and that they receive full training in data protection matters.

The *DPA 1998* was introduced largely to promote openness and transparency of information held about individuals in filing systems, whether manual or computerised, and to provide a specific entitlement for individuals to gain access to any information held about them. The eight data protection principles contained in the *DPA 1998* underpin an employer's duties and obligations to process all personal data in a fair and proper way and ensure information is collected and retained about employees (and job applicants) only where it is necessary for the business. Employers are, irrespective of their size or business sector, required to determine the purposes for which they obtain and use personal information about their employees and ensure the information is not subsequently used for any incompatible purposes. Employers must also ensure personal information is held securely and not disclosed without authority. Other obligations include the duty to ensure that the information held about employees is accurate, is not excessive in relation to its purpose and is not retained for any longer than it is legitimately needed. All these issues will need to be managed and handled by HR.

The Act, and the accompanying Employment Practices Data Protection Code, aim to encourage employers to strike a balance between their reasonable need to create, keep and use records about their staff and the rights of employees to respect for their private lives. The Code of Practice, although not legally binding, represents the Information Commissioner's recommendations as to how employers should fulfil their legal requirements under the *DPA 1998*. In the event of a legal challenge, a court or tribunal can take the Code into account, and any evidence that the employer has not complied with the recommendations contained in the Code are almost certain to operate to their detriment. Much of the Code is concerned with proportionality, ie whether a particular course of action carried out by the employer is appropriate and necessary for the achievement of a legitimate aim when balanced against the needs of the individual, including the right to privacy.

Awareness of data protection issues and the taking of the necessary steps to ensure compliance with the law come into play in a number of key HR activities, starting with recruitment and selection, which, inevitably, will represent one of HR's most important responsibilities.

In order to comply with the *DPA 1998* during the process of recruitment, employers should, for example, be upfront about disclosing their identity (ie not seek to conceal their identity from job applicants); use different application forms to ensure the information they collect about job applicants is restricted to that which is relevant to the job in question; ensure applicants' consent is obtained before conducting any checks, for example reference checks or checks on qualifications; and ensure the security of all job applications, including those sent in online. At the end of the recruitment exercise, employers should notify any applicants whose details they wish to retain on file, giving them the option to ask the employer not to retain them, and in general retain recruitment records for as short a period of time as necessary, based on stated business needs. Clearly it is advisable for HR to devise and implement a policy on the handling, retention and disposal of job applications, including unsolicited applications, so that every aspect of the *DPA 1998* can be fully complied with.

The creation and maintenance of employment records will form the foundation of effective people management, irrespective of the size of the business. If employment records are structured, well-organised and incorporate only information that is appropriate and relevant to the employer's needs, they will serve the employer well and aid compliance with the *DPA 1998*. HR should therefore devise and implement a clear and comprehensive policy on employment records, including, for example, a statement as to whether records should be held only by HR department, or whether line managers may also hold certain types of records about their staff. It may be helpful also for the HR department to conduct an exercise to establish what personal information about employees exists within the organisation other than in the HR department, where it is held and who is responsible for it. Security of records, both manual and computerised will be another important responsibility, often shared amongst the HR department, IT staff and line managers.

Other key points for HR in relation to employment records are to ensure all new staff are informed about what records are to be held about them; the source(s) of any information held about them; the purpose for which the records are to be held; how the information will be used; who it will be disclosed to; and what their rights are under the *DPA 1998*. Furthermore, it is a sound idea for all employers to devise a policy that will ensure the efficient handling of subject access requests.

With regard to the specific retention periods for different types of employment records, proper policy decisions should be made, for example the length of time that leavers' files and recruitment files will be retained. Once such policy decisions have been made, they should be consistently adhered to and HR should have in place a system to ensure the regular clearing out of records both from files held manually and from their computer systems. The decision as to how long to retain employment records should be based on business needs and should be made objectively. Records should not be maintained 'just in case' they might be needed at some future point in time.

Employers will need to pay particular heed to the provisions of the *DPA 1998* (and the provisions contained in *Article 8* of the *Human Rights Act 1998*, ie the right to respect for one's private life) when considering any form of monitoring within the workplace. Equal opportunities monitoring, for example, represents a valid and useful tool for identifying and tackling discrimination and promoting equal opportunities, but the investigation and record keeping associated with monitoring is controversial as some people may object to being asked questions about (for example) their ethnic origins or religion. Nevertheless, the collection of certain types of information may be required by law; for example, it may be necessary for an employer to collect and retain data about a disabled employee's condition and its effects if they are to be in a position to fulfil their duty under the *Disability Discrimination Act 1995* to make reasonable adjustments for that employee.

Other types of monitoring may prove to be even more controversial, for example drugs and alcohol screening, or where an employer operates a policy of monitoring employees' use of email and/or the internet. Such monitoring will need to comply with legislation such as the *Human Rights Act 1998* and (in the case of email/internet monitoring) the *Lawful Business Practice Regulations 2000*, as well as with the *DPA 1998*, assuming a record is kept of what was monitored. Nevertheless, it can be argued that some monitoring is a necessity for many employers in order to protect their interests, together with those of their staff and their clients.

The main aim in designing monitoring should be to strike a reasonable balance between the need to monitor as judged against employees' rights in contract, including the mutual duty of trust and confidence, and the right to privacy under the *Human Rights Act 1998*. Once again, HR should plan to carry out an impact assessment before any decision is made on a policy of monitoring. The impact assessment should be used to establish whether there is justification for monitoring in a general sense and also to review whether or not monitoring in specific circumstances would be justifiable.

One key issue in relation to the prospective monitoring of employee communications will be to decide whether monitoring will be designed primarily to highlight internet access rates (as a spot check on possible problem areas) or to monitor actual content. Essentially, monitoring should be carried out only where it is necessary and relevant to the business, and where the legitimate business needs of the employer outweigh the inevitable intrusion into employees' private lives. Even where it has been established that a degree of monitoring is a business necessity, steps should be taken to minimise the level of intrusion into employees' private lives whenever possible.

Health Records 10.6

Any records that relate to an employee's physical or mental health held in the context of employment will have to be treated with particular care and respect, taking into account the duty of confidentiality owed by employers to their employees. Data about an individual's physical or mental health is one of the categories of information that is regarded as 'sensitive data' under the *DPA 1998* and must be treated accordingly, taking into account the need to minimise any intrusion into employees' privacy.

In general, employers should consider carefully whether they actually need to collect and hold information about their employees' health and if so, what level of detail is genuinely necessary to ensure their business interests. Some basic data will be held simply to support the payment of Statutory Sick Pay, whilst specific information about employees' health or illness may be needed to administer occupational health schemes. More detailed information may be gathered as a result of medical examination and testing.

It is strongly advisable to separate information about employees' health from information about absence. For example, it will only be necessary, when deciding whether to pay sick pay, to record the fact that the employee is unfit for work under his or her contract; the nature of the sickness will be immaterial to the question of whether to make payment. It may also be useful to segregate the health data that is held into two types: that which the employee may volunteer (such as the information needed to join the employer's occupational pension scheme) and that which the employer gathers compulsorily.

The best way to establish whether there is justification for holding information about employees' health is to conduct an impact assessment, in particular in relation to information that is gathered compulsorily from employees. This task would normally fall to the HR department to organise and coordinate. An impact assessment should aim to identify the purpose(s) for which health information is to be collected and held, and the potential health-related risks to the organisation. Any adverse impact on employees that is likely to be caused by the collection and use of health information should also be established, as well as any possible alternatives (ie alternative ways of addressing the risks other than the collection of health information about employees). Ultimately, the impact assessment will enable the employer to decide whether or not collecting and holding health information is justified, taking into account the obligations that arise out of the collection and holding of such information. If justification exists, the employer should still aim to keep the collection and retention of health information to a minimum.

The employer should of course, use properly qualified staff to undertake the collection of health information. For medical examinations and testing, it will be essential to use health professionals who will adhere to their own codes of conduct and ethical standards. Furthermore, suitably qualified health professionals should be employed to interpret health information and judge an employee's fitness for his or her particular job.

It is also advisable to limit access to health records so that only health professionals with a need to know are able to access personal health information. Employers should avoid holding health data in employees' general personal files and should instead use a separate system whenever possible. Health data should be retained only for as long as it is needed. For example, once samples for testing have been examined and the results established, the samples themselves should be destroyed. If the testing was implemented in order to enforce an organisational rule on drug and alcohol abstinence, negative results can and should be destroyed. If an audit trail is needed, the employer should use the test administration rather than the medical data gathered as evidence that the testing was in fact carried out.

Similarly, local managers should not be allowed to gather any health data on their own initiative and should be clearly instructed to pass on any health data which they obtain quickly and confidentially to the right person in the organisation.

To ensure the competent handling of health, sickness and attendance data, the employer should draw up procedures for the handling of health records, ranging from sickness certificates through to information obtained as a result of medical examinations. The procedure should include details of where and how particular records are to be held, eg in payroll, HR or within the occupational health department.

Employees will of course expect all their health data to be treated with the same high levels of privacy and confidentiality as they receive from their own general practitioner.

Payroll   10.7

The main purpose of any payroll function is to pay employees on time and accurately, so the prime focus of payroll is the employee and thus much personal data about employees is used for payroll purposes. Most employees within the payroll function understand the need for confidentiality and privacy of the personal data that they handle routinely as part of the many payroll processes. For their part, employees will expect a high level of confidentiality of their payroll information as the norm. If there are sound procedures in place for the payroll function, these will meet most of the needs of the *DPA 1998*. However, as the payroll function will have been in existence as long as the organisation has been an employer, the procedures may pre-date data protection legislation. It would therefore be wise from time to time to conduct an assessment of the payroll policies and procedures as measured against the law and the Employment Practices Data Protection Code.

Data protection issues can be classified into two sets:

- the security of the personal data while it is processed in the payroll function; and

- disclosure of the information, whether internally or to external sources.

The first of these two points is a matter for the whole of the organisation. Individual employees themselves generate much payroll-related data. The passage of that data from the employee to the payroll function whenever it uses the employer's facilities must happen securely. The payroll office and any systems used for payroll data must be secure.

Disclosure of payroll-related data outside the payroll function is a continuous, frequent, regular and occasional activity. Disclosure may be required for internal reporting, ranging from the costs of overtime and bonuses to the costs of occupational sick pay. If the information is reported in a way that does not identify individuals by, say, reporting only at cost centre levels, there are few data protection issues. Where, however, data that clearly refer to one individual employee are distributed to one or more other parts of an organisation, this must be done within the requirements of the *DPA 1998*. Extra care must be taken where personal data are transferred outside the EEA. The concept of 'binding company rules' was emerging at the beginning of 2004 but has yet to be established as a satisfactory solution for internal, international transfers.

Disclosures outside an organisation are common in the payroll function. Examples include those required by law, such as annual returns to the Inland Revenue, those required under contract such as returns to pension providers or those instigated by the employees themselves, such as confirmation of earnings for mortgage applications. Employers must ensure that they have the proper authority to justify any disclosure if it is to constitute fair and lawful processing. Adequate security – both technical and organisational – will be needed to prevent unauthorised access or disclosure.

Payroll will also handle sensitive personal data in the course of its work, for example data on employees' trade union membership and health information (unless this is processed by a specialist health unit). This will mean that the employer will have to meet the additional data protection conditions applicable to sensitive personal data.

Many employers make use of a third party to manage and handle some elements of the payroll function. Whatever the degree of processing carried out by the third party, the responsibility for data protection remains with the employer. In particular, the contract for the processing of payroll must be in writing and must restrict the data processor (as the third party is called) to processing personal data only on the instructions of the data controller (as the employer is called). The data controller must use a data processor with adequate security and ensure that the data processor does indeed have the required level of technical and organisational security. Any obligations imposed on the data controller by law cannot be delegated to the data processor. Thus it is the data controller who must instruct the data processor to make disclosures on behalf of the employer and specify when and how the disclosures are to be made.

In terms of complying with data protection legislation in all the areas mentioned above, the key to staying within the law whilst at the same time ensuring fairness, is to:

- adhere to the data protection principles and the recommendations contained in the Employment Practices Data Protection Code; and

- aim to strike a reasonable balance between the needs of the business to operate efficiently and lawfully, and the rights of employees to enjoy privacy and to be treated with respect.

The *DPA 1998* creates many responsibilities and liabilities for HR and payroll practitioners, and it is hoped that this book has improved understanding of the many complex and important issues associated with data protection in the workplace.

Index